# Bake!

# Bake!
## The
## QUICK-LOOK COOKBOOK

GABRIELA SCOLIK + TEAM / INFOGRAPHICS: NO.PARKING

weldonowen

# tools, tips, and techniques

# basic batters and doughs

# cakes and quick breads

## pies and tarts

# muffins and cupcakes

# cookies and bars

# specialty desserts

# soufflés and custards

# sauces, glazes, and toppings

# Bon Appétit!

Do you want to bake the chewiest cookies? Impress your friends with a homemade cheesecake (# 058) or your family with a towering black forest cake (# 065)? Or surprise your kids with homemade apple crumble bars (# 195) for their lunchboxes?

**058** make ricotta-lemon cheesecake

**065** make black forest cake

Look no further! In BAKE! THE QUICK-LOOK COOKBOOK, you'll learn step-by-step everything you need to know to bake the best sweet and savory treats. Our team of expert bakers and graphic artists have created hundreds of fully illustrated recipes to create sweet treats for every taste and every occasion.

Whether you are a pastry chef or a new baker, this is the book for you! Just put on your apron, mix up some dough, and make your home smell delicious with treats baked with love.

In these pages, you'll discover hundreds of new favorites and classic desserts as well as loads of decorating tips that will make your creations look like they came from the bakery, like how to create sugar flower petals (# 026) or chocolate lace (# 033). Simple step-by-step instructions and clear illustrations will guide you through each recipe, so you can be sure to succeed. Our tips and tricks will help you make beautiful and enticing baked goods every single time.

So start stirring, kneading, decorating, and baking your way to delightful cakes, pies, cupcakes and cookies! Bon appétit!

**234** make apple crumble bars

**026** make sugared flower petals

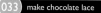

**033** make chocolate lace

**BAKE! THE QUICK-LOOK COOKBOOK** is divided into 9 chapters, organized by types of sweet treats. Look something up in the respective category or just flip through the book for inspiration!

### tools, tips, and techniques

Here you will find all the equipment you need, and their functions. In addition, fundamental techniques are explained and there are plenty of tips for successful baking.

### basic batters and doughs

These basic batters and doughs are ones that you will use again and again.

### cakes and quickbreads

Classics and special cakes and quickbreads, from Sacher Torte to carrot cake to pound cake and more.

### pies and tarts

Find simple and delicious seasonal pies, tarts, tartlets or crisps and cobblers here!

### muffins and cupcakes

Treat your loved ones or yourself to tender breakfast muffins or create party-worthy cupcakes!

### cookies and bars

You'll find a world of cookies and brownies for any occasion here, from Christmas to a tea party. Be inspired by creative decorating ideas and impress with classic macarons!

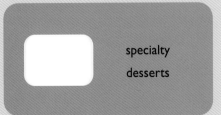

### specialty desserts

Here you'll find delicate fruit strudel, international specialties, and even colorful cake pops for a kid's birthday party.

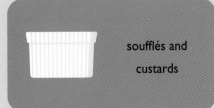

### soufflés and custards

Soufflés don't have to be hard, with a little practice you'll always succeed! Find that and plenty of delightful puddings and custards here.

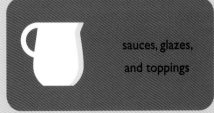

### sauces, glazes, and toppings

Sauces, glazes, and toppings will help refine your cakes, macarons and other desserts, and take them over the top!

The recipes in **BAKE! THE QUICK-LOOK COOKBOOK** are presented graphically. All recipes have a number – so you can find them easily. Should you be looking for a particular recipe or keyword, you can find it in the index at the back of the book which is sorted in alphabetical order.

**TIPS** You can find tips and tricks or additional information marked with an *.

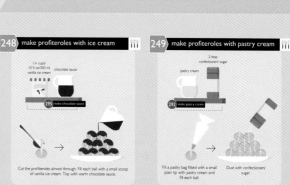

**247**  make choux profiteroles

**248**  make profiteroles with ice cream

Cut the profiteroles almost through. Fill each ball with a small scoop of vanilla ice cream. Top with warm chocolate sauce.

**249**  make profiteroles with pastry cream

Fill a pastry bag fitted with a small plain tip with pastry cream and fill each ball. Dust with confectioners' sugar.

**250**  make profiteroles with jam filling

Stir together the jam and lemon juice. Fill a pastry bag fitted with a small plain tip with the jam mixture and fill each ball. Dust with confectioners' sugar.

**251**  make profiteroles with baileys cream

Gently stir the Baileys into the whipped cream. Fill a pastry bag fitted with a small plain tip with Baileys cream and fill each ball.

**ZOOMS** Close-up views show important details.

**250**  **SUB-RECIPES** Some recipes can be varied – they are marked with a number in an arrow.

**CROSS REFERENCES** Sometimes one thing leads to another. Follow the cross reference for techniques, other recipes or useful techniques. In the circle you find the number of the entry.

**015**  whip cream

## ICON GUIDE:

Whisks stand for the level of difficulty:

easy

medium

difficult

Store in an airtight container.

Serve immediately, eat within three days from preparation.

Quick recipes that you can prepare in less than 30 minutes (excluding baking time).

**LIST OF INGREDIENTS** On the cutting board you find the list of ingredients, how much you need and how to prepare them (e.g. 1 apple, peeled, cored and sliced). The list of ingredients is at the same time your shopping list. The dotted lines mark the different working steps. In the boxes with dashed lines you find the tools that you will need for the specific recipe.

**SYMBOL GUIDE** Many symbols point to important aspects of a recipe, including cooking time, heat or temperature. Here are the symbols you will find throughout the book:

The kitchen timer shows the cooking, cooling, or resting time.

Shows the temperature of the oven or the deep-frying oil. If you have a convection oven deduct 50°F/20°C from the indicated heat.

How hot? Cook at low, medium, or high temperature – that applies to electric, gas, or induction stoves.

Let chill in the refrigerator or freezer.

## USEFUL TIPS

- Always read the recipe closely before you start.

- Gather all kitchen equipment you need before starting (including oven gloves and a dish towel).

- Prepare the ingredients as shown in the recipe. With good preparation (mise en place) baking will be easier!

- Weigh and measure all ingredients carefully - baking requires precision!

- Don't work too fast, take your time.

- If necessary, draw templates on parchment paper. Turn it over before use.

- When making cookies, scones, biscuits, etc. be sure to divide the dough into evenly-sized portions so that they bake in the same amount of time. Different sizes will bake more quickly or slowly.

- Some baked goods need to be spaced slightly apart on the baking sheet as they expand during baking. Leave enough space between each portion before baking.

- If you are using refrigerated ingredients, let stand at room temperature before using them, unless otherwise directed. That especially applies to butter and eggs.

- When separating eggs, use 3 bowls: one to separate the first white into, one for all of the yolks, one for all of the clean whites once you ensure there is no yolk or shells in the white.

- Always beat egg whites in a grease-free dish, or they will not whip into voluminous peaks.

- Never add beaten egg whites to the batter all at once. Gently fold in one-third to lighten the dough, then fold in the remainder.

- Adjust the amount of sugar to your personal taste.

- Instead of using an immersion blender, you can also use an electric blender.

- If ingredients need to be whisked for a long time, you can use a handheld electric mixer or a stand mixer with beaters instead of a hand-held whisk.

- If using the peel of citrus fruits, buy organic produce and wash it before usage.

- Some mixtures, like custards, will become lumpy if overheated or heated too quickly: watch the temperature or use a double boiler.

- Strain sauces, custards, curds, dissolved gelatin mixtures, and fruit purees through a fine-mesh sieve set over a bowl to remove lumps or small seeds.

- Cover doughs and batters tightly before putting them into the refrigerator, as they can easily take on an odor.

- Some baked goods are well suited for storage or are best stored before eating. Keep them in airtight containers.

tools,
tips, and
techniques

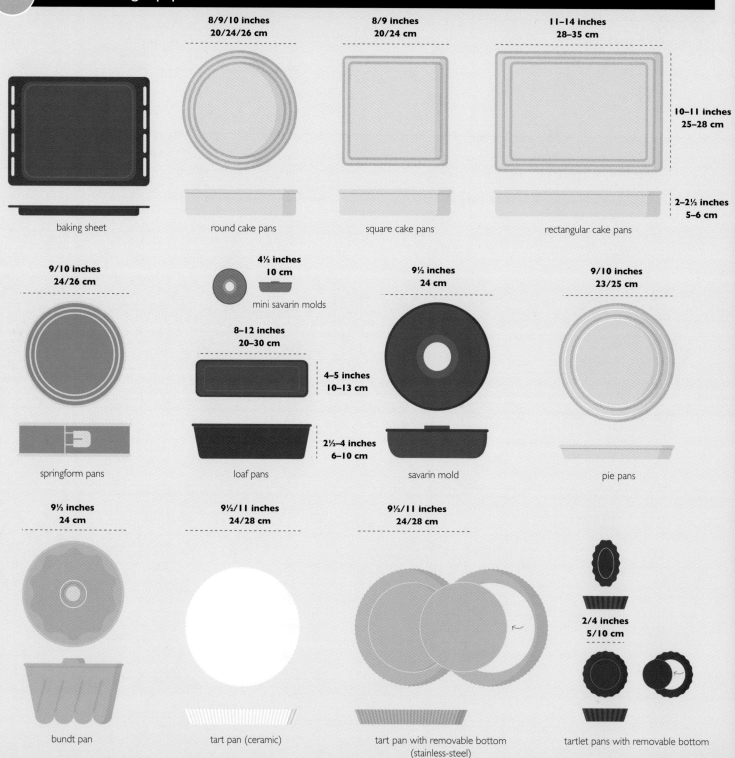

**8/9/10 inches**
**20/24/26 cm**

**8/9 inches**
**20/24 cm**

**11–14 inches**
**28–35 cm**

**10–11 inches**
**25–28 cm**

**2–2½ inches**
**5–6 cm**

baking sheet

round cake pans

square cake pans

rectangular cake pans

**9/10 inches**
**24/26 cm**

**4½ inches**
**10 cm**

mini savarin molds

**9½ inches**
**24 cm**

**9/10 inches**
**23/25 cm**

**8–12 inches**
**20–30 cm**

**4–5 inches**
**10–13 cm**

**2½–4 inches**
**6–10 cm**

springform pans

loaf pans

savarin mold

pie pans

**9½ inches**
**24 cm**

**9½/11 inches**
**24/28 cm**

**9½/11 inches**
**24/28 cm**

**2/4 inches**
**5/10 cm**

bundt pan

tart pan (ceramic)

tart pan with removable bottom
(stainless-steel)

tartlet pans with removable bottom

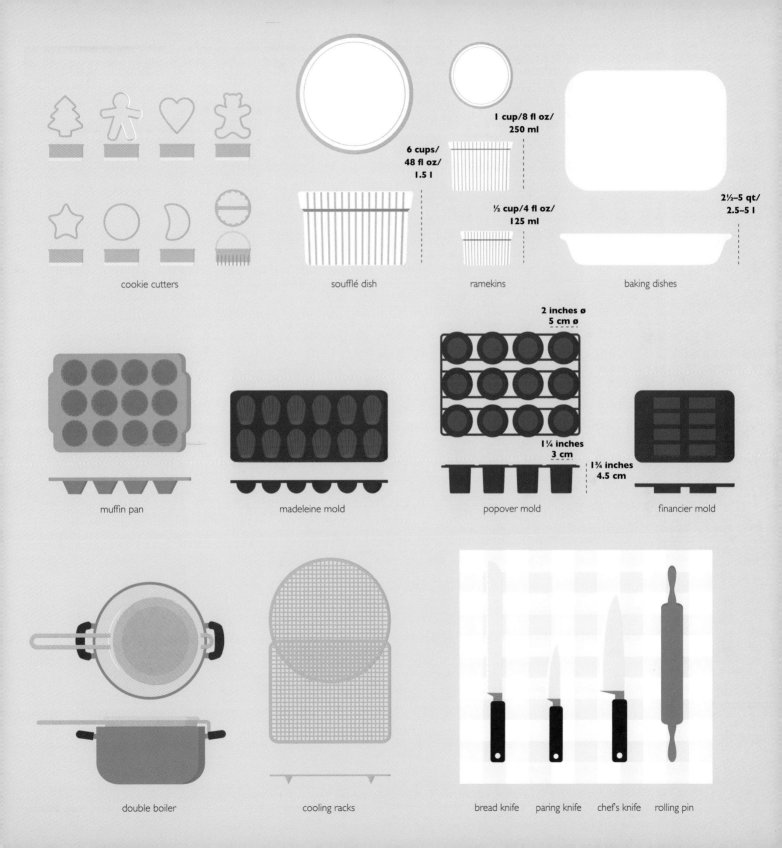

cookie cutters

souufflé dish

6 cups/
48 fl oz/
1.5 l

ramekins

1 cup/8 fl oz/
250 ml

½ cup/4 fl oz/
125 ml

baking dishes

2½–5 qt/
2.5–5 l

muffin pan

madeleine mold

popover mold

2 inches ø
5 cm ø

1¼ inches
3 cm

1¾ inches
4.5 cm

financier mold

double boiler

cooling racks

bread knife    paring knife    chef's knife    rolling pin

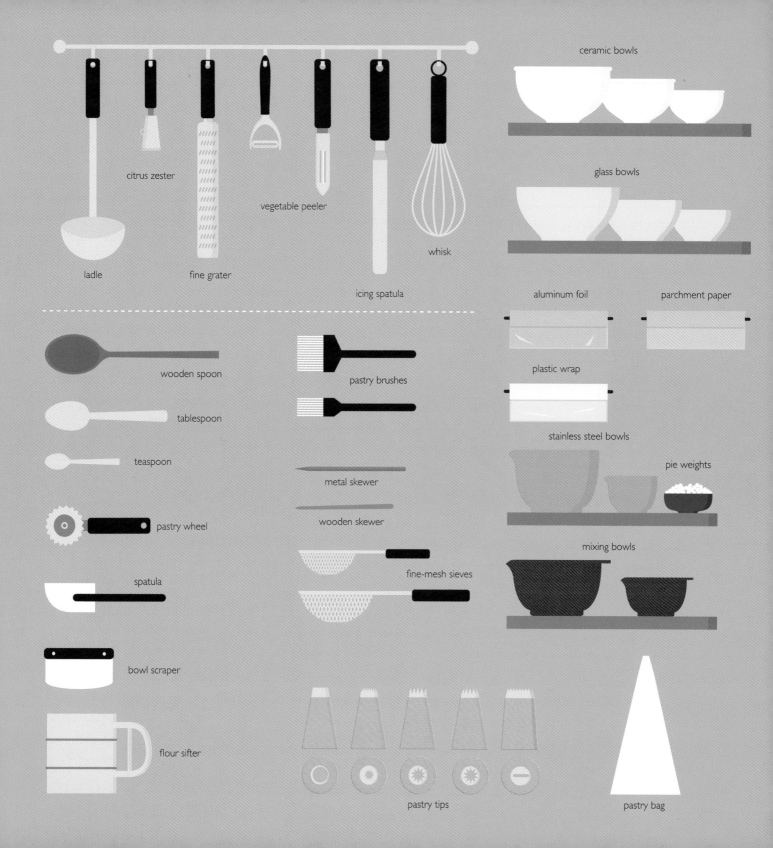

citrus zester

ladle

fine grater

vegetable peeler

icing spatula

whisk

ceramic bowls

glass bowls

aluminum foil

parchment paper

plastic wrap

stainless steel bowls

pie weights

mixing bowls

wooden spoon

pastry brushes

tablespoon

teaspoon

metal skewer

wooden skewer

pastry wheel

spatula

fine-mesh sieves

bowl scraper

flour sifter

pastry tips

pastry bag

whipped cream maker

kitchen torch

liquid measuring cup

kitchen scale

measuring spoons

blender

handheld mixer with beaters
and dough hooks

immersion
blender

measuring cups

timer

stand mixer

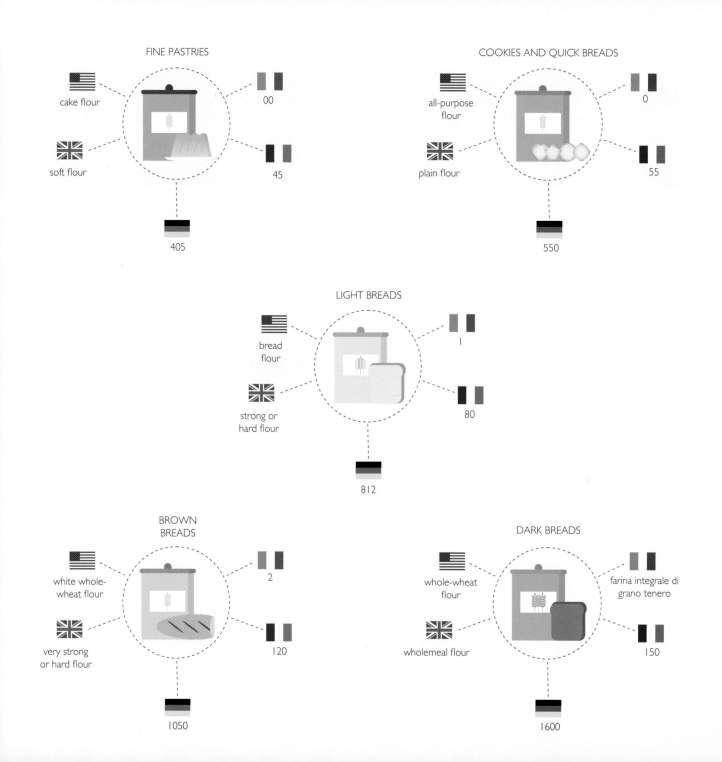

FINE PASTRIES

cake flour

soft flour

00

45

405

COOKIES AND QUICK BREADS

all-purpose flour

plain flour

0

55

550

LIGHT BREADS

bread flour

strong or hard flour

1

80

812

BROWN BREADS

white whole-wheat flour

very strong or hard flour

2

120

1050

DARK BREADS

whole-wheat flour

wholemeal flour

farina integrale di grano tenero

150

1600

## 005 | test doneness with a metal skewer

To test whether a cake is done, stick a metal skewer into the center of the cake and pull it back out.

The temperature of the skewer should be the same all over.

## 006 | test doneness with a wooden skewer

To test whether a cake is done, stick a wooden skewer into the center of the cake and pull it back out.

The cake is done when the skewer comes out clean.

## 007 | test doneness with your fingertip

Gently press the surface of a cake with your fingertip.

If it is not firm enough, bake for another couple of minutes.

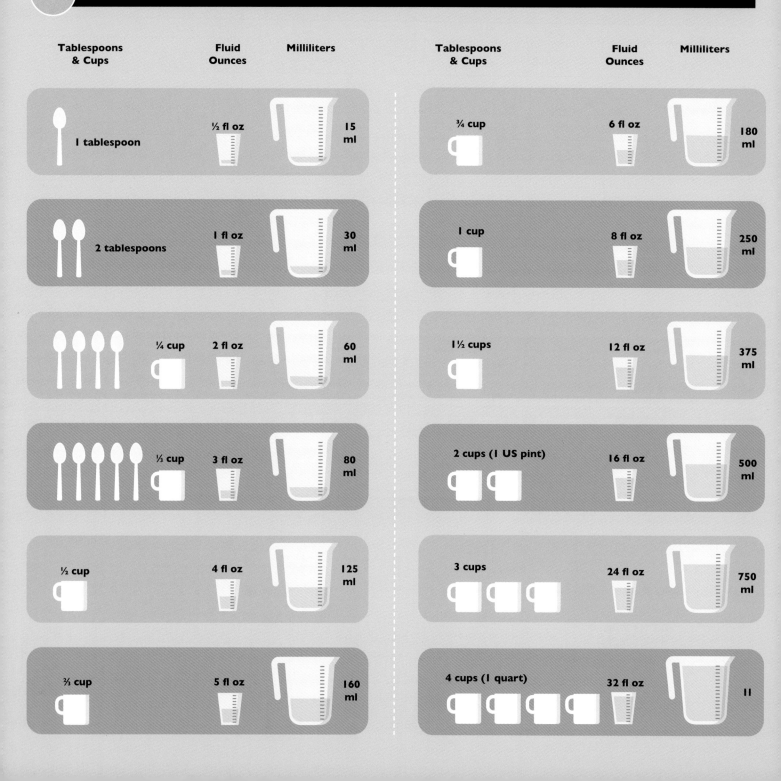

| Tablespoons & Cups | Fluid Ounces | Milliliters |
|---|---|---|
| 1 tablespoon | ½ fl oz | 15 ml |
| 2 tablespoons | 1 fl oz | 30 ml |
| ¼ cup | 2 fl oz | 60 ml |
| ⅓ cup | 3 fl oz | 80 ml |
| ½ cup | 4 fl oz | 125 ml |
| ⅔ cup | 5 fl oz | 160 ml |

| Tablespoons & Cups | Fluid Ounces | Milliliters |
|---|---|---|
| ¾ cup | 6 fl oz | 180 ml |
| 1 cup | 8 fl oz | 250 ml |
| 1½ cups | 12 fl oz | 375 ml |
| 2 cups (1 US pint) | 16 fl oz | 500 ml |
| 3 cups | 24 fl oz | 750 ml |
| 4 cups (1 quart) | 32 fl oz | 1 l |

# 009 convert weight

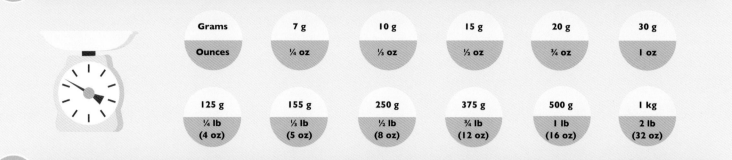

| Grams | 7 g | 10 g | 15 g | 20 g | 30 g |
|---|---|---|---|---|---|
| Ounces | ¼ oz | ⅓ oz | ½ oz | ¾ oz | 1 oz |
| 125 g | 155 g | 250 g | 375 g | 500 g | 1 kg |
| ¼ lb (4 oz) | ⅓ lb (5 oz) | ½ lb (8 oz) | ¾ lb (12 oz) | 1 lb (16 oz) | 2 lb (32 oz) |

# 010 convert temperature

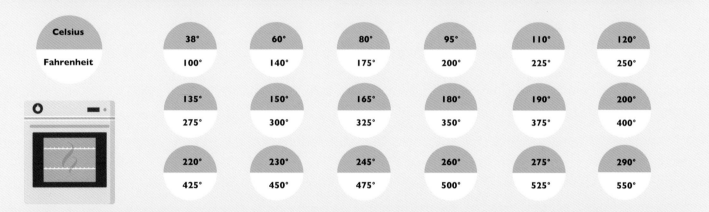

| Celsius | 38° | 60° | 80° | 95° | 110° | 120° |
|---|---|---|---|---|---|---|
| Fahrenheit | 100° | 140° | 175° | 200° | 225° | 250° |
| 135° | 150° | 165° | 180° | 190° | 200° |
| 275° | 300° | 325° | 350° | 375° | 400° |
| 220° | 230° | 245° | 260° | 275° | 290° |
| 425° | 450° | 475° | 500° | 525° | 550° |

# 011 convert length

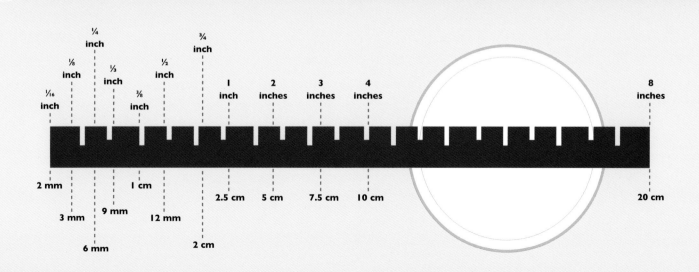

1/16 inch · ⅛ inch · ¼ inch · ⅓ inch · ⅜ inch · ½ inch · ¾ inch · 1 inch · 2 inches · 3 inches · 4 inches · 8 inches

2 mm · 3 mm · 6 mm · 9 mm · 1 cm · 12 mm · 2 cm · 2.5 cm · 5 cm · 7.5 cm · 10 cm · 20 cm

## 012 separate an egg

✳ Use fresh eggs. Make sure no yolk gets into the whites, otherwise the whites will not whip up.

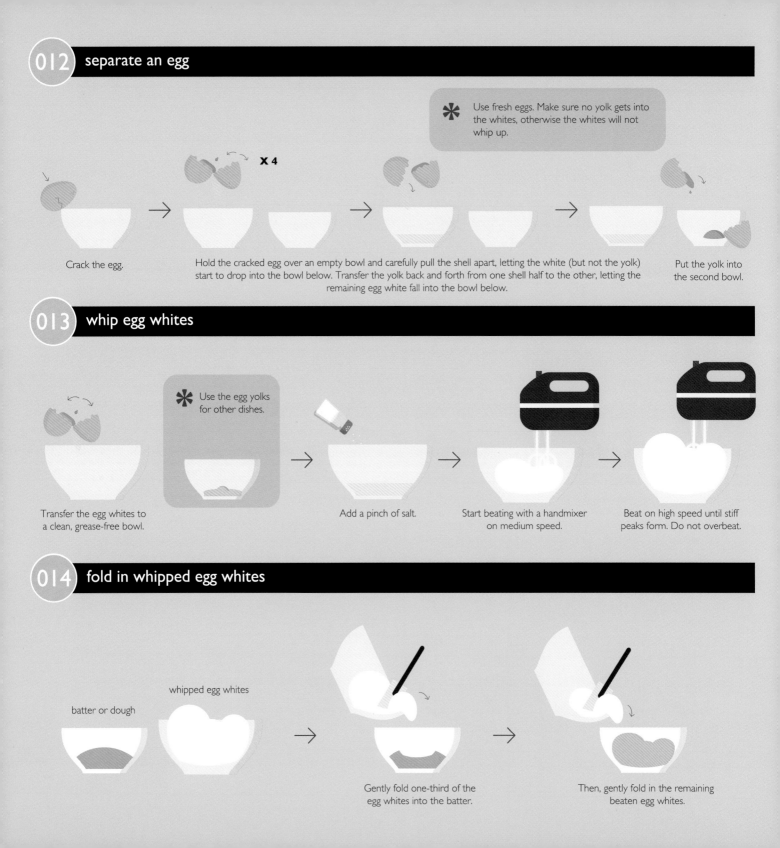

Crack the egg.

Hold the cracked egg over an empty bowl and carefully pull the shell apart, letting the white (but not the yolk) start to drop into the bowl below. Transfer the yolk back and forth from one shell half to the other, letting the remaining egg white fall into the bowl below.

Put the yolk into the second bowl.

## 013 whip egg whites

Transfer the egg whites to a clean, grease-free bowl.

✳ Use the egg yolks for other dishes.

Add a pinch of salt.

Start beating with a handmixer on medium speed.

Beat on high speed until stiff peaks form. Do not overbeat.

## 014 fold in whipped egg whites

batter or dough

whipped egg whites

Gently fold one-third of the egg whites into the batter.

Then, gently fold in the remaining beaten egg whites.

## whip cream

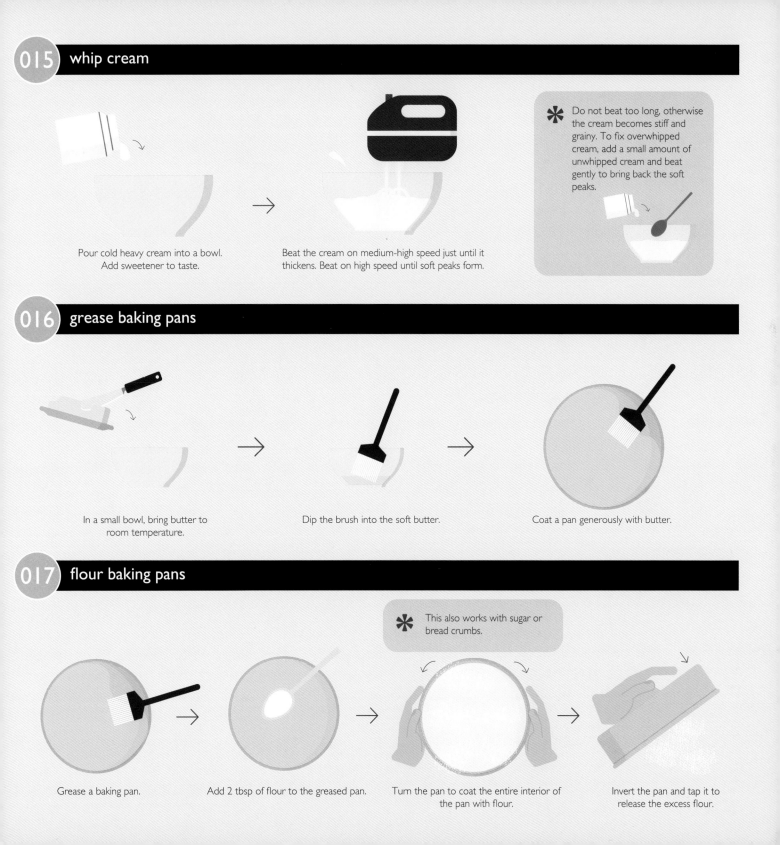

Pour cold heavy cream into a bowl. Add sweetener to taste.

Beat the cream on medium-high speed just until it thickens. Beat on high speed until soft peaks form.

**✳** Do not beat too long, otherwise the cream becomes stiff and grainy. To fix overwhipped cream, add a small amount of unwhipped cream and beat gently to bring back the soft peaks.

## grease baking pans

In a small bowl, bring butter to room temperature.

Dip the brush into the soft butter.

Coat a pan generously with butter.

## flour baking pans

**✳** This also works with sugar or bread crumbs.

Grease a baking pan.

Add 2 tbsp of flour to the greased pan.

Turn the pan to coat the entire interior of the pan with flour.

Invert the pan and tap it to release the excess flour.

## 018 cream butter and sugar

¾ cup/6 oz/ 185 g unsalted butter

¾ cup/6 oz/ 185 g sugar

Put the butter and sugar into a mixing bowl.

Start beating on medium speed.

3 min — Beat on high speed until the mixture becomes creamy and pale yellow.

5 min — Test with your fingertips. You should not feel the sugar crystals.

## 019 use gelatin

5 min — Soak sheets of gelatin in cold water.

Wring the sheets gently to remove any excess water.

Sprinkle powdered gelatin over cold water, stir, and let soften until opaque.

5 min

Heat the gelatin with a liquid according to your recipe, stirring, until the gelatin dissolves. Do not boil.

Strain through a fine-mesh sieve into the mixture you are using in the recipe, and stir well to combine.

2 sheets gelatin (3.5 g/⅛ oz) = 1 tsp unflavored powdered gelatin → Dissolve in 2 tbsp water.

4 sheets gelatin (7 g/¼ oz) = 1 tbsp unflavored powdered gelatin → Dissolve in 4 tbsp water.

6 sheets gelatin (10 g/⅓ oz) = 1½ tbsp unflavored powdered gelatin → Dissolve in 6 tbsp water.

## 020  work with vanilla beans

Use a paring knife to cut down the center of the bean lengthwise.

Scrape out the seeds with the back of the knife.

## 021  make your own vanilla sugar

✷ You can replace vanilla extract with homemade vanilla sugar – 1 tsp vanilla extract equals 1½ tsp/¼ oz/7 g vanilla sugar. Reduce the amount of sugar in the recipe accordingly.

1 cup/7 oz/ 220 g sugar

glass jar with lid

vanilla bean pod without seeds

Put the sugar into the glass jar.

Add the vanilla bean pod and seal the jar.

Let sit for 2 weeks before using.

## 022  weave a lattice-top pie

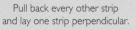

On a floured work surface roll out pie dough into a circle about ⅛ inch/3 mm thick, then cut into 1-inch/2,5-cm strips

Lay half of the strips on top in the same direction.

Pull back every other strip and lay one strip perpendicular.

Repeat with the remaining strips until covered.

## 023 release a cake after baking

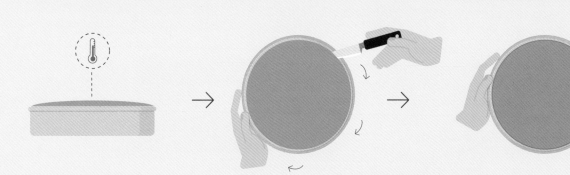

Let the cake cool.

Run a thin knife along the inside edge of the pan.

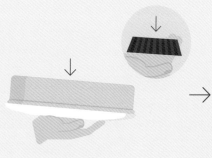
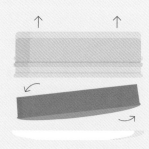

Invert a plate over the top of the pan.

Invert the pan and plate together.

Rotate the cake so it is right-side up.

## 024 cut a cake into layers

Place the cake on a flat surface. Hold a long, thin serrated knife parallel to the working surface.

Slowly rotating the cake, trace a line around the cake halfway up the side.

Following the line, split the cake horizontally into 2 layers. Repeat as necessary.

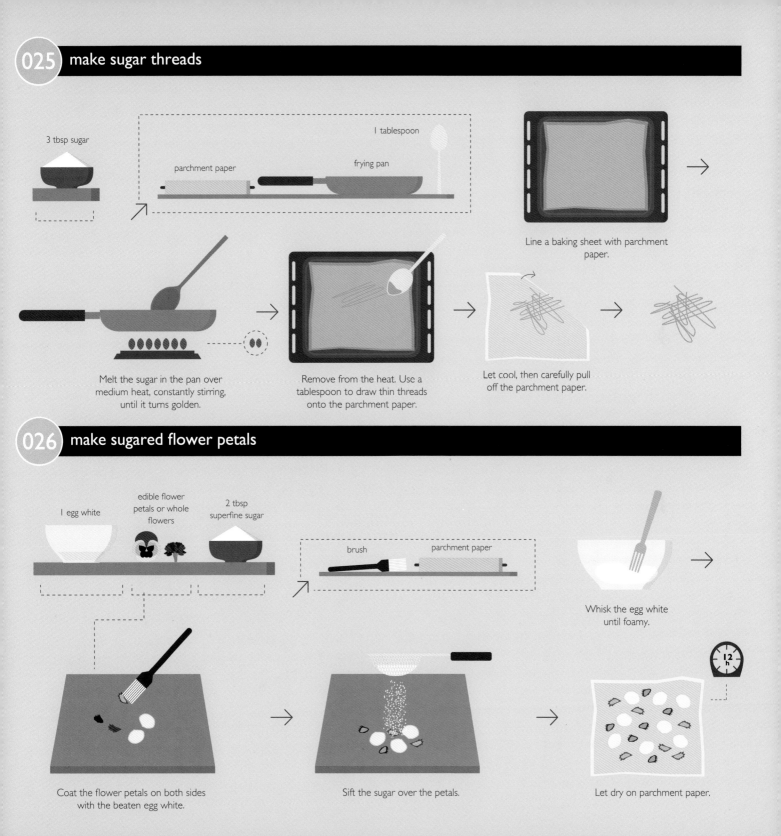

## 025 make sugar threads

3 tbsp sugar

parchment paper

1 tablespoon

frying pan

Line a baking sheet with parchment paper.

Melt the sugar in the pan over medium heat, constantly stirring, until it turns golden.

Remove from the heat. Use a tablespoon to draw thin threads onto the parchment paper.

Let cool, then carefully pull off the parchment paper.

## 026 make sugared flower petals

1 egg white

edible flower petals or whole flowers

2 tbsp superfine sugar

brush

parchment paper

Whisk the egg white until foamy.

Coat the flower petals on both sides with the beaten egg white.

Sift the sugar over the petals.

Let dry on parchment paper.

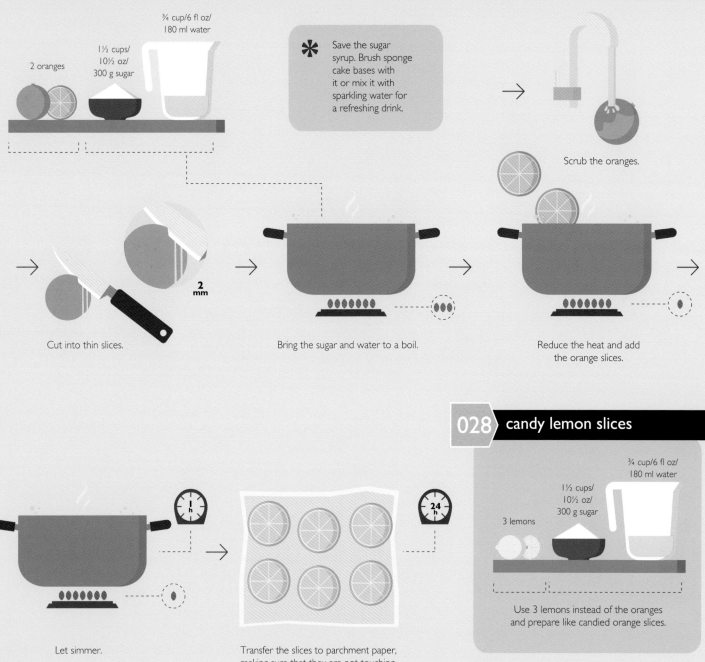

2 oranges

1½ cups/
10½ oz/
300 g sugar

¾ cup/6 fl oz/
180 ml water

Save the sugar syrup. Brush sponge cake bases with it or mix it with sparkling water for a refreshing drink.

Scrub the oranges.

2 mm

Cut into thin slices.

Bring the sugar and water to a boil.

Reduce the heat and add the orange slices.

Let simmer.

Transfer the slices to parchment paper, making sure that they are not touching. Let dry at room temperature.

## 028  candy lemon slices

3 lemons

1½ cups/
10½ oz/
300 g sugar

¾ cup/6 fl oz/
180 ml water

Use 3 lemons instead of the oranges and prepare like candied orange slices.

# 029 candy orange zest

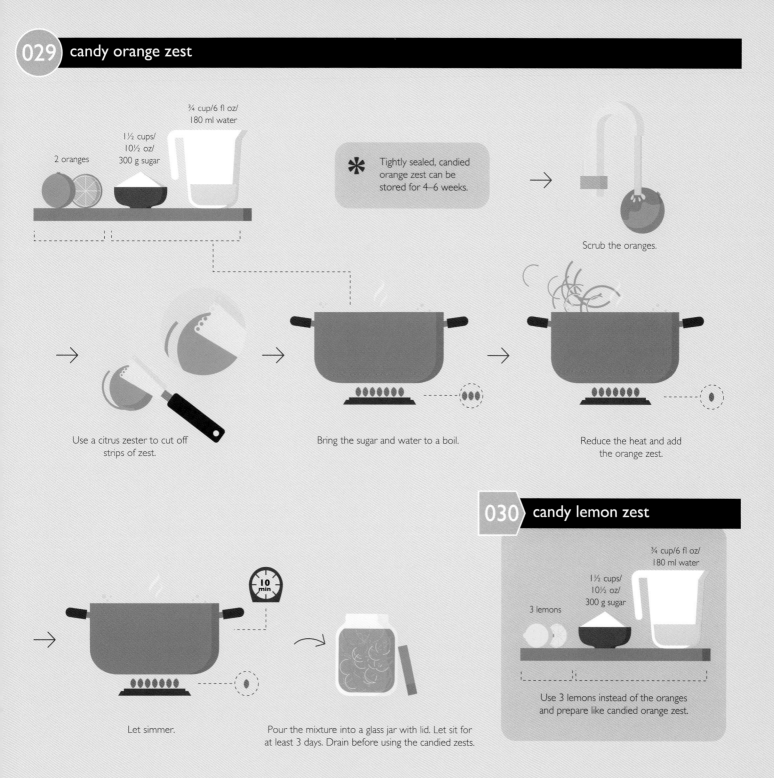

2 oranges

1½ cups/
10½ oz/
300 g sugar

¾ cup/6 fl oz/
180 ml water

＊ Tightly sealed, candied orange zest can be stored for 4–6 weeks.

Scrub the oranges.

Use a citrus zester to cut off strips of zest.

Bring the sugar and water to a boil.

Reduce the heat and add the orange zest.

Let simmer.

Pour the mixture into a glass jar with lid. Let sit for at least 3 days. Drain before using the candied zests.

# 030 candy lemon zest

¾ cup/6 fl oz/
180 ml water

1½ cups/
10½ oz/
300 g sugar

3 lemons

Use 3 lemons instead of the oranges and prepare like candied orange zest.

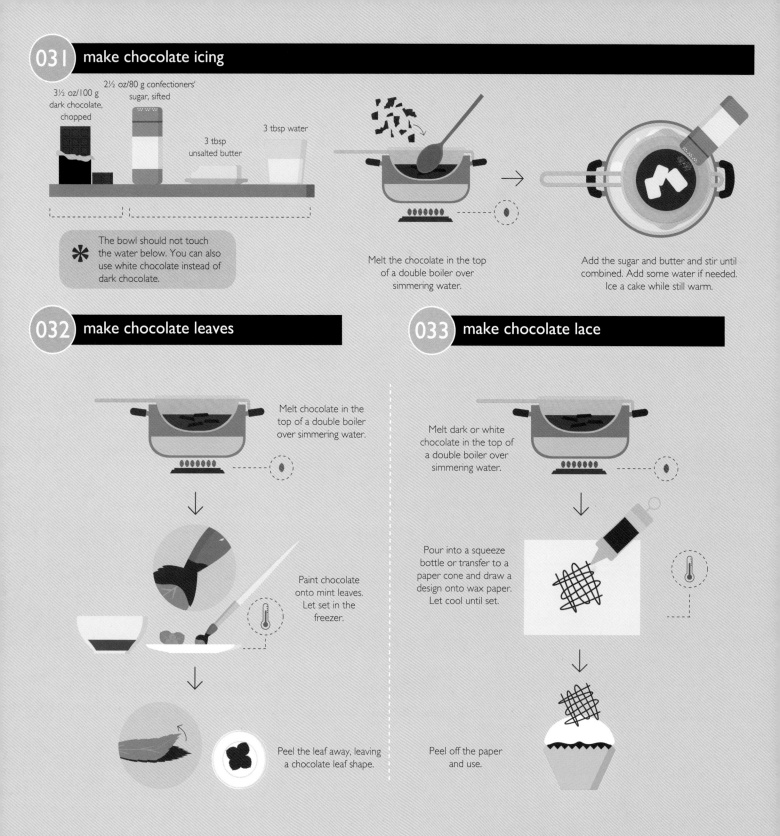

## 031 make chocolate icing

3½ oz/100 g
dark chocolate,
chopped

2½ oz/80 g confectioners'
sugar, sifted

3 tbsp
unsalted butter

3 tbsp water

**✱** The bowl should not touch the water below. You can also use white chocolate instead of dark chocolate.

Melt the chocolate in the top of a double boiler over simmering water.

Add the sugar and butter and stir until combined. Add some water if needed. Ice a cake while still warm.

## 032 make chocolate leaves

Melt chocolate in the top of a double boiler over simmering water.

Paint chocolate onto mint leaves. Let set in the freezer.

Peel the leaf away, leaving a chocolate leaf shape.

## 033 make chocolate lace

Melt dark or white chocolate in the top of a double boiler over simmering water.

Pour into a squeeze bottle or transfer to a paper cone and draw a design onto wax paper. Let cool until set.

Peel off the paper and use.

Trim a cooled cake to create a level surface.

Set on a cardboard round on a cake turntable.

Pour a thin coat of icing over the top of the cake, then spread to an even layer. Let the icing dry in the refrigerator.

Add more icing; spread over the whole cake.

Smooth from the edge to the center. Cover the sides with icing.

Hold the spatula under hot water.

Hold the edge of the spatula to the cake and rotate the cake turntable to smooth the icing.

Lay a stencil onto a cooled and iced cake.

Sift confectioners' sugar over the stencil.

Remove the stencil carefully.

## 036 shave chocolate

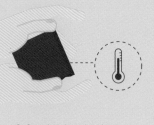

Soften the chocolate by rubbing it with your hands.

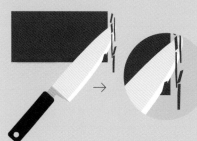

Slide a knife over the narrow side of the bar to shave the chocolate.

## 037 curl chocolate

Use a vegetable peeler to scrape curls off the edge of a chocolate bar.

## 038 chop chocolate

Using a sharp knife, cut slices off the edge of a chocolate bar.

Chop into smaller pieces.

**decorate with a pastry bag**

**decorate with whipped cream**

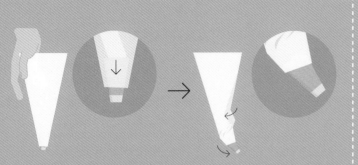

Push a tip into the small hole of a pastry bag.

Fold the pastry bag once just behind the tip to close it.

**decorate with chocolate buttercream**

Put the pastry bag into a tall mug or a glass.

Fold down the top of the bag to form a cuff.

Fill the pastry bag.

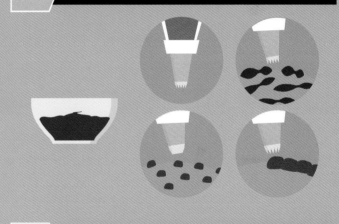

**decorate with meringue**

Unfold the cuff.

Remove the pastry bag from the mug and twist the open end to close.

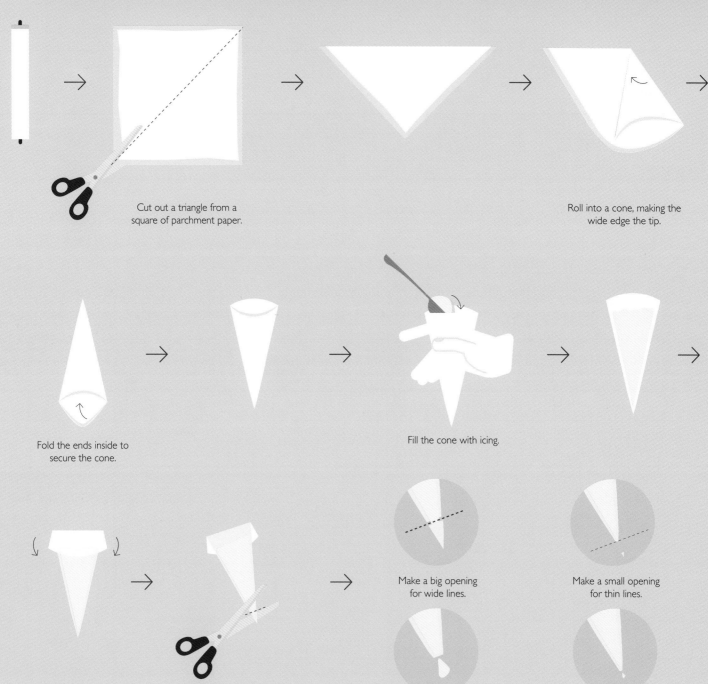

Cut out a triangle from a square of parchment paper.

Roll into a cone, making the wide edge the tip.

Fold the ends inside to secure the cone.

Fill the cone with icing.

Fold the top over.

Snip a small bit off the end.

Make a big opening for wide lines.

Make a small opening for thin lines.

Draw lines in decorative patterns.

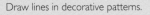

Outline the edges.

Flood the center inside the outlined edges.

Make dots.

Write on a cake.

Draw waves.

Divide icing between multiple small bowls.
Color the icing with food coloring.
Use more than one color.

# basic batters
# and doughs

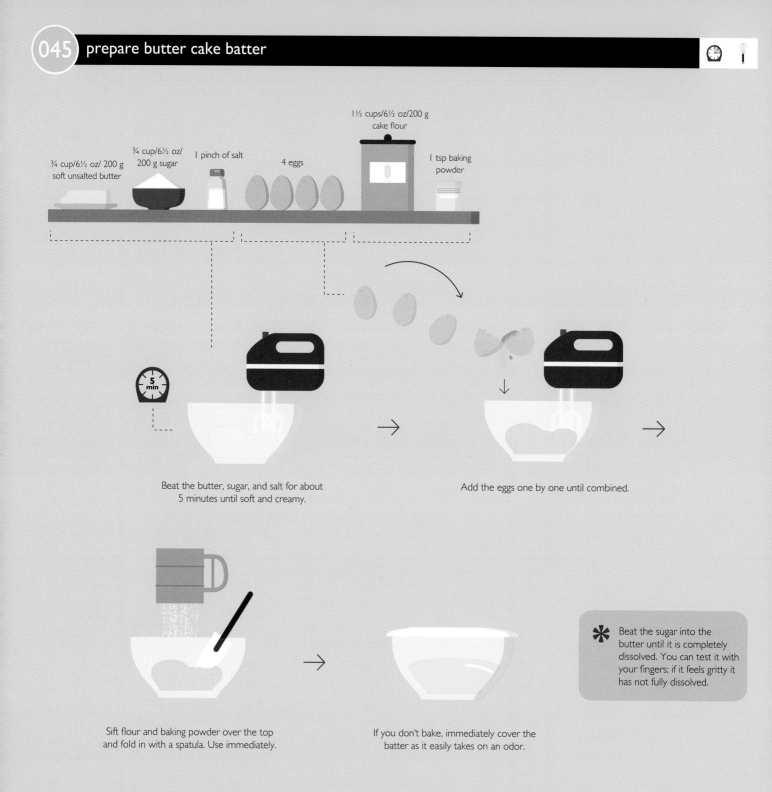

1½ cups/6½ oz/200 g cake flour

¾ cup/6½ oz/ 200 g sugar

1 pinch of salt

4 eggs

¾ cup/6½ oz/ 200 g soft unsalted butter

1 tsp baking powder

5 min

Beat the butter, sugar, and salt for about 5 minutes until soft and creamy.

Add the eggs one by one until combined.

Sift flour and baking powder over the top and fold in with a spatula. Use immediately.

If you don't bake, immediately cover the batter as it easily takes on an odor.

Beat the sugar into the butter until it is completely dissolved. You can test it with your fingers; if it feels gritty it has not fully dissolved.

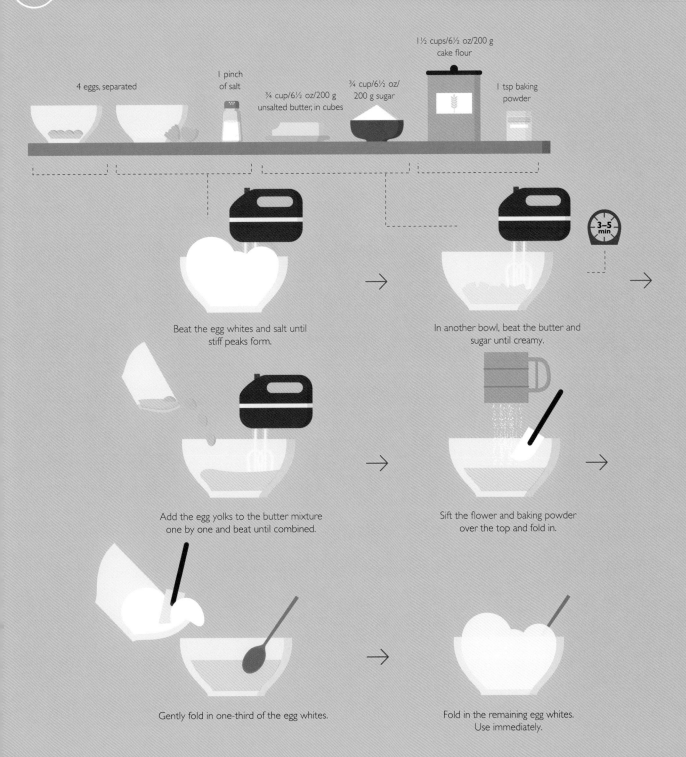

1½ cups/6½ oz/200 g
cake flour

4 eggs, separated

I pinch
of salt

¾ cup/6½ oz/200 g
unsalted butter, in cubes

¾ cup/6½ oz/
200 g sugar

I tsp baking
powder

3–5
min

Beat the egg whites and salt until
stiff peaks form.

In another bowl, beat the butter and
sugar until creamy.

Add the egg yolks to the butter mixture
one by one and beat until combined.

Sift the flower and baking powder
over the top and fold in.

Gently fold in one-third of the egg whites.

Fold in the remaining egg whites.
Use immediately.

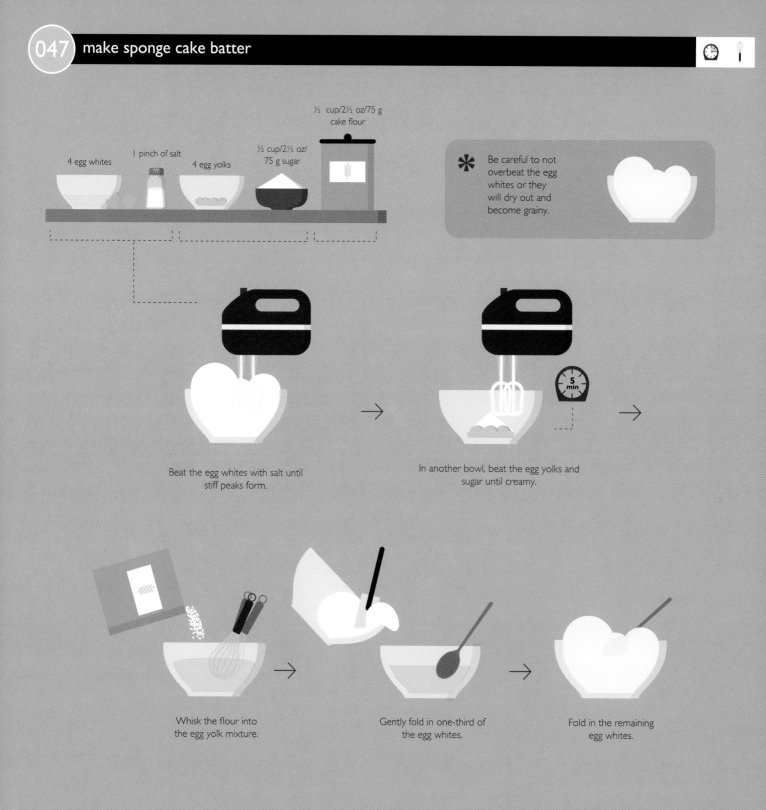

4 egg whites

1 pinch of salt

4 egg yolks

½ cup/2½ oz/75 g sugar

½ cup/2½ oz/75 g cake flour

* Be careful to not overbeat the egg whites or they will dry out and become grainy.

Beat the egg whites with salt until stiff peaks form.

In another bowl, beat the egg yolks and sugar until creamy.

5 min

Whisk the flour into the egg yolk mixture.

Gently fold in one-third of the egg whites.

Fold in the remaining egg whites.

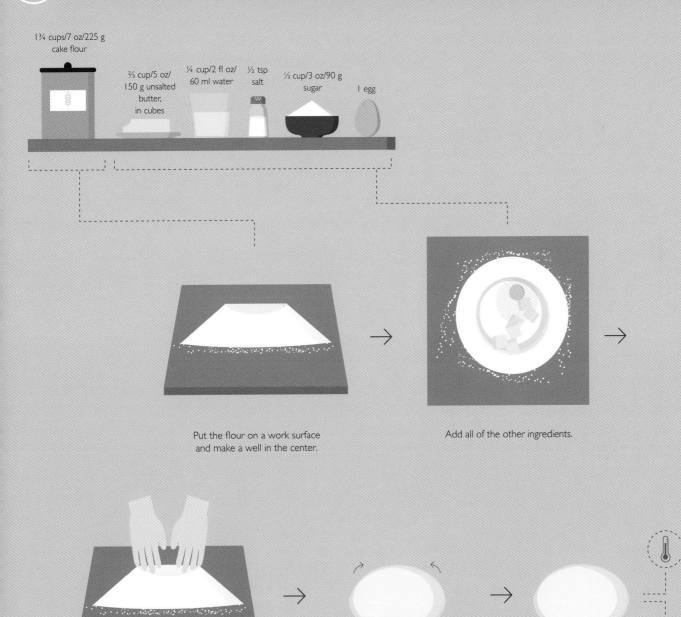

1¾ cups/7 oz/225 g cake flour

⅔ cup/5 oz/150 g unsalted butter, in cubes

¼ cup/2 fl oz/60 ml water

½ tsp salt

⅓ cup/3 oz/90 g sugar

1 egg

Put the flour on a work surface and make a well in the center.

Add all of the other ingredients.

Knead together from the inside to the outside until a smooth dough forms.

Wrap tightly with plastic wrap.

Let it rest in the refrigerator.

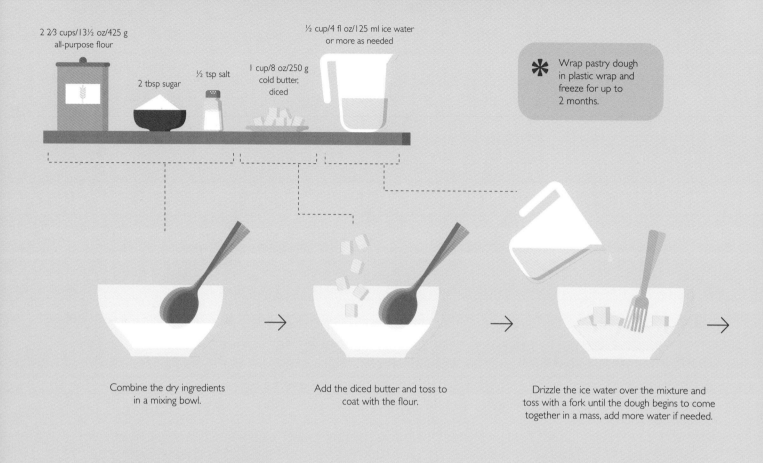

2 2/3 cups/13½ oz/425 g
all-purpose flour

2 tbsp sugar

½ tsp salt

1 cup/8 oz/250 g
cold butter,
diced

½ cup/4 fl oz/125 ml ice water
or more as needed

✳ Wrap pastry dough
in plastic wrap and
freeze for up to
2 months.

Combine the dry ingredients
in a mixing bowl.

Add the diced butter and toss to
coat with the flour.

Drizzle the ice water over the mixture and
toss with a fork until the dough begins to come
together in a mass, add more water if needed.

Transfer the dough to a work surface,
pat into a ball and flatten into a disk.

Wrap with plastic wrap and let rest in
the refrigerator.

30
min

Roll out the dough as directed.

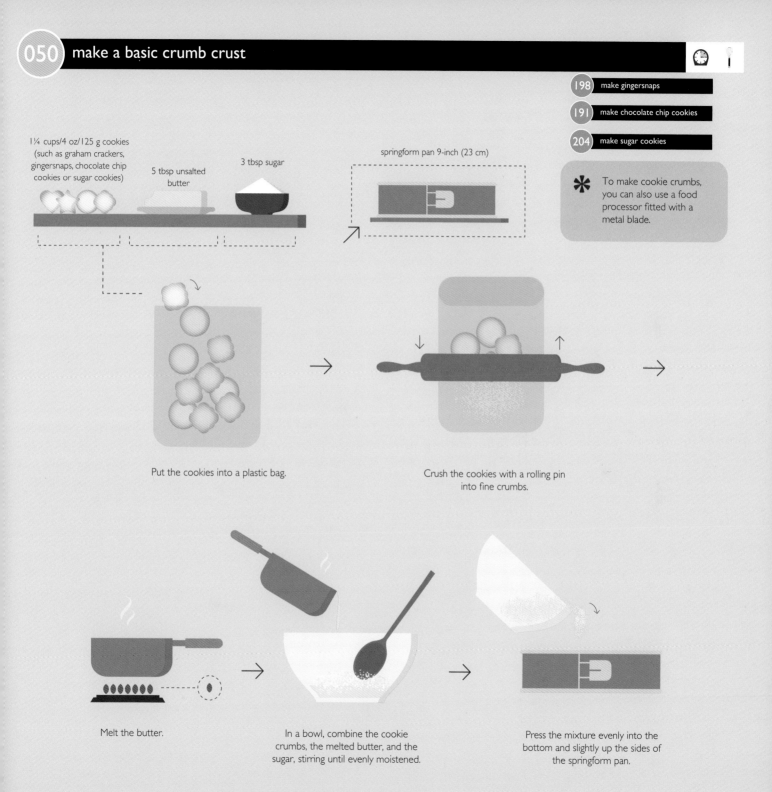

1¼ cups/4 oz/125 g cookies (such as graham crackers, gingersnaps, chocolate chip cookies or sugar cookies)

5 tbsp unsalted butter

3 tbsp sugar

springform pan 9-inch (23 cm)

* To make cookie crumbs, you can also use a food processor fitted with a metal blade.

Put the cookies into a plastic bag.

Crush the cookies with a rolling pin into fine crumbs.

Melt the butter.

In a bowl, combine the cookie crumbs, the melted butter, and the sugar, stirring until evenly moistened.

Press the mixture evenly into the bottom and slightly up the sides of the springform pan.

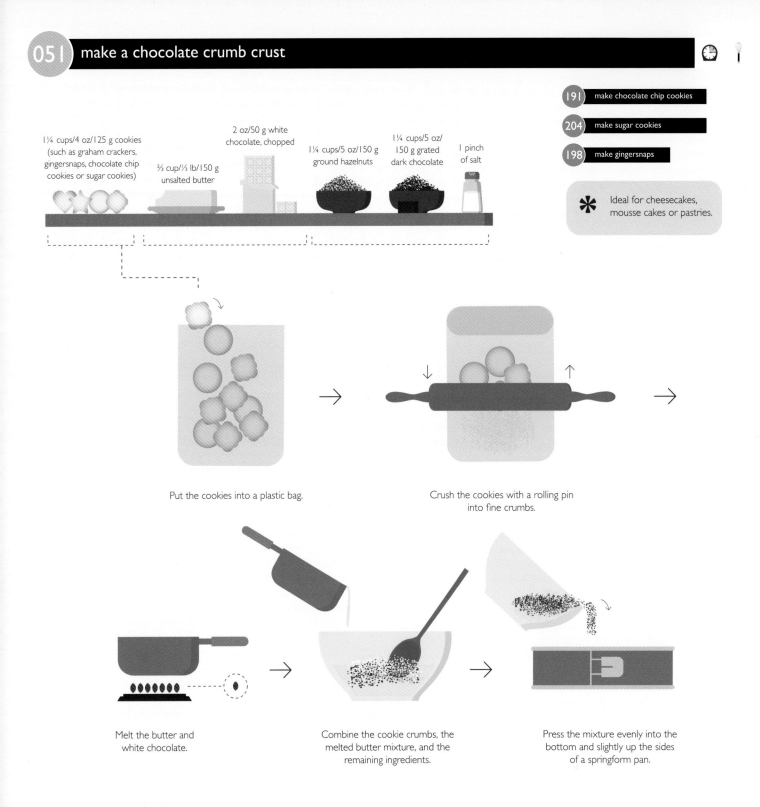

1¼ cups/4 oz/125 g cookies (such as graham crackers, gingersnaps, chocolate chip cookies or sugar cookies)

⅔ cup/⅓ lb/150 g unsalted butter

2 oz/50 g white chocolate, chopped

1¼ cups/5 oz/150 g ground hazelnuts

1¼ cups/5 oz/150 g grated dark chocolate

1 pinch of salt

191 make chocolate chip cookies

204 make sugar cookies

198 make gingersnaps

Ideal for cheesecakes, mousse cakes or pastries.

Put the cookies into a plastic bag.

Crush the cookies with a rolling pin into fine crumbs.

Melt the butter and white chocolate.

Combine the cookie crumbs, the melted butter mixture, and the remaining ingredients.

Press the mixture evenly into the bottom and slightly up the sides of a springform pan.

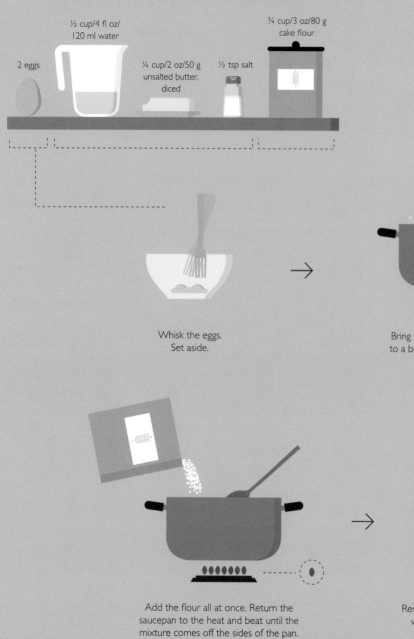

2 eggs

½ cup/4 fl oz/
120 ml water

¼ cup/2 oz/50 g
unsalted butter,
diced

½ tsp salt

¾ cup/3 oz/80 g
cake flour

Whisk the eggs.
Set aside.

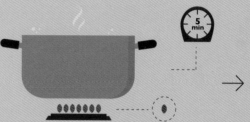

Bring the water, butter, and salt
to a boil; remove from the heat.

Add the flour all at once. Return the
saucepan to the heat and beat until the
mixture comes off the sides of the pan.

Remove from the heat; gradually beat in the
whisked eggs. Use the paste right away.

1 cup/8 fl oz/250 ml whole milk

3 tbsp sugar

2 tbsp unsalted butter

2¼ tsp active dry yeast

3¼ cups/17½ oz/500 g all-purpose flour

3 eggs

1 tsp salt

1 tsp canola oil

✱ Instead of active dry yeast you can use 2¼ tsp/7 g instant yeast. If using instant yeast, mix together all of the ingredients to form a dough, knead the dough, then let it rise for 1 hour.

Warm the milk, sugar, and butter.

Pour into a bowl and let cool to 105°–115°F (40°–46°C).

105°F

Sprinkle the yeast over the milk mixture and whisk it in with 3 tbsp of the flour.

10 min

Let stand until foamy.

Put the remaining flour in a bowl and make a well in the center.

Add the yeast mixture along with the eggs and salt and stir until a soft, sticky dough forms.

10 min

Turn the dough out onto a floured work surface and knead it until it is smooth, elastic, and no longer sticky.

Coat a bowl with the oil, add the dough and cover with plastic wrap.

1 h

Let the dough rise in a warm place until doubled.

1 cup/8 fl oz/250 ml
whole milk

3 tbsp sugar

2 tbsp unsalted
butter

2¼ tsp active
dry yeast

3¼ cups/17½ oz/500 g
all-purpose flour

5 egg yolks

2 eggs

1 tsp
salt

1 tsp canola
oil

Instead of active dry yeast you can use 2¼ tsp/7 g instant yeast. If using instant yeast, mix together all of the ingredients to form a dough, knead the dough, then let it rise for 1 hour.

105°F

Warm the milk, sugar, and butter.

Pour into a bowl and let cool to 105°–115°F (40°–46°C).

Sprinkle the yeast over the milk mixture and whisk in the yeast and 3 tbsp flour.

10 min

Let stand until foamy.

Put the remaining flour in a bowl and make a well in the center.

Add the yeast mixture, butter, egg yolks, eggs, and salt and stir until a soft, sticky dough forms.

10 min

Turn the dough out onto a floured work surface and knead it until it is smooth, elastic, and no longer sticky.

Coat a bowl with the oil, add the dough and cover with plastic wrap.

1 h

Let the dough rise in a warm place until doubled.

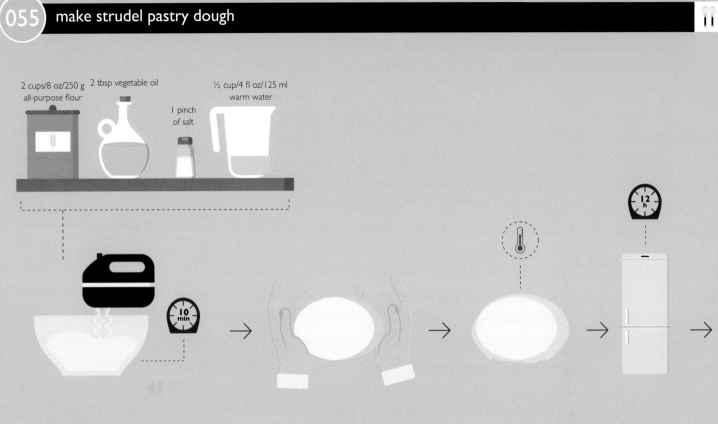

2 cups/8 oz/250 g
all-purpose flour

2 tbsp vegetable oil

1 pinch
of salt

½ cup/4 fl oz/125 ml
warm water

Beat together all ingredients
to form a smooth dough.

Take the dough out of the bowl
and form a ball.

Cover with plastic wrap and chill overnight
in the refrigerator.

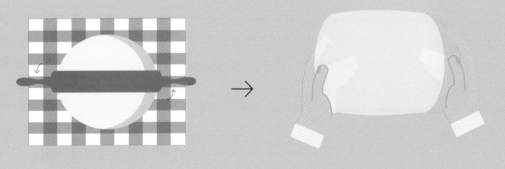

Roll out the dough on a clean,
damp dish towel.

Pull the dough over your hand and stretch it
as thin as possible.

6 egg whites

1¼ cups/10 oz/ 300 g sugar

1 pinch of salt

292 make pastry cream

300 make wine sabayon

✳ Use the egg yolks to make pastry cream or wine sabayon. You can keep them in the refrigerator for a maximum of 1 day.

Whisk together the egg whites, 2 tbsp sugar and the salt.

→

Beat at medium speed until medium peaks form.

→

Slowly add the remaining sugar. Continue to beat until the mixture is thick and glossy.

2–4 drops food coloring

6 egg whites

1¼ cups/10 oz/ 300 g sugar

1 pinch of salt

Whisk together the egg whites, 2 tbsp sugar, and the salt.

→

3 min

Beat at medium speed until medium peaks form.

→

10 min

Slowly add the remaining sugar. Continue to beat until the mixture is thick and glossy. Add 2–4 drops food coloring.

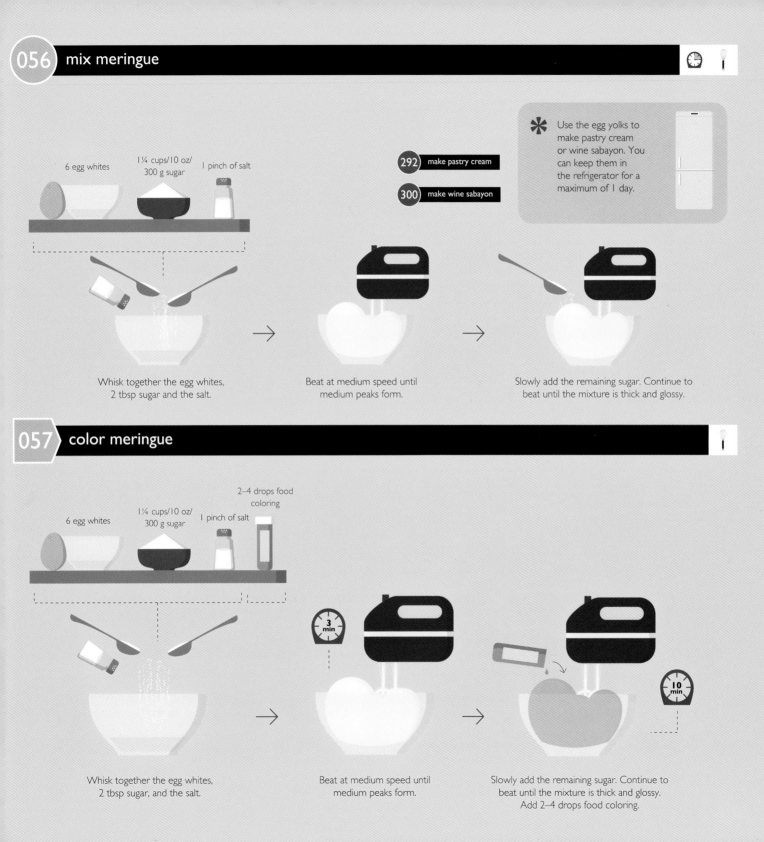

cakes
and
quick breads

I tbsp flour

basic crumb crust

1 cup/8 oz/250 g
cream cheese

1 cup/7 oz/
220 g sugar

2 tbsp vanilla
sugar

4 cups/2 lb/
1 kg ricotta

6 eggs

1 tbsp finely
grated
lemon zest

For a chocolate
crumb crust add
2 tbsps cocoa
to the cookie
crumbs

050 make a basic crumb crust

021 make your own vanilla sugar

springform pan (9½ inches/24 cm),
greased

Press the crumb crust mixture evenly
into the bottom and all the way up the
sides of the springform pan.

2 h

Refrigerate until
well chilled.

350°F/180°C

Preheat the oven.

3 min

For the filling, beat the cream cheese
and both sugars until smooth.

Add the ricotta and beat to combine.

Add the eggs, one at a time,
beating after each addition.

Add the flour and lemon zest
and beat to combine.

Pour the filling into the prepared
crust and spread it evenly.

1 h

350°F/180°C

Bake until the filling
is set and the edges
are slightly puffed.

3 h

Let cool, then cover and refrigerate until
chilled. To serve, unclasp the pan, remove the
sides, and transfer the cake to a serving plate.

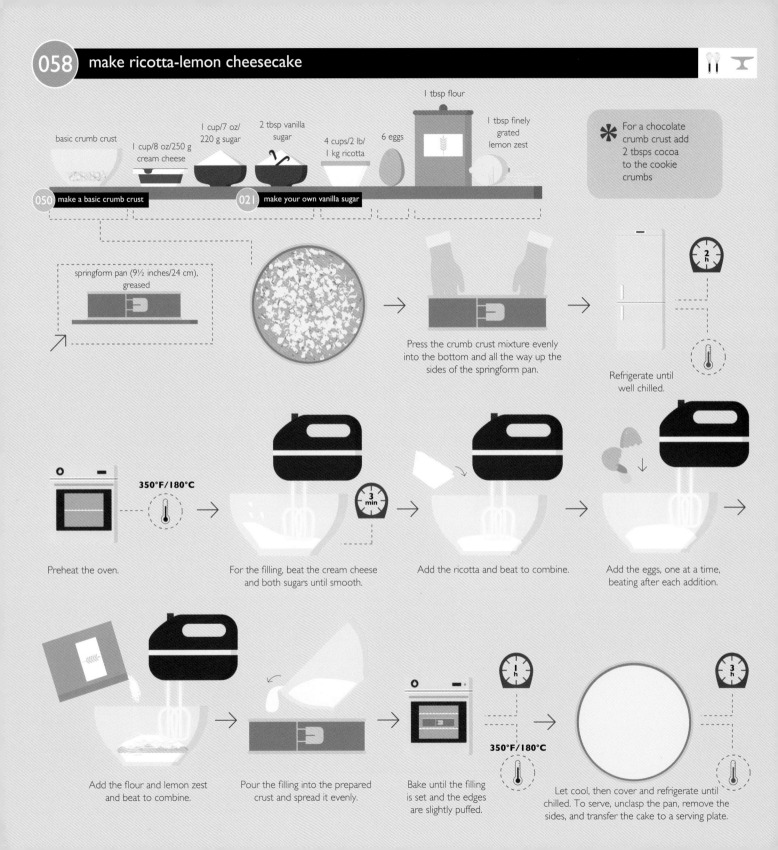

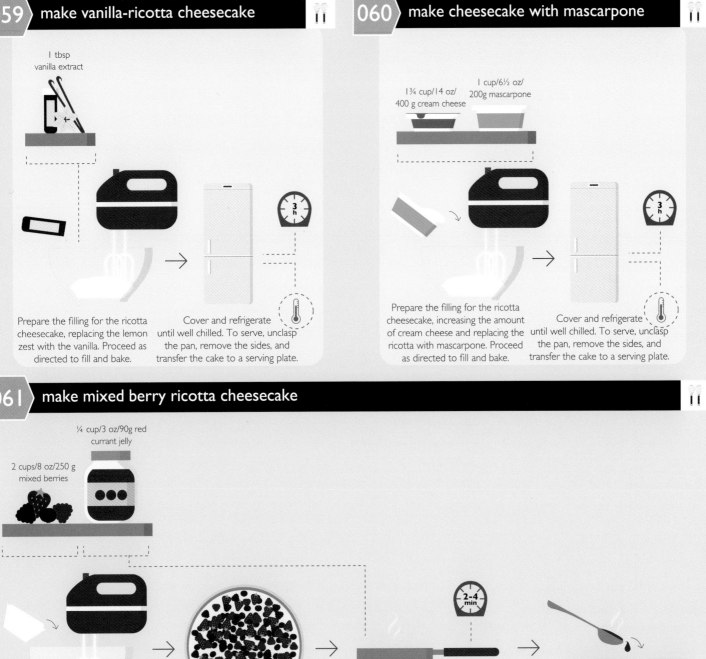

1 tbsp
vanilla extract

Prepare the filling for the ricotta cheesecake, replacing the lemon zest with the vanilla. Proceed as directed to fill and bake.

Cover and refrigerate until well chilled. To serve, unclasp the pan, remove the sides, and transfer the cake to a serving plate.

1¾ cup/14 oz/
400 g cream cheese

1 cup/6½ oz/
200g mascarpone

Prepare the filling for the ricotta cheesecake, increasing the amount of cream cheese and replacing the ricotta with mascarpone. Proceed as directed to fill and bake.

Cover and refrigerate until well chilled. To serve, unclasp the pan, remove the sides, and transfer the cake to a serving plate.

¼ cup/3 oz/90g red
currant jelly

2 cups/8 oz/250 g
mixed berries

Prepare the ricotta-lemon cheesecake as directed.

Arrange the berries on top of the baked and cooled cheesecake.

Heat the currant jelly until it melts.

Drizzle the jelly over the berries, giving the cake a glossy finish. To serve, unclasp the pan, remove the sides, and transfer the cake to a serving plate.

basic crumb crust

ricotta-cream cheese-filling

2 tbsp unsalted butter

4 cups/1 lb/500 g cherries, pitted

2 tbsp lemon juice

¼ cup/2 oz/ 60 g sugar

1 tbsp amaretto

1 tbsp unsalted butter

⅓ cup/ 1½ oz/45 g sliced almonds

1 cup/8 oz/ 225 g sour cream

¼ cup/2 oz/ 60 g sugar

1 tsp vanilla extract

1 tsp almond extract

050 make a basic crumb crust

058 ricotta-cheesecake

Press the crumb crust mixture evenly into the bottom and all the way up the sides of the springform pan; refrigerate until chilled. Prepare the filling for the ricotta-lemon cheesecake, then set aside.

Melt the 2 tbsp butter. Add the cherries, lemon juice, ¼ cup sugar, and the amaretto. Let come to a boil briefly, then reduce the heat and let simmer.

5-7 min

Preheat the oven.

350°F/180°C

Transfer the cherry mixture to a bowl and let cool completely.

15 min

Pour the cherry mixture into the prepared crust and spread it evenly. Add the ricotta-lemon filling and spread it to the pan edges.

Bake until the filling is set and the edges are slightly puffed.

1 h

350°F/180°C

Melt the 1 tbsp butter. Add the sliced almonds and toast until golden.

Beat together the sour cream, ¼ cup sugar, vanilla, and almond extract.

Spread the topping over the warm cheesecake.

Sprinkle the cake with the toasted almonds.

Bake until the topping looks slightly set.

8 min

320°F/160°C

Cover and refrigerate until well chilled. To serve, unclasp the pan, remove the sides and transfer the cake to a serving plate.

3 h

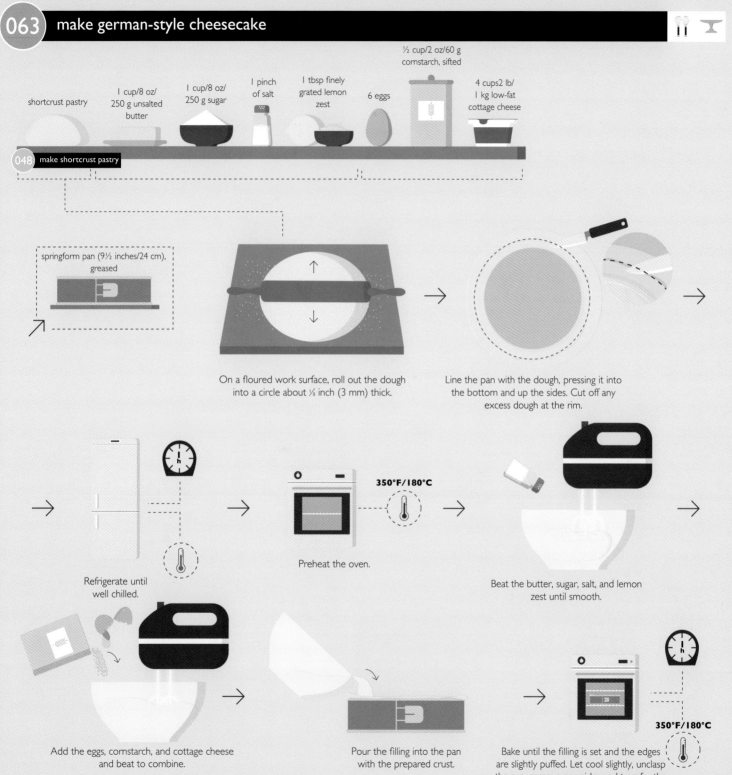

shortcrust pastry

I cup/8 oz/ 250 g unsalted butter

I cup/8 oz/ 250 g sugar

I pinch of salt

I tbsp finely grated lemon zest

6 eggs

½ cup/2 oz/60 g cornstarch, sifted

4 cups2 lb/ I kg low-fat cottage cheese

048 make shortcrust pastry

springform pan (9½ inches/24 cm), greased

On a floured work surface, roll out the dough into a circle about ⅛ inch (3 mm) thick.

Line the pan with the dough, pressing it into the bottom and up the sides. Cut off any excess dough at the rim.

Refrigerate until well chilled.

**350°F/180°C**

Preheat the oven.

Beat the butter, sugar, salt, and lemon zest until smooth.

Add the eggs, cornstarch, and cottage cheese and beat to combine.

Pour the filling into the pan with the prepared crust.

Bake until the filling is set and the edges are slightly puffed. Let cool slightly, unclasp the pan, remove pan sides and transfer the cake to a serving plate. Refrigerate until chilled.

**350°F/180°C**

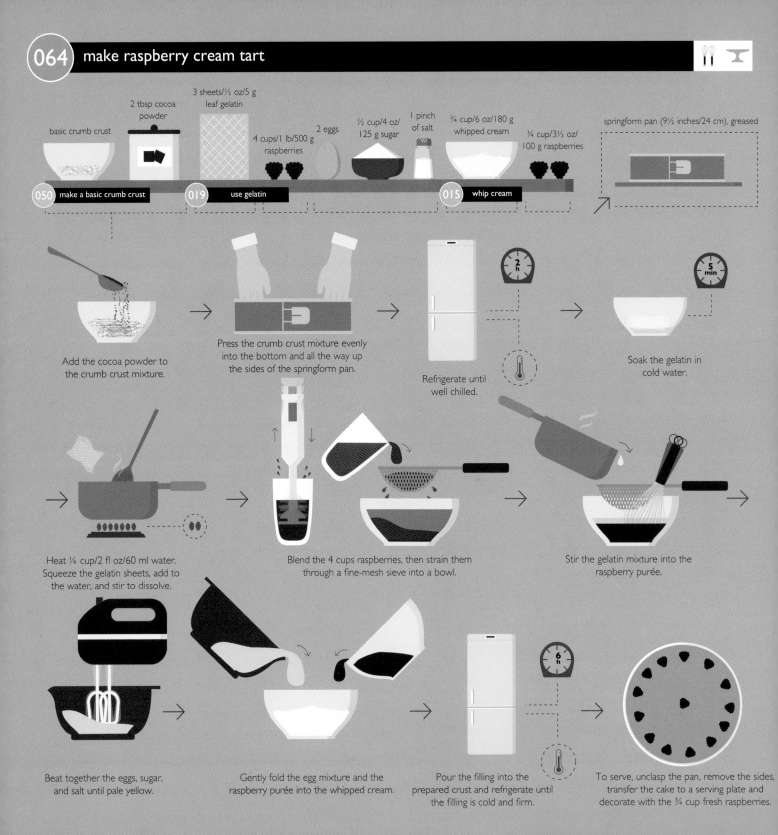

basic crumb crust

2 tbsp cocoa powder

3 sheets/½ oz/5 g leaf gelatin

4 cups/1 lb/500 g raspberries

2 eggs

½ cup/4 oz/ 125 g sugar

1 pinch of salt

¾ cup/6 oz/180 g whipped cream

¾ cup/3½ oz/ 100 g raspberries

springform pan (9½ inches/24 cm), greased

050 make a basic crumb crust

019 use gelatin

015 whip cream

Add the cocoa powder to the crumb crust mixture.

Press the crumb crust mixture evenly into the bottom and all the way up the sides of the springform pan.

Refrigerate until well chilled.

2 h

5 min

Soak the gelatin in cold water.

Heat ¼ cup/2 fl oz/60 ml water. Squeeze the gelatin sheets, add to the water, and stir to dissolve.

Blend the 4 cups raspberries, then strain them through a fine-mesh sieve into a bowl.

Stir the gelatin mixture into the raspberry purée.

Beat together the eggs, sugar, and salt until pale yellow.

Gently fold the egg mixture and the raspberry purée into the whipped cream.

Pour the filling into the prepared crust and refrigerate until the filling is cold and firm.

6 h

To serve, unclasp the pan, remove the sides, transfer the cake to a serving plate and decorate with the ¾ cup fresh raspberries.

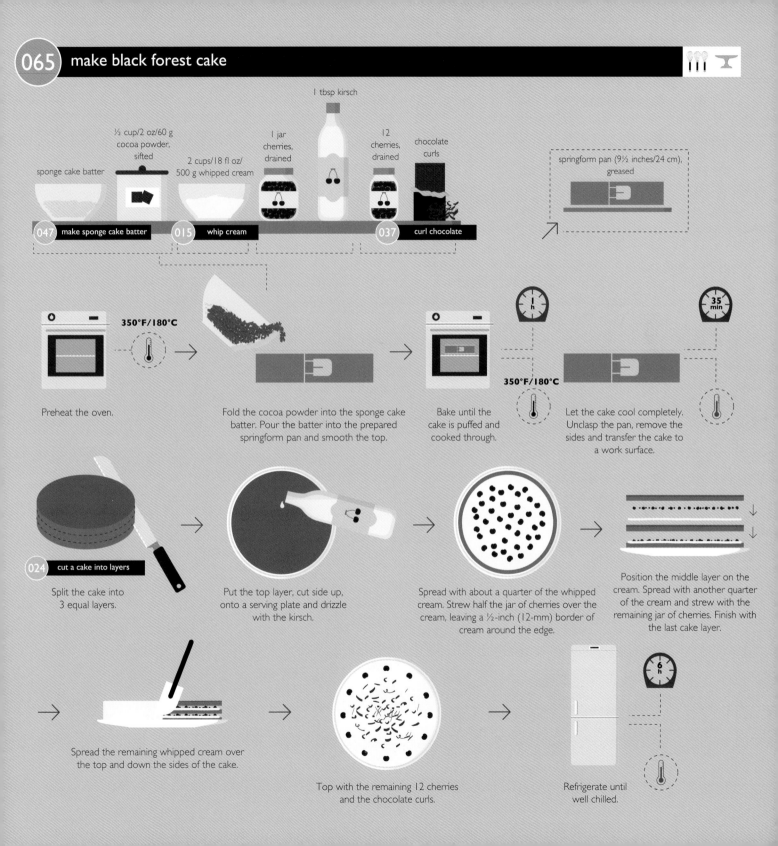

1 tbsp kirsch

½ cup/2 oz/60 g
cocoa powder,
sifted

2 cups/18 fl oz/
500 g whipped cream

1 jar
cherries,
drained

12
cherries,
drained

chocolate
curls

sponge cake batter

springform pan (9½ inches/24 cm),
greased

047 make sponge cake batter

015 whip cream

037 curl chocolate

350°F/180°C

Preheat the oven.

Fold the cocoa powder into the sponge cake
batter. Pour the batter into the prepared
springform pan and smooth the top.

Bake until the
cake is puffed and
cooked through.

1 h

35 min

350°F/180°C

Let the cake cool completely.
Unclasp the pan, remove the
sides and transfer the cake to
a work surface.

024 cut a cake into layers

Split the cake into
3 equal layers.

Put the top layer, cut side up,
onto a serving plate and drizzle
with the kirsch.

Spread with about a quarter of the whipped
cream. Strew half the jar of cherries over the
cream, leaving a ½-inch (12-mm) border of
cream around the edge.

Position the middle layer on the
cream. Spread with another quarter
of the cream and strew with the
remaining jar of cherries. Finish with
the last cake layer.

Spread the remaining whipped cream over
the top and down the sides of the cake.

Top with the remaining 12 cherries
and the chocolate curls.

6 h

Refrigerate until
well chilled.

½ cup/4 fl oz/125 ml framboise

20 ladyfingers

4 sheets/¼ oz/ 7 g sheets leaf gelatin

3 cups/ 12 oz/375 g raspberries

2 cups/ 8 oz/250 g strawberries, hulled

½ cup/4 oz/ 60 g sugar, plus 3 tbsp

3 egg yolks

1 cup/8 fl oz/ 250 ml whipped cream

**217** make classic ladyfingers | **019** use gelatin | **015** whip cream

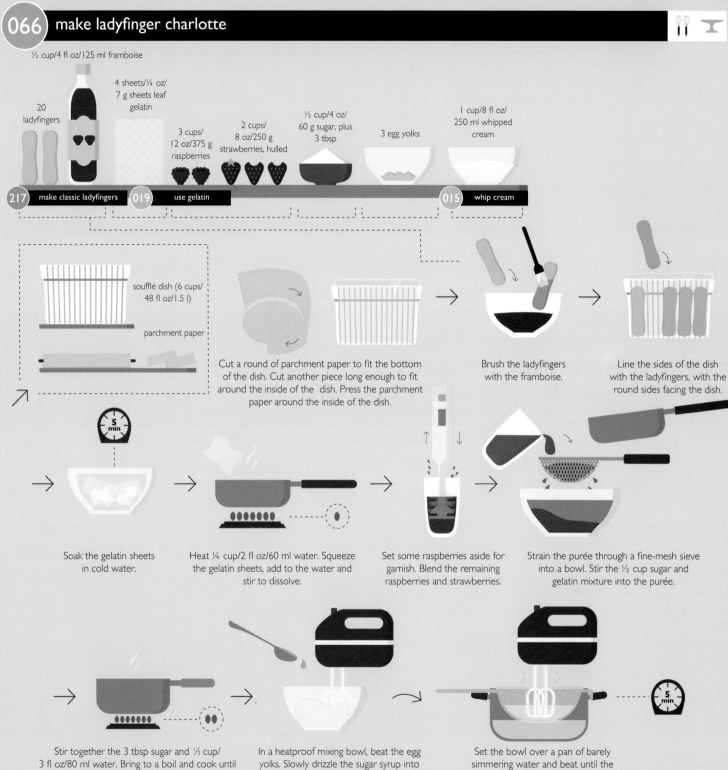

soufflé dish (6 cups/ 48 fl oz/1.5 l)

parchment paper

Cut a round of parchment paper to fit the bottom of the dish. Cut another piece long enough to fit around the inside of the dish. Press the parchment paper around the inside of the dish.

Brush the ladyfingers with the framboise.

Line the sides of the dish with the ladyfingers, with the round sides facing the dish.

Soak the gelatin sheets in cold water.

Heat ¼ cup/2 fl oz/60 ml water. Squeeze the gelatin sheets, add to the water and stir to dissolve.

Set some raspberries aside for garnish. Blend the remaining raspberries and strawberries.

Strain the purée through a fine-mesh sieve into a bowl. Stir the ½ cup sugar and gelatin mixture into the purée.

Stir together the 3 tbsp sugar and ⅓ cup/ 3 fl oz/80 ml water. Bring to a boil and cook until the sugar dissolves and becomes syrupy.

In a heatproof mixing bowl, beat the egg yolks. Slowly drizzle the sugar syrup into the egg yolks while beating.

Set the bowl over a pan of barely simmering water and beat until the mixture is thick and pale yellow.

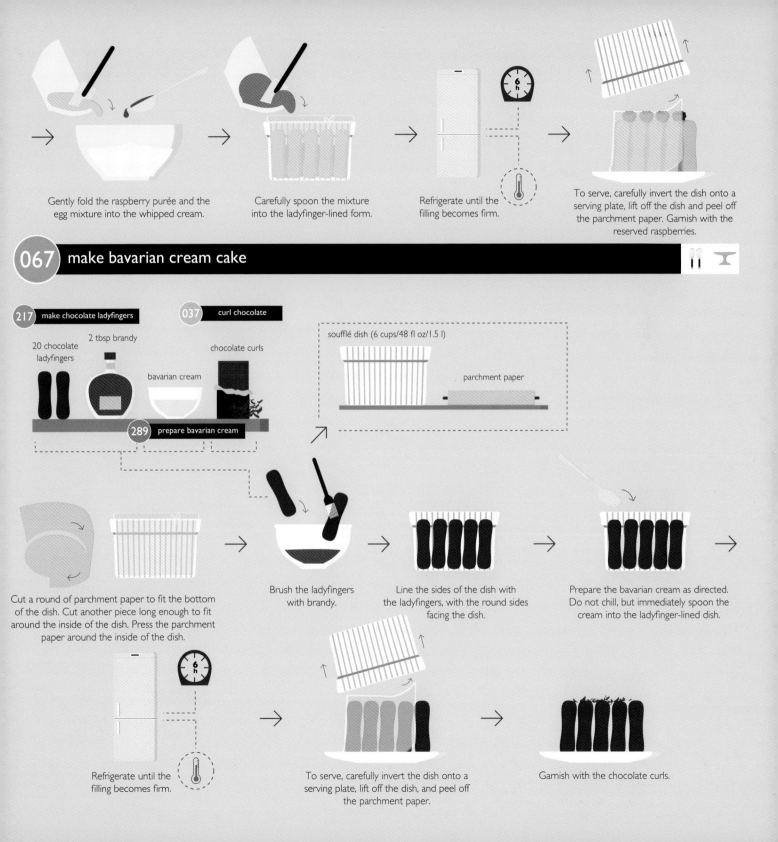

Gently fold the raspberry purée and the egg mixture into the whipped cream.

Carefully spoon the mixture into the ladyfinger-lined form.

Refrigerate until the filling becomes firm.

To serve, carefully invert the dish onto a serving plate, lift off the dish and peel off the parchment paper. Garnish with the reserved raspberries.

## 067 make bavarian cream cake

**217** make chocolate ladyfingers

**037** curl chocolate

20 chocolate ladyfingers

2 tbsp brandy

chocolate curls

bavarian cream

**289** prepare bavarian cream

soufflé dish (6 cups/48 fl oz/1.5 l)

parchment paper

Cut a round of parchment paper to fit the bottom of the dish. Cut another piece long enough to fit around the inside of the dish. Press the parchment paper around the inside of the dish.

Brush the ladyfingers with brandy.

Line the sides of the dish with the ladyfingers, with the round sides facing the dish.

Prepare the bavarian cream as directed. Do not chill, but immediately spoon the cream into the ladyfinger-lined dish.

Refrigerate until the filling becomes firm.

To serve, carefully invert the dish onto a serving plate, lift off the dish, and peel off the parchment paper.

Garnish with the chocolate curls.

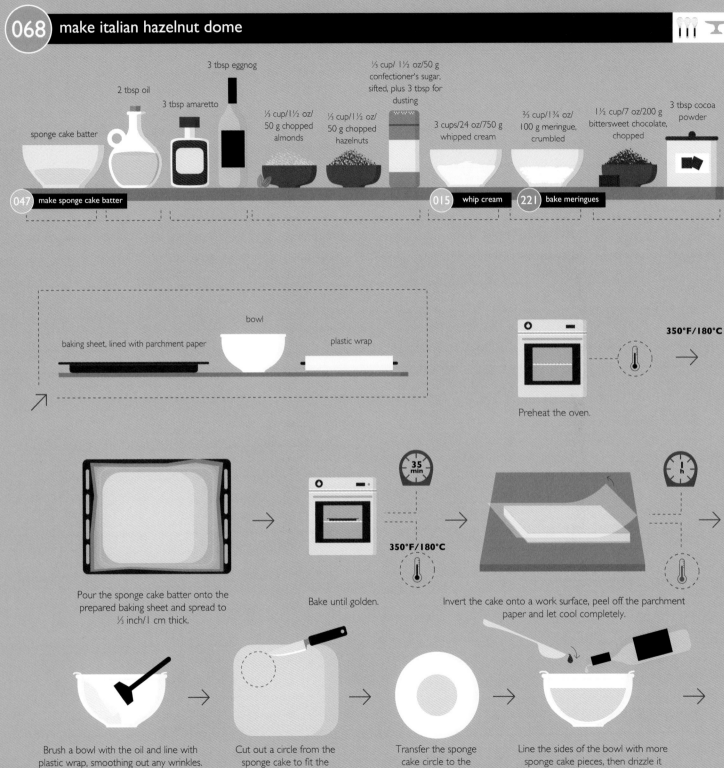

3 tbsp eggnog

2 tbsp oil

3 tbsp amaretto

⅓ cup/ 1½ oz/50 g confectioner's sugar, sifted, plus 3 tbsp for dusting

⅓ cup/1½ oz/ 50 g chopped almonds

⅓ cup/1½ oz/ 50 g chopped hazelnuts

3 cups/24 oz/750 g whipped cream

⅔ cup/1¾ oz/ 100 g meringue, crumbled

1½ cup/7 oz/200 g bittersweet chocolate, chopped

3 tbsp cocoa powder

sponge cake batter

047 make sponge cake batter

015 whip cream

221 bake meringues

baking sheet, lined with parchment paper

bowl

plastic wrap

350°F/180°C

Preheat the oven.

Pour the sponge cake batter onto the prepared baking sheet and spread to ⅓ inch/1 cm thick.

35 min

350°F/180°C

Bake until golden.

Invert the cake onto a work surface, peel off the parchment paper and let cool completely.

Brush a bowl with the oil and line with plastic wrap, smoothing out any wrinkles.

Cut out a circle from the sponge cake to fit the bottom of the bowl.

Transfer the sponge cake circle to the plastic wrap-lined bowl.

Line the sides of the bowl with more sponge cake pieces, then drizzle it with the amaretto and eggnog.

Lightly toast the almonds and hazelnuts, then stir in the ⅓ cup confectioner's sugar. Let cool.

Gently fold the nut mixture into the whipped cream.

Divide the nut-cream mixture evenly between two bowls.

Melt half of the chopped chocolate. Let cool slightly.

Gently fold the melted chocolate and the remaining chopped chocolate into one part of the nut-cream mixture.

Stir the meringue crumbs into the other half.

Alternately spread light and dark cream layers into the sponge cake-lined form. Finish with one layer of sponge cake

Refrigerate until well chilled.

To serve, carefully invert the dish onto a serving plate and lift off the dish.

Carefully peel off the plastic wrap.

Mix the cocoa powder and 3 tbsp confectioner's sugar.

Dust the hazelnut dome with the cocoa sugar.

* Finish the cake with chocolate icing instead of dusting with cocoa.

031 make chocolate icing

I cup/8 fl oz/ 250 ml rum

I ¾ cup/7 oz/200 g confectioner's sugar, sifted

sponge cake batter

⅔ cup/5 oz/ 150 g sugar

¾ cup/6 oz/ 185 g unsalted butter

4 egg yolks

I ½ cups/6 oz/ 180 g ground almonds

¾ cup/5 oz/ 150 g heavy cream

20 ladyfingers

I cup/8 oz/250 ml whipped cream

047 make sponge cake batter

217 make classic ladyfingers

015 whip cream

ladyfingers for garnishing

chocolate curls

I pastry bag with star tip

springform pan (9½ inches/24 cm), greased

037 curl chocolate

350°F/180°C

Preheat the oven.

Pour the sponge cake batter into the prepared springform pan.

35 min

350°F/180°C

Bake until golden.

024 cut a cake into layers

Unmold the cake, put on a work surface, and split into 2 equal layers.

2-4 min

Heat the sugar together with ⅔ cup/ 5 fl oz/150 ml water, stirring until the sugar dissolves. Add the rum.

Beat the butter and confectioners' sugar until smooth. Add the egg yolks, one at a time, beating well after each addition.

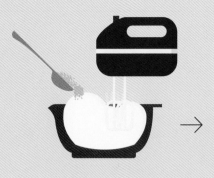

Add the ground almonds and heavy cream and beat until a stiff batter forms.

Place one cake layer into a greased springform pan. Drizzle with some of the rum syrup and spread with one-third of the almond-cream mixture.

Brush the ladyfingers with rum syrup.

Layer half of the ladyfingers side by side onto the almond-cream mixture. Repeat with another layer of the almond-cream mixture and the remaining ladyfingers.

Finish with the remaining almond-cream mixture.

Top with the second sponge cake layer.

Cover and refrigerate until well chilled.

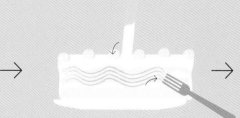

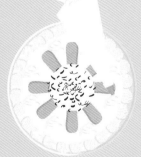

To serve, unclasp the pan, remove the sides, and transfer the cake to a serving plate.

Frost the cake with about two thirds of the whipped cream, spreading over the top and down the sides. Use a fork to draw a wave pattern on the sides of the cake.

Fill a pastry bag fitted with a star tip with the remaining whipped cream and pipe rosettes around the border of the cake. Decorate the top with halved ladyfingers and chocolate curls.

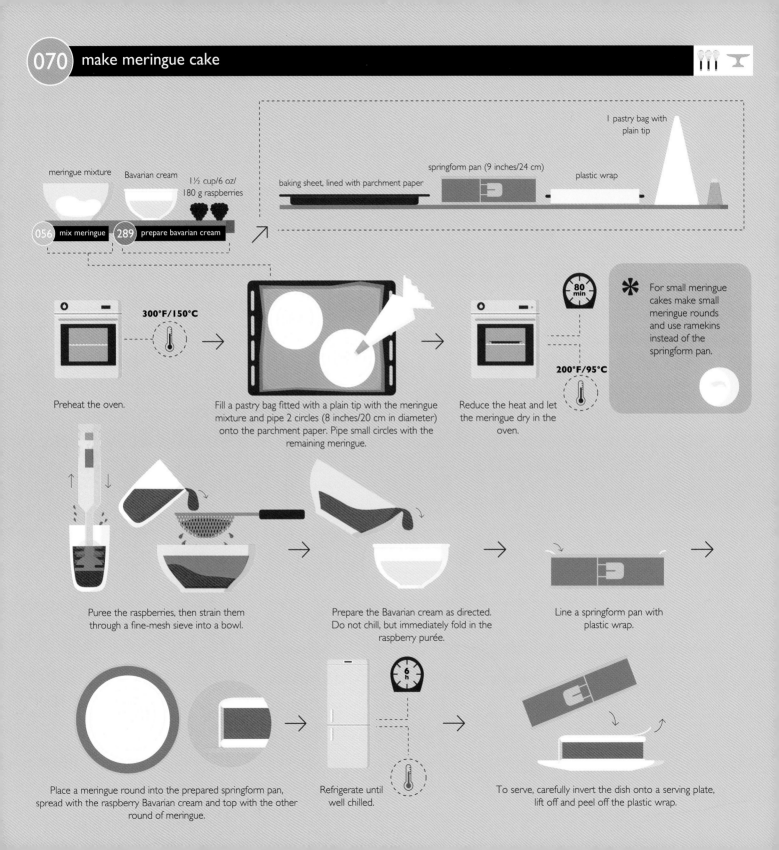

meringue mixture

Bavarian cream

1 ½ cup/6 oz/ 180 g raspberries

056 mix meringue

289 prepare bavarian cream

baking sheet, lined with parchment paper

springform pan (9 inches/24 cm)

plastic wrap

1 pastry bag with plain tip

**300°F/150°C**

Preheat the oven.

Fill a pastry bag fitted with a plain tip with the meringue mixture and pipe 2 circles (8 inches/20 cm in diameter) onto the parchment paper. Pipe small circles with the remaining meringue.

**80 min**

Reduce the heat and let the meringue dry in the oven.

**200°F/95°C**

* For small meringue cakes make small meringue rounds and use ramekins instead of the springform pan.

Puree the raspberries, then strain them through a fine-mesh sieve into a bowl.

Prepare the Bavarian cream as directed. Do not chill, but immediately fold in the raspberry purée.

Line a springform pan with plastic wrap.

Place a meringue round into the prepared springform pan, spread with the raspberry Bavarian cream and top with the other round of meringue.

**6 h**

Refrigerate until well chilled.

To serve, carefully invert the dish onto a serving plate, lift off and peel off the plastic wrap.

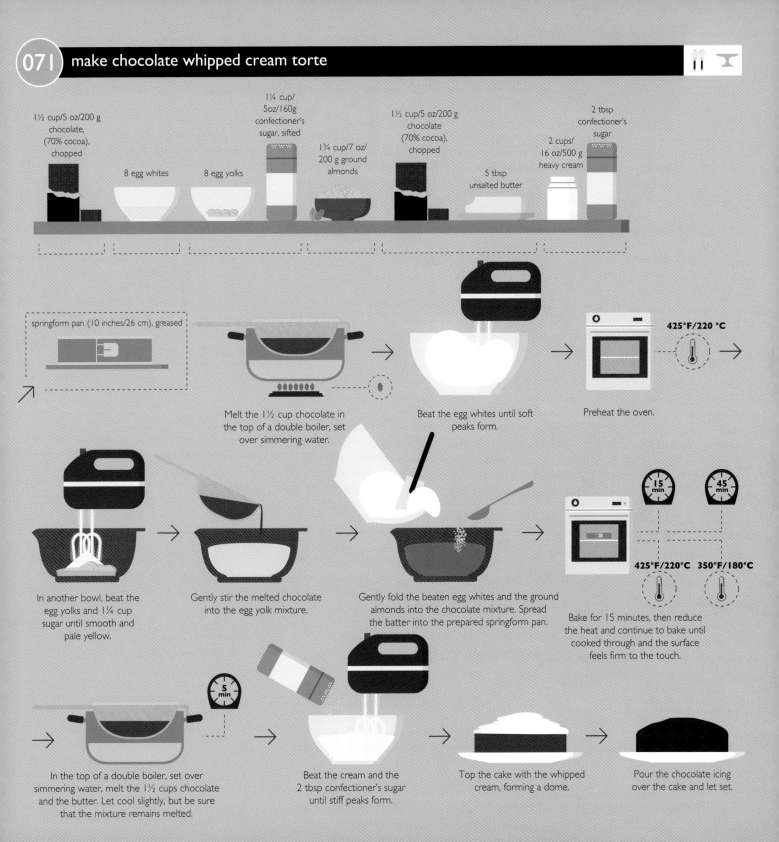

1½ cup/5 oz/200 g chocolate, (70% cocoa), chopped

8 egg whites

8 egg yolks

1¼ cup/ 5oz/160g confectioner's sugar, sifted

1¾ cup/7 oz/ 200 g ground almonds

1½ cup/5 oz/200 g chocolate (70% cocoa), chopped

5 tbsp unsalted butter

2 cups/ 16 oz/500 g heavy cream

2 tbsp confectioner's sugar

springform pan (10 inches/26 cm), greased

Melt the 1½ cup chocolate in the top of a double boiler, set over simmering water.

Beat the egg whites until soft peaks form.

425°F/220 °C

Preheat the oven.

In another bowl, beat the egg yolks and 1¼ cup sugar until smooth and pale yellow.

Gently stir the melted chocolate into the egg yolk mixture.

Gently fold the beaten egg whites and the ground almonds into the chocolate mixture. Spread the batter into the prepared springform pan.

15 min

45 min

425°F/220°C   350°F/180°C

Bake for 15 minutes, then reduce the heat and continue to bake until cooked through and the surface feels firm to the touch.

In the top of a double boiler, set over simmering water, melt the 1½ cups chocolate and the butter. Let cool slightly, but be sure that the mixture remains melted.

5 min

Beat the cream and the 2 tbsp confectioner's sugar until stiff peaks form.

Top the cake with the whipped cream, forming a dome.

Pour the chocolate icing over the cake and let set.

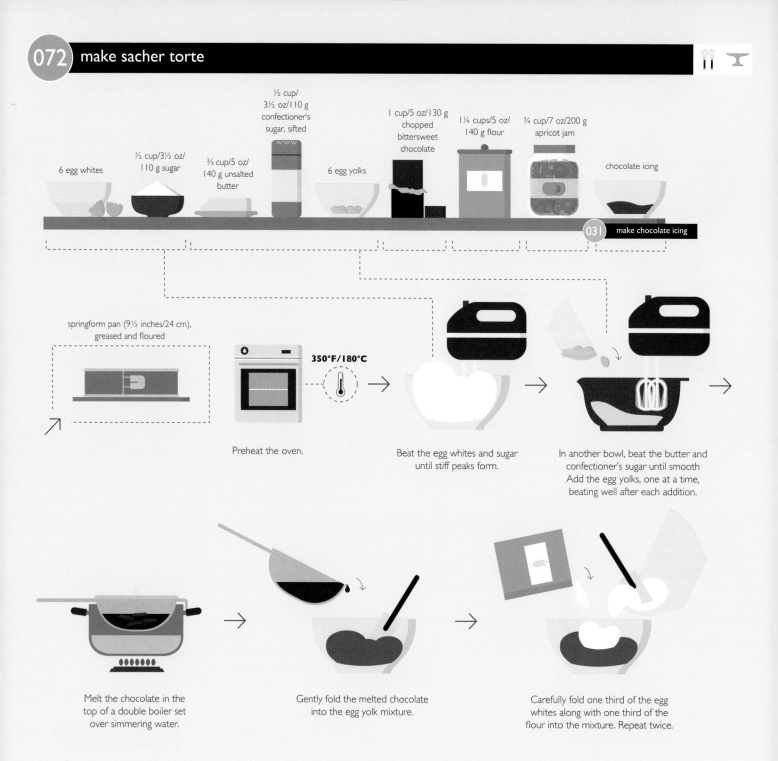

½ cup/
3½ oz/110 g
confectioner's
sugar, sifted

1 cup/5 oz/130 g
chopped
bittersweet
chocolate

1¼ cups/5 oz/
140 g flour

¾ cup/7 oz/200 g
apricot jam

½ cup/3½ oz/
110 g sugar

⅔ cup/5 oz/
140 g unsalted
butter

chocolate icing

6 egg whites

6 egg yolks

031 make chocolate icing

springform pan (9½ inches/24 cm),
greased and floured

350°F/180°C

Preheat the oven.

Beat the egg whites and sugar
until stiff peaks form.

In another bowl, beat the butter and
confectioner's sugar until smooth
Add the egg yolks, one at a time,
beating well after each addition.

Melt the chocolate in the
top of a double boiler set
over simmering water.

Gently fold the melted chocolate
into the egg yolk mixture.

Carefully fold one third of the egg
whites along with one third of the
flour into the mixture. Repeat twice.

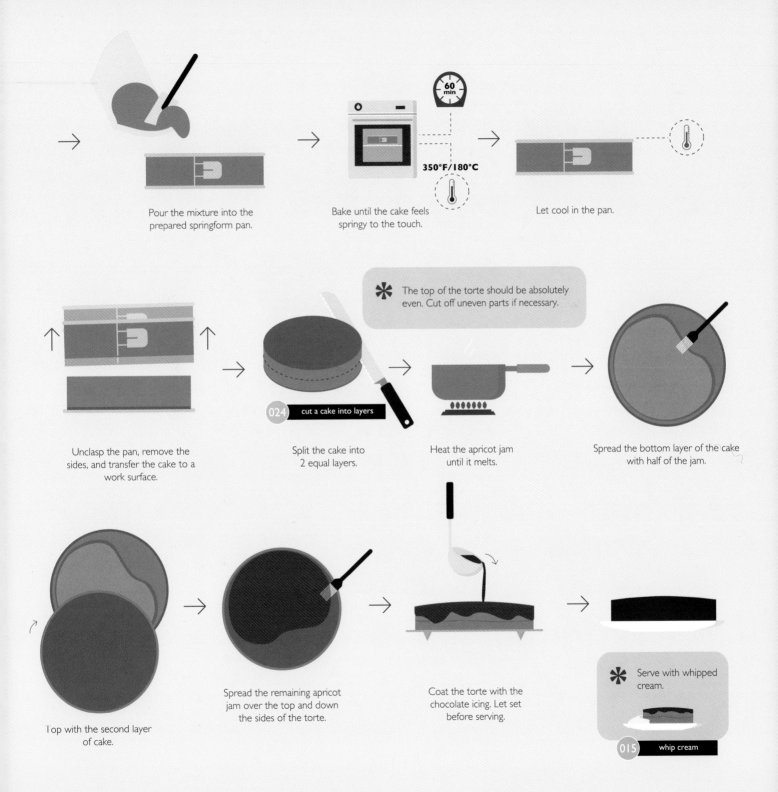

Pour the mixture into the prepared springform pan.

Bake until the cake feels springy to the touch.

350°F/180°C

Let cool in the pan.

Unclasp the pan, remove the sides, and transfer the cake to a work surface.

The top of the torte should be absolutely even. Cut off uneven parts if necessary.

024 cut a cake into layers

Split the cake into 2 equal layers.

Heat the apricot jam until it melts.

Spread the bottom layer of the cake with half of the jam.

Top with the second layer of cake.

Spread the remaining apricot jam over the top and down the sides of the torte.

Coat the torte with the chocolate icing. Let set before serving.

Serve with whipped cream.

015 whip cream

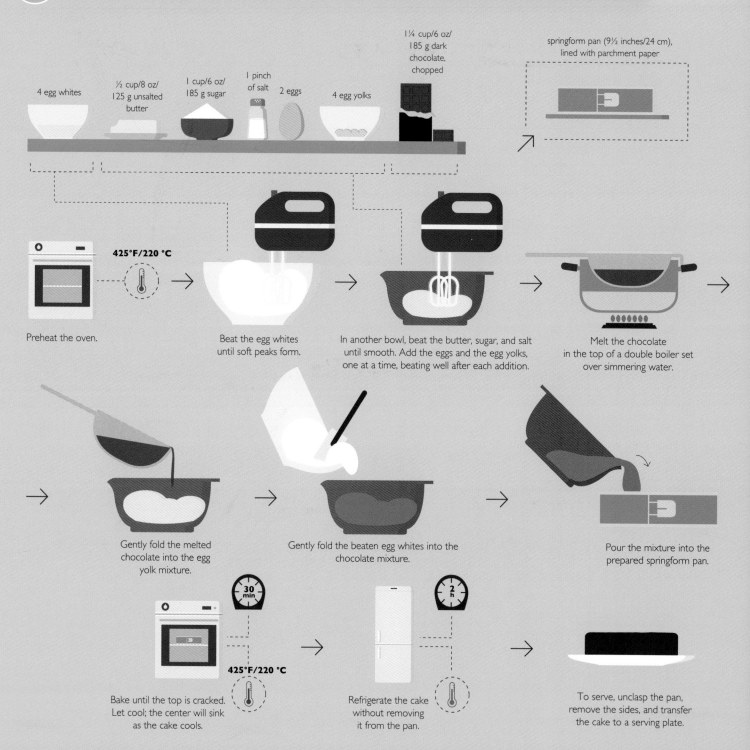

4 egg whites

½ cup/8 oz/ 125 g unsalted butter

1 cup/6 oz/ 185 g sugar

1 pinch of salt

2 eggs

4 egg yolks

1¼ cup/6 oz/ 185 g dark chocolate, chopped

springform pan (9½ inches/24 cm), lined with parchment paper

**425°F/220 °C**

Preheat the oven.

Beat the egg whites until soft peaks form.

In another bowl, beat the butter, sugar, and salt until smooth. Add the eggs and the egg yolks, one at a time, beating well after each addition.

Melt the chocolate in the top of a double boiler set over simmering water.

Gently fold the melted chocolate into the egg yolk mixture.

Gently fold the beaten egg whites into the chocolate mixture.

Pour the mixture into the prepared springform pan.

30 min

Bake until the top is cracked. Let cool; the center will sink as the cake cools.

**425°F/220 °C**

2 h

Refrigerate the cake without removing it from the pan.

To serve, unclasp the pan, remove the sides, and transfer the cake to a serving plate.

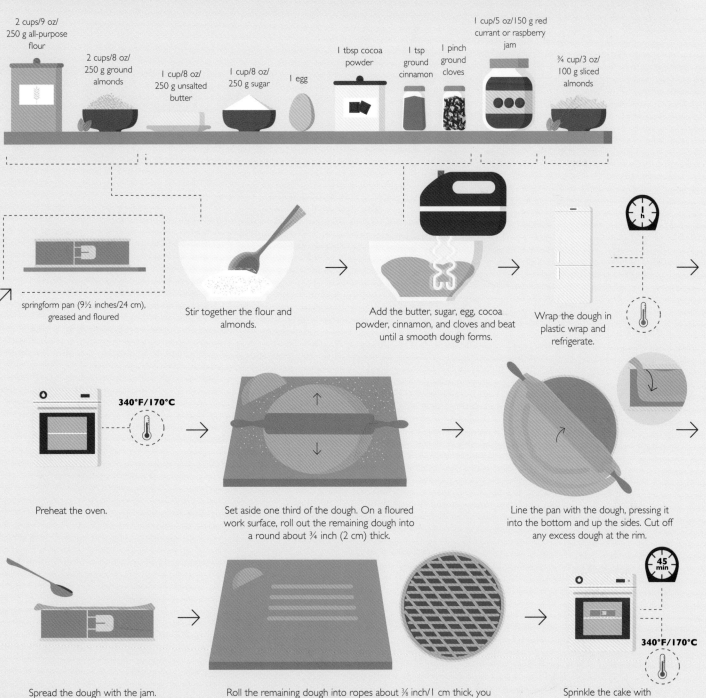

2 cups/9 oz/ 250 g all-purpose flour

2 cups/8 oz/ 250 g ground almonds

1 cup/8 oz/ 250 g unsalted butter

1 cup/8 oz/ 250 g sugar

1 egg

1 tbsp cocoa powder

1 tsp ground cinnamon

1 pinch ground cloves

1 cup/5 oz/150 g red currant or raspberry jam

¾ cup/3 oz/ 100 g sliced almonds

springform pan (9½ inches/24 cm), greased and floured

Stir together the flour and almonds.

Add the butter, sugar, egg, cocoa powder, cinnamon, and cloves and beat until a smooth dough forms.

Wrap the dough in plastic wrap and refrigerate.

340°F/170°C

Preheat the oven.

Set aside one third of the dough. On a floured work surface, roll out the remaining dough into a round about ¾ inch (2 cm) thick.

Line the pan with the dough, pressing it into the bottom and up the sides. Cut off any excess dough at the rim.

Spread the dough with the jam.

Roll the remaining dough into ropes about ⅜ inch/1 cm thick, you should have 16–20. Use the ropes to weave a lattice-top.

45 min

340°F/170°C

Sprinkle the cake with sliced almonds and bake until golden brown.

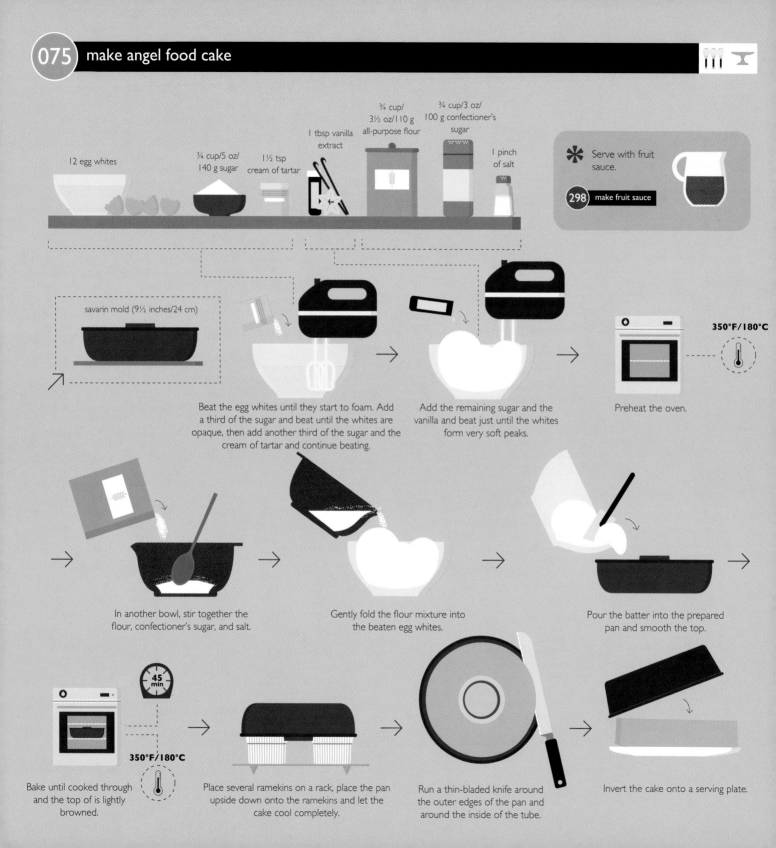

12 egg whites

¾ cup/5 oz/ 140 g sugar

1½ tsp cream of tartar

1 tbsp vanilla extract

¾ cup/ 3½ oz/110 g all-purpose flour

¾ cup/3 oz/ 100 g confectioner's sugar

1 pinch of salt

Serve with fruit sauce.

298 make fruit sauce

savarin mold (9½ inches/24 cm)

Beat the egg whites until they start to foam. Add a third of the sugar and beat until the whites are opaque, then add another third of the sugar and the cream of tartar and continue beating.

Add the remaining sugar and the vanilla and beat just until the whites form very soft peaks.

350°F/180°C

Preheat the oven.

In another bowl, stir together the flour, confectioner's sugar, and salt.

Gently fold the flour mixture into the beaten egg whites.

Pour the batter into the prepared pan and smooth the top.

45 min

350°F/180°C

Bake until cooked through and the top of is lightly browned.

Place several ramekins on a rack, place the pan upside down onto the ramekins and let the cake cool completely.

Run a thin-bladed knife around the outer edges of the pan and around the inside of the tube.

Invert the cake onto a serving plate.

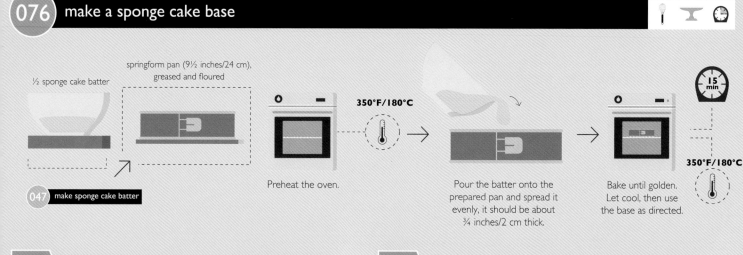

½ sponge cake batter

springform pan (9½ inches/24 cm),
greased and floured

350°F/180°C

15 min

047 make sponge cake batter

Preheat the oven.

Pour the batter onto the prepared pan and spread it evenly, it should be about ¾ inches/2 cm thick.

Bake until golden. Let cool, then use the base as directed.

350°F/180°C

## 077 make berry-topped cake

½ recipe pastry cream

3¼ cups/14 oz/ 400 g mixed berries

¾ cup/5 oz/150 g whipped cream

292 make pastry cream

015 whip cream

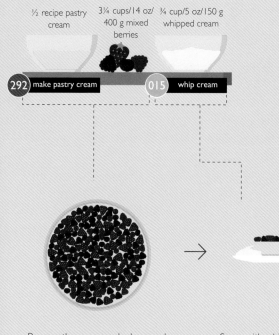

Prepare the sponge cake base and bake as directed. Spread the cooled cake with the pastry cream and top with the mixed berries.

Serve with whipped cream.

## 078 make peach chocolate cake

chocolate buttercream

4 peaches, cored, peeled and cut into slices

2 tbsp lemon juice

291 make chocolate buttercream

Prepare the sponge cake base and bake as directed. Spread the cooled cake with the chocolate buttercream.

Sprinkle the peach slices with lemon juice.

Arrange the peach slices decoratively on top of the buttercream.

✳ Decorate with the peaches just before serving to avoid them becoming brown.

## 079 make a jelly roll

sponge cake batter

¾ cup/9 oz/250 g apricot or other fruit jam

047 make sponge cake batter

dish towel

baking sheet, lined with parchment paper

**\*** If you want to fill the sponge cake roll with whipped cream or buttercream it should be completely cooled. Use a damp dish towel so that the sponge cake doesn't crack.

Pour the batter onto the prepared baking sheet and spread it evenly. It should be about ¾ inches/2 cm thick.

**10 min**

**350°F/180°C**

Bake until golden. Test with a toothpick. If it comes out clean the cake is done.

Invert the sponge cake onto the dish towel and peel off the parchment paper.

Let cool before filling.

Spread the sponge cake with the jam.

Roll it into a log with the help of the dish towel.

Let cool completely before serving.

## 080 make blackberry roulade

½ cup/4 oz/ 125 g whipped cream

½ cup/ 2 oz/60 g confectioner's sugar, sifted

1 cup/4 oz/125 g blackberries

015 whip cream

Prepare the sponge cake base as directed in the jelly roll recipe. Stir together the whipped cream and confectioner's sugar.

Spread the cooled sponge cake base with whipped cream. Scatter the berries over of the cream.

**45 min**

Roll into a log. Refrigerate until well chilled.

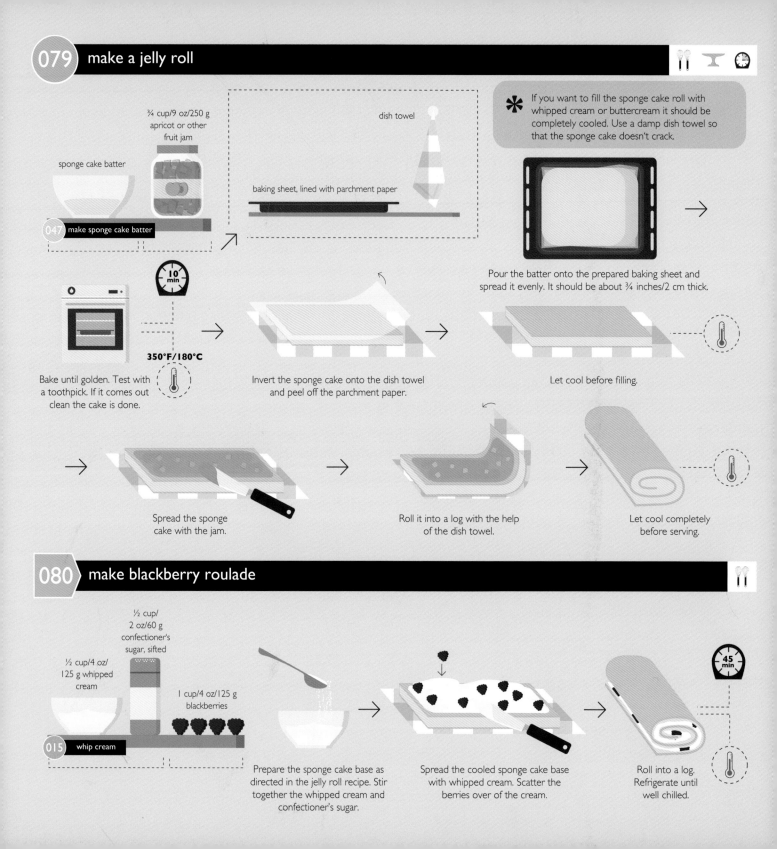

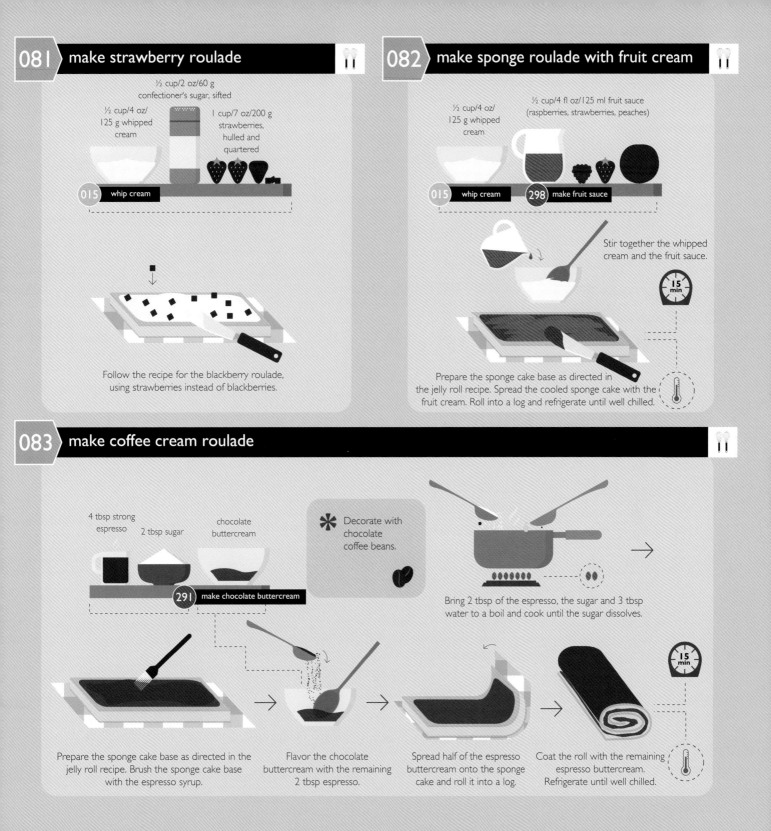

## 081   make strawberry roulade

½ cup/4 oz/ 125 g whipped cream

½ cup/2 oz/60 g confectioner's sugar, sifted

1 cup/7 oz/200 g strawberries, hulled and quartered

**015**   whip cream

Follow the recipe for the blackberry roulade, using strawberries instead of blackberries.

## 082   make sponge roulade with fruit cream

½ cup/4 oz/ 125 g whipped cream

½ cup/4 fl oz/125 ml fruit sauce (raspberries, strawberries, peaches)

**015**   whip cream    **298**   make fruit sauce

Stir together the whipped cream and the fruit sauce.

15 min

Prepare the sponge cake base as directed in the jelly roll recipe. Spread the cooled sponge cake with the fruit cream. Roll into a log and refrigerate until well chilled.

## 083   make coffee cream roulade

4 tbsp strong espresso

2 tbsp sugar

chocolate buttercream

**291**   make chocolate buttercream

✳ Decorate with chocolate coffee beans.

Bring 2 tbsp of the espresso, the sugar and 3 tbsp water to a boil and cook until the sugar dissolves.

Prepare the sponge cake base as directed in the jelly roll recipe. Brush the sponge cake base with the espresso syrup.

Flavor the chocolate buttercream with the remaining 2 tbsp espresso.

Spread half of the espresso buttercream onto the sponge cake and roll it into a log.

Coat the roll with the remaining espresso buttercream. Refrigerate until well chilled.

15 min

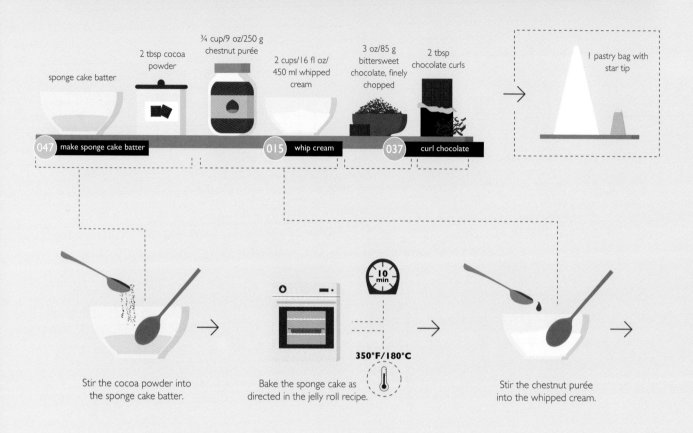

sponge cake batter

2 tbsp cocoa powder

¾ cup/9 oz/250 g chestnut purée

2 cups/16 fl oz/ 450 ml whipped cream

3 oz/85 g bittersweet chocolate, finely chopped

2 tbsp chocolate curls

1 pastry bag with star tip

047 make sponge cake batter

015 whip cream

037 curl chocolate

Stir the cocoa powder into the sponge cake batter.

Bake the sponge cake as directed in the jelly roll recipe.

350°F/180°C

10 min

Stir the chestnut purée into the whipped cream.

Spread the cooled sponge cake base with half of the chestnut cream, sprinkle with the chopped bittersweet chocolate and roll it into a log.

Fill a pastry bag fitted with a star tip with the remaining chestnut cream and pipe long lines onto the log from end to end. Decorate with chocolate curls.

Refrigerate until well chilled.

2 tbsp coffee liqueur

10 oz/315 g bittersweet chocolate, finely chopped

2¼ cups/18 fl oz/ 560 ml heavy cream

1 tsp vanilla extract

sponge cake batter

⅓ cup/3 oz/ 90 g sugar

2 tbsp chocolate curls

047 make sponge cake batter

037 curl chocolate

Melt chocolate and cream in the top of a double boiler set over simmering water.

Transfer the chocolate mixture to a bowl and refrigerate until well chilled. Then stir in the vanilla extract.

2 h

Bake the sponge cake as directed in the jelly roll recipe.

10 min

350°F/180°C

Bring the sugar, coffee liqueur, and ⅓ cup/ 3 fl oz/80 ml water to a simmer, stirring until the sugar dissolves. Do not boil.

Brush the sponge cake with the coffee syrup.

Beat the chocolate cream until soft peaks form.

Spread the sponge cake with half of the chocolate cream and roll it into a log.

Cut two wedges off the ends of the cake at a 45 degrees angle.

Attach the wedges on diagonally opposite sides of the log. Cover the bûche with the remaining chocolate cream, fixing the small pieces with it.

Use a fork to create a wave pattern.

Garnish with chocolate curls.

6½ oz/200 g bittersweet chocolate , chopped

¾ cup/6½ oz/ 200 g unsalted butter

⅔ cup/5 oz/ 150 g sugar

2½ cups/10 oz/ 300 g ground almonds

1 tbsp vanilla sugar

5 eggs

springform pan (9½ inches/24 cm), greased

350°F/180°C

021 make your own vanilla sugar

Preheat the oven.

Melt the chocolate in the top of a double boiler set over simmering water.

Beat the butter and sugar until combined.

Add the remaining ingredients. Stir to combine, then pour the batter into the prepared pan.

40 min

350°F/180°C

Bake until the cake feels springy to the touch.

½ cup/4 oz/ 125 g unsalted butter

1 cup/8 oz/250 g brown sugar

2 eggs

2¼ cups/9 oz/ 300 g flour

¾ cup/4 oz/ 115 g molasses

1 cup/8 fl oz/ 250 ml milk

1 tbsp ginger, ground

1 tbsp cinnamon, ground

2 tbsp baking powder

½ tsp baking soda

loaf pan (8½ by 4½ inch/ 21.5 by 11.5 cm), greased

350°F/180°C

Preheat the oven.

Beat the butter, sugar, and eggs until smooth.

Add the remaining ingredients. Stir to combine, then pour the batter into the prepared pan.

30 min

350°F/180°C

Bake until cooked through and puffed.

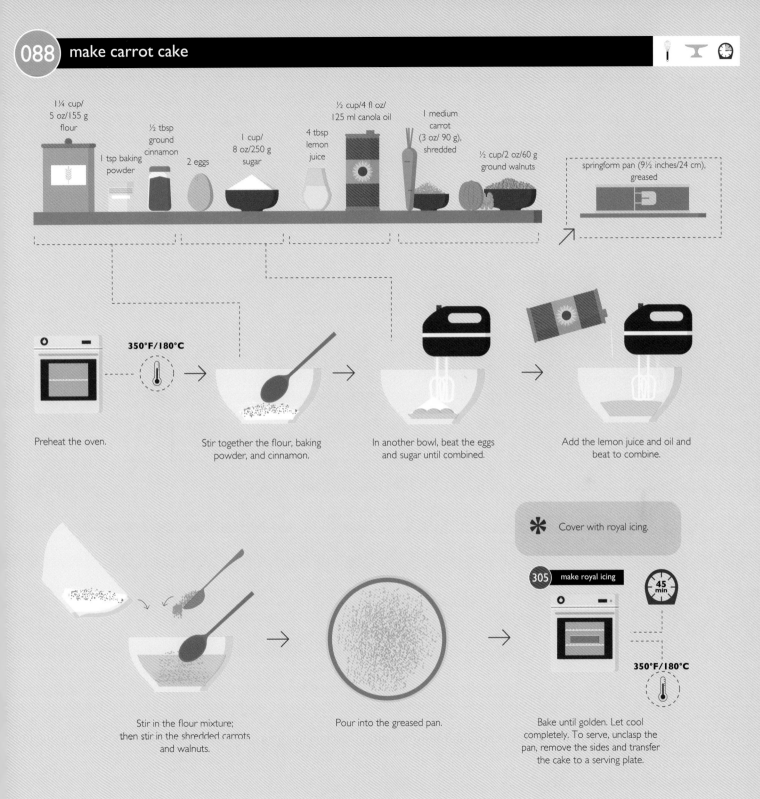

1¼ cup/ 5 oz/155 g flour

1 tsp baking powder

½ tbsp ground cinnamon

2 eggs

1 cup/ 8 oz/250 g sugar

4 tbsp lemon juice

½ cup/4 fl oz/ 125 ml canola oil

1 medium carrot (3 oz/ 90 g), shredded

½ cup/2 oz/60 g ground walnuts

springform pan (9½ inches/24 cm), greased

350°F/180°C

Preheat the oven.

Stir together the flour, baking powder, and cinnamon.

In another bowl, beat the eggs and sugar until combined.

Add the lemon juice and oil and beat to combine.

Stir in the flour mixture; then stir in the shredded carrots and walnuts.

Pour into the greased pan.

❋ Cover with royal icing.

305 make royal icing

45 min

350°F/180°C

Bake until golden. Let cool completely. To serve, unclasp the pan, remove the sides and transfer the cake to a serving plate.

⅔ cup/5 oz/ 155 g unsalted butter

⅔ cup/5 oz/ 155 g sugar

3 eggs

4 ripe bananas

1 tbsp vanilla extract

2¼ cup/11½ oz/ 360 g all-purpose flour

2 tsp baking powder

1 pinch of salt

⅔ cup/2½ oz/ 75 g chopped walnuts

loaf pan (8½ by 4½ inch/ 21.5 by 11.5 cm), greased

**350°F/180°C**

Preheat the oven.

Beat the butter and sugar until smooth. Add the eggs, one at a time, beating well after each addition.

In another bowl, mash the bananas coarsely with a fork.

Add the mashed bananas and the vanilla to the butter mixture.

In a clean bowl, stir together the flour, baking powder and salt.

Stir the flour mixture into the banana mixture.

Pour the mixture into the prepared loaf pan and bake until golden and cooked through.

**350°F/180°C**

**55 min**

Test with a wooden skewer. If it comes out clean the bread is done.

Let cool slightly, then invert the bread.

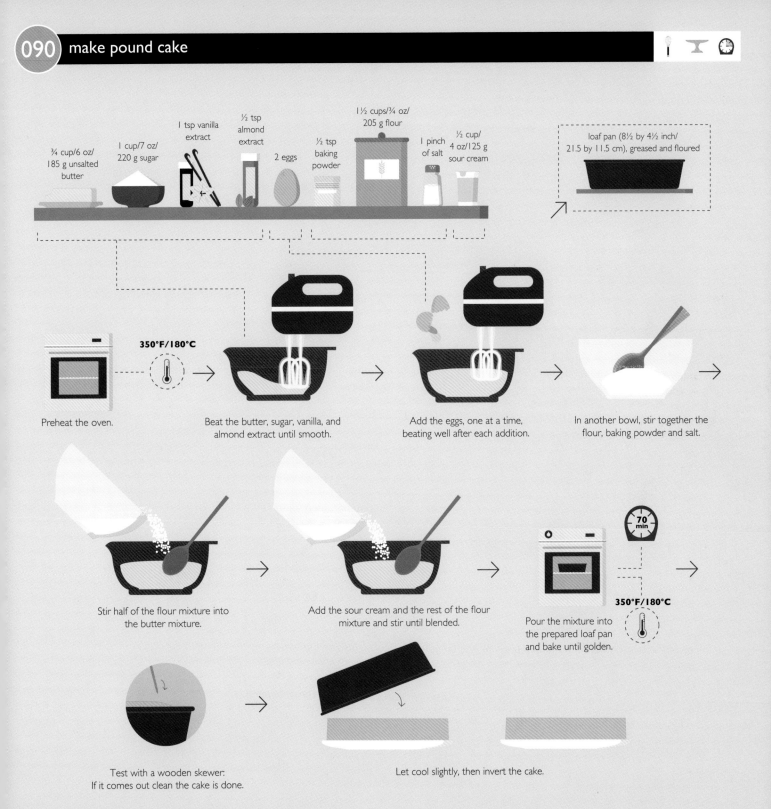

¾ cup/6 oz/ 185 g unsalted butter

1 cup/7 oz/ 220 g sugar

1 tsp vanilla extract

½ tsp almond extract

2 eggs

½ tsp baking powder

1½ cups/¾ oz/ 205 g flour

1 pinch of salt

½ cup/ 4 oz/125 g sour cream

loaf pan (8½ by 4½ inch/ 21.5 by 11.5 cm), greased and floured

350°F/180°C

Preheat the oven.

Beat the butter, sugar, vanilla, and almond extract until smooth.

Add the eggs, one at a time, beating well after each addition.

In another bowl, stir together the flour, baking powder and salt.

Stir half of the flour mixture into the butter mixture.

Add the sour cream and the rest of the flour mixture and stir until blended.

70 min

350°F/180°C

Pour the mixture into the prepared loaf pan and bake until golden.

Test with a wooden skewer: If it comes out clean the cake is done.

Let cool slightly, then invert the cake.

## 091 make poppy seed pound cake

3 tbsp poppy seeds

loaf pan (8½ by 4½ inch/ 21.5 by 11.5 cm), greased and floured

70 min

350°F/180°C

Prepare the pound cake batter, adding the poppy seeds to the batter. Proceed as directed.

## 092 make lemon pound cake

2 tbsp lemon juice

1 tbsp finely grated lemon zest

loaf pan (8½ by 4½ inch/ 21.5 by 11.5 cm), greased and floured

70 min

350°F/180°C

Prepare the pound cake batter, adding the lemon juice and grated lemon zest to the batter. Proceed as directed.

## 093 make espresso pound cake

1 tbsp ground espresso

loaf pan (8½ by 4½ inch/ 21.5 by 11.5 cm), greased and floured

70 min

350°F/180°C

Prepare the pound cake batter, adding the ground espresso to the batter. Proceed as directed.

## 094 make coconut pound cake ring

1 cup/4 oz/120 g unsweetened shredded coconut

savarin mold (9½ inches/24 cm diameter), greased and floured

55 min

350°F/180°C

Prepare the pound cake batter, adding the shredded coconut to the flour mixture. Proceed as directed.

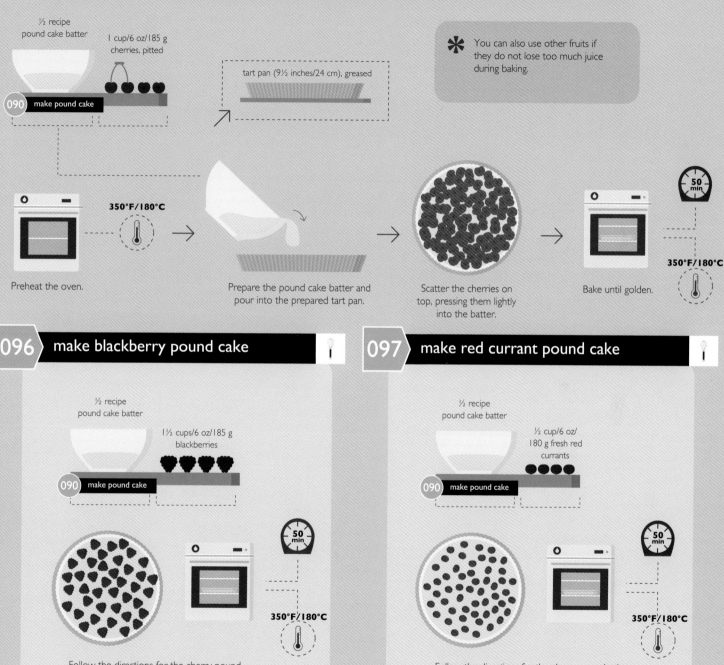

## 095 make cherry pound cake

½ recipe pound cake batter

1 cup/6 oz/185 g cherries, pitted

**090** make pound cake

tart pan (9½ inches/24 cm), greased

✳ You can also use other fruits if they do not lose too much juice during baking.

**350°F/180°C**

Preheat the oven.

Prepare the pound cake batter and pour into the prepared tart pan.

Scatter the cherries on top, pressing them lightly into the batter.

Bake until golden.

50 min

**350°F/180°C**

## 096 make blackberry pound cake

½ recipe pound cake batter

1½ cups/6 oz/185 g blackberries

**090** make pound cake

50 min

**350°F/180°C**

Follow the directions for the cherry pound cake, using blackberries instead of the cherries.

## 097 make red currant pound cake

½ recipe pound cake batter

½ cup/6 oz/ 180 g fresh red currants

**090** make pound cake

50 min

**350°F/180°C**

Follow the directions for the cherry pound cake, using red currants instead of the cherries.

make bundt cake

1 cup/8 oz/
250 g unsalted
butter

1 cup/7 oz/
200 g sugar

1 pinch
of salt

1 tsp vanilla
extract

4 eggs

3¼ cups/16½ oz/
510 g flour

1 tbsp baking
powder

½ cup/4 fl oz/
125 ml milk

1 cup/6 oz/
185 g raisins

2 tbsp
confectioner's
sugar

bundt pan (9½ inches/24 cm),
greased

Preheat the oven.

350°F/180°C

Beat the butter, sugar, salt, and vanilla extract
until smooth. Add the eggs, one at a time,
beating well after each addition.

Stir the flour, baking powder,
and milk into the mixture.

Stir in the raisins.

Pour the mixture into the
prepared pan.

Bake until golden.

350°F/180°C

60 min

Let cool slightly, then invert the
cake onto a serving plate.

Sprinkle with confectioners'
sugar before serving.

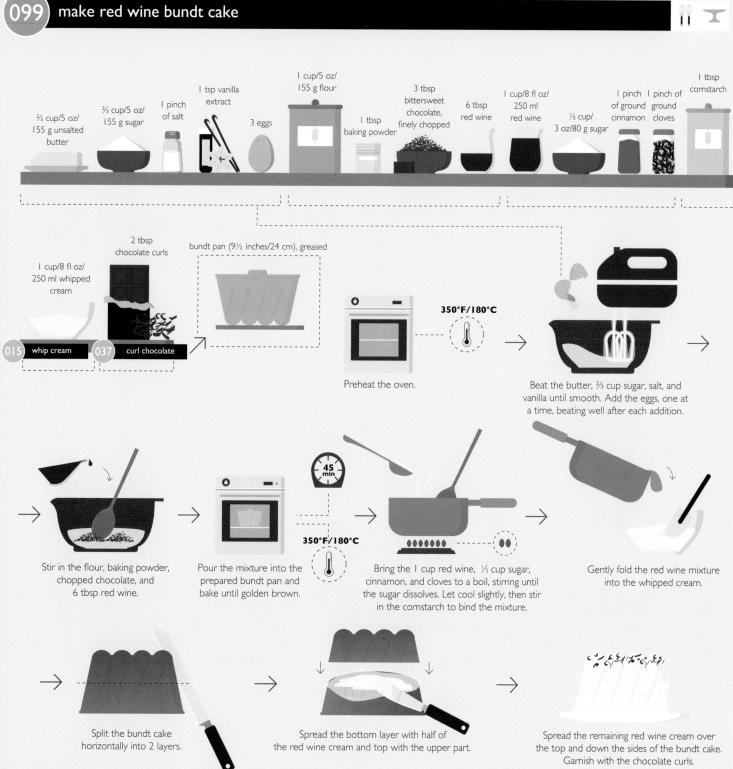

⅔ cup/5 oz/ 155 g unsalted butter

⅔ cup/5 oz/ 155 g sugar

1 pinch of salt

1 tsp vanilla extract

3 eggs

1 cup/5 oz/ 155 g flour

1 tbsp baking powder

3 tbsp bittersweet chocolate, finely chopped

6 tbsp red wine

1 cup/8 fl oz/ 250 ml red wine

⅓ cup/ 3 oz/80 g sugar

1 pinch of ground cinnamon

1 pinch of ground cloves

1 tbsp cornstarch

1 cup/8 fl oz/ 250 ml whipped cream

2 tbsp chocolate curls

bundt pan (9½ inches/24 cm), greased

015 whip cream

037 curl chocolate

350°F/180°C

Preheat the oven.

Beat the butter, ⅔ cup sugar, salt, and vanilla until smooth. Add the eggs, one at a time, beating well after each addition.

Stir in the flour, baking powder, chopped chocolate, and 6 tbsp red wine.

350°F/180°C

Pour the mixture into the prepared bundt pan and bake until golden brown.

45 min

Bring the 1 cup red wine, ⅓ cup sugar, cinnamon, and cloves to a boil, stirring until the sugar dissolves. Let cool slightly, then stir in the cornstarch to bind the mixture.

Gently fold the red wine mixture into the whipped cream.

Split the bundt cake horizontally into 2 layers.

Spread the bottom layer with half of the red wine cream and top with the upper part.

Spread the remaining red wine cream over the top and down the sides of the bundt cake. Garnish with the chocolate curls.

## 100 make marble cake

butter cake batter

1 tbsp cocoa powder

045 prepare butter cake batter

loaf pan (8½ by 4½ inch/ 21.5 by 11.5 cm), greased and floured

350°F/180°C

Preheat the oven.

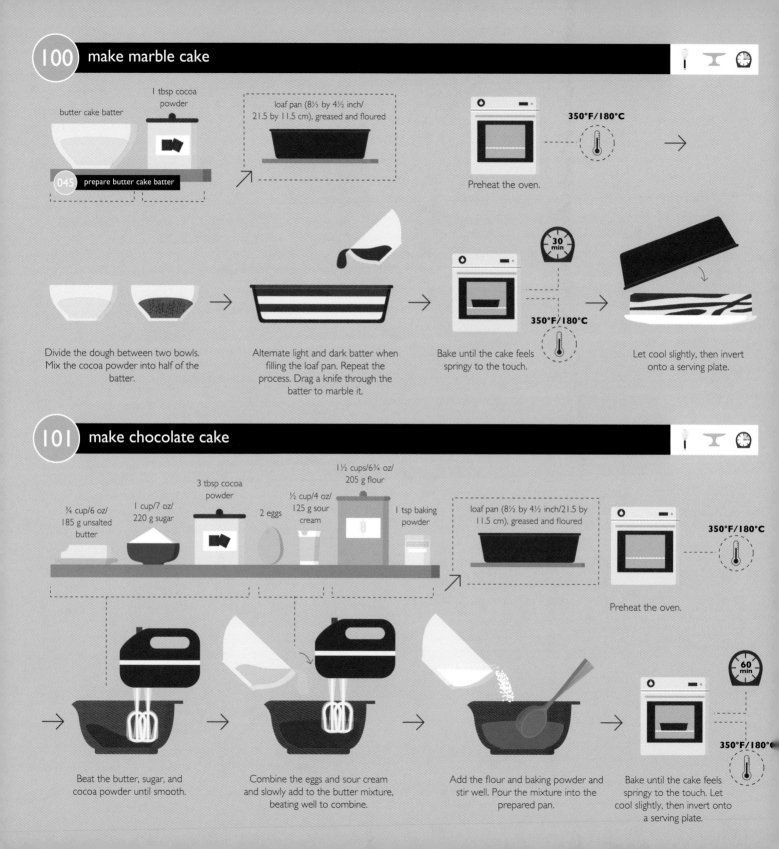

Divide the dough between two bowls. Mix the cocoa powder into half of the batter.

Alternate light and dark batter when filling the loaf pan. Repeat the process. Drag a knife through the batter to marble it.

350°F/180°C

Bake until the cake feels springy to the touch.

30 min

Let cool slightly, then invert onto a serving plate.

## 101 make chocolate cake

¾ cup/6 oz/ 185 g unsalted butter

1 cup/7 oz/ 220 g sugar

3 tbsp cocoa powder

2 eggs

½ cup/4 oz/ 125 g sour cream

1½ cups/6¾ oz/ 205 g flour

1 tsp baking powder

loaf pan (8½ by 4½ inch/21.5 by 11.5 cm), greased and floured

350°F/180°C

Preheat the oven.

Beat the butter, sugar, and cocoa powder until smooth.

Combine the eggs and sour cream and slowly add to the butter mixture, beating well to combine.

Add the flour and baking powder and stir well. Pour the mixture into the prepared pan.

60 min

350°F/180°C

Bake until the cake feels springy to the touch. Let cool slightly, then invert onto a serving plate.

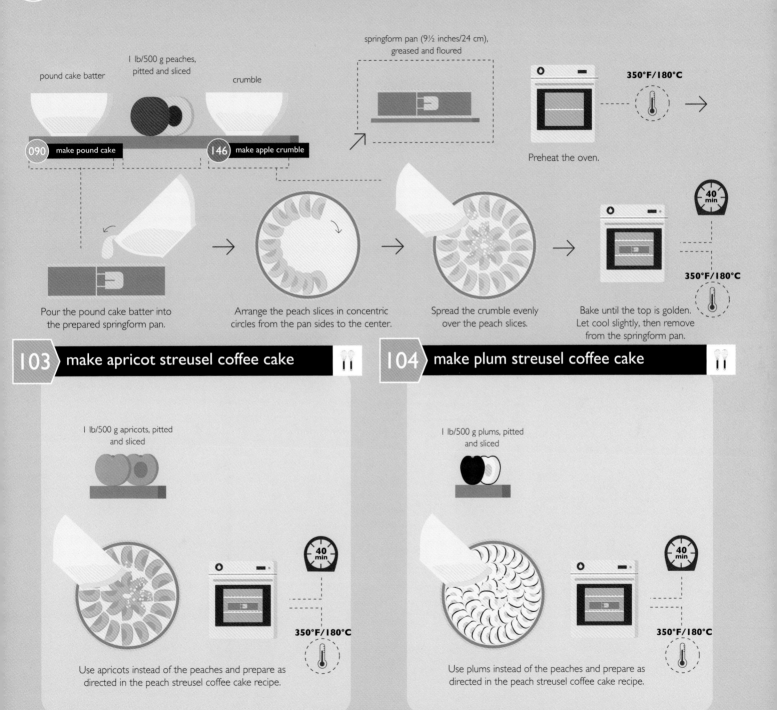

## 102 make peach streusel coffee cake

pound cake batter

1 lb/500 g peaches, pitted and sliced

crumble

090 make pound cake

146 make apple crumble

springform pan (9½ inches/24 cm), greased and floured

350°F/180°C

Preheat the oven.

Pour the pound cake batter into the prepared springform pan.

Arrange the peach slices in concentric circles from the pan sides to the center.

Spread the crumble evenly over the peach slices.

40 min

350°F/180°C

Bake until the top is golden. Let cool slightly, then remove from the springform pan.

## 103 make apricot streusel coffee cake

1 lb/500 g apricots, pitted and sliced

40 min

350°F/180°C

Use apricots instead of the peaches and prepare as directed in the peach streusel coffee cake recipe.

## 104 make plum streusel coffee cake

1 lb/500 g plums, pitted and sliced

40 min

350°F/180°C

Use plums instead of the peaches and prepare as directed in the peach streusel coffee cake recipe.

2 eggs

1 cup/7 oz/ 200 g sugar

1 pinch of salt

1 cup/8 oz/ 225 g yogurt

1 tsp almond extract

¼ cup/2 oz/ 60 g unsalted butter

2 cups/9 oz/ 250 g all-purpose flour

2 tbsp baking powder

1 pinch of salt

springform pan (9½ inches/24 cm), greased and floured

**350°F/180°C**

Preheat the oven.

Beat the eggs, sugar, and salt until well combined.

Add the yogurt and almond extract and beat well to combine.

Melt the butter.

Add the melted butter to the batter, beating well to combine.

Fold the flour, baking powder, and salt into the mixture.

Pour the mixture into the prepared pan.

**40 min**

**350°F/180°C**

Bake until golden.

Test with a wooden skewer: If it comes out clean the cake is done. Let cool slightly, then remove from the springform pan.

✳ Serve with fruit sauce.

298 make fruit sauce

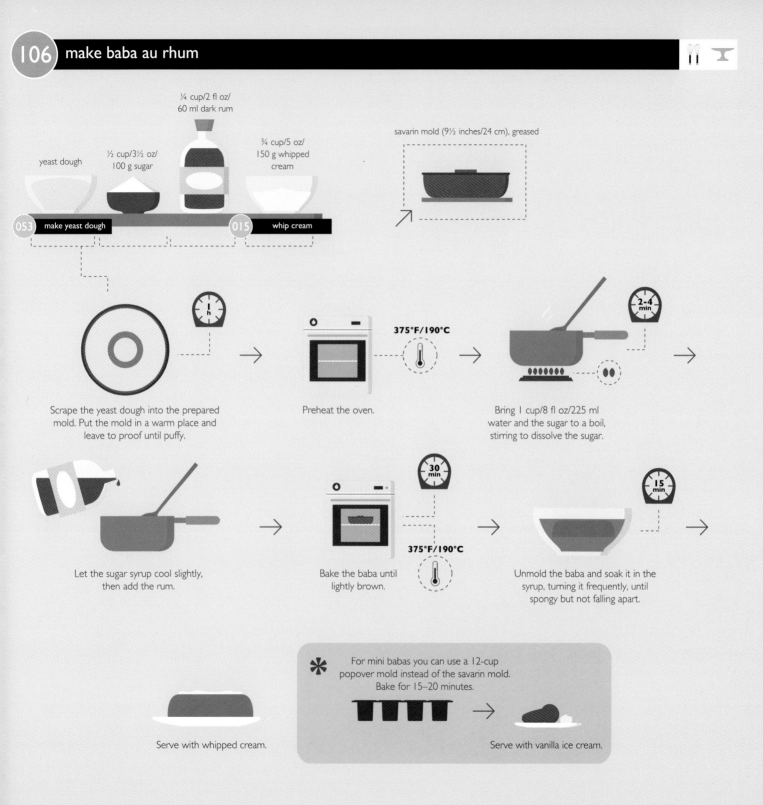

¼ cup/2 fl oz/ 60 ml dark rum

½ cup/3½ oz/ 100 g sugar

¾ cup/5 oz/ 150 g whipped cream

yeast dough

savarin mold (9½ inches/24 cm), greased

053 make yeast dough

015 whip cream

1 h

Scrape the yeast dough into the prepared mold. Put the mold in a warm place and leave to proof until puffy.

Preheat the oven.

375°F/190°C

Bring 1 cup/8 fl oz/225 ml water and the sugar to a boil, stirring to dissolve the sugar.

2-4 min

Let the sugar syrup cool slightly, then add the rum.

Bake the baba until lightly brown.

30 min

375°F/190°C

Unmold the baba and soak it in the syrup, turning it frequently, until spongy but not falling apart.

15 min

Serve with whipped cream.

✳ For mini babas you can use a 12-cup popover mold instead of the savarin mold. Bake for 15–20 minutes.

Serve with vanilla ice cream.

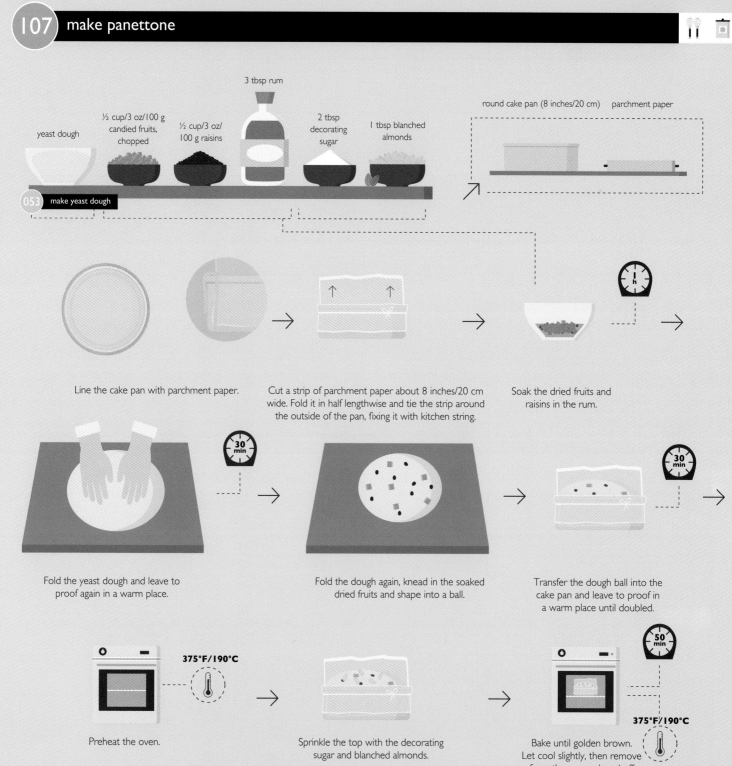

3 tbsp rum

yeast dough

½ cup/3 oz/100 g candied fruits, chopped

½ cup/3 oz/ 100 g raisins

2 tbsp decorating sugar

1 tbsp blanched almonds

round cake pan (8 inches/20 cm)    parchment paper

053 make yeast dough

Line the cake pan with parchment paper.

Cut a strip of parchment paper about 8 inches/20 cm wide. Fold it in half lengthwise and tie the strip around the outside of the pan, fixing it with kitchen string.

Soak the dried fruits and raisins in the rum.

Fold the yeast dough and leave to proof again in a warm place.

Fold the dough again, knead in the soaked dried fruits and shape into a ball.

Transfer the dough ball into the cake pan and leave to proof in a warm place until doubled.

375°F/190°C

Preheat the oven.

Sprinkle the top with the decorating sugar and blanched almonds.

375°F/190°C

Bake until golden brown. Let cool slightly, then remove from the pan and peel off the parchment paper.

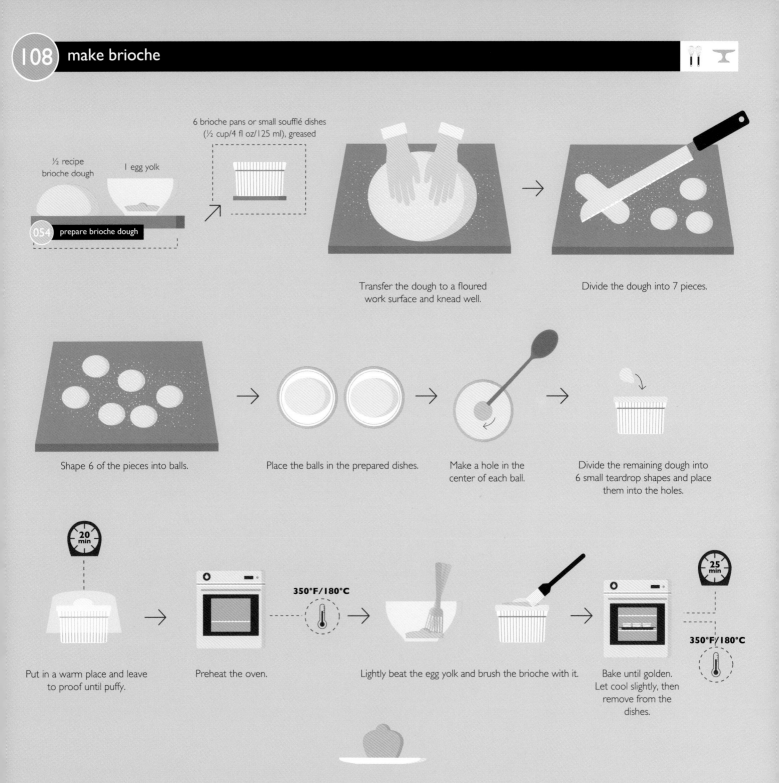

½ recipe brioche dough

I egg yolk

054   prepare brioche dough

6 brioche pans or small soufflé dishes (½ cup/4 fl oz/125 ml), greased

Transfer the dough to a floured work surface and knead well.

Divide the dough into 7 pieces.

Shape 6 of the pieces into balls.

Place the balls in the prepared dishes.

Make a hole in the center of each ball.

Divide the remaining dough into 6 small teardrop shapes and place them into the holes.

20 min

Put in a warm place and leave to proof until puffy.

Preheat the oven.

350°F/180°C

Lightly beat the egg yolk and brush the brioche with it.

Bake until golden. Let cool slightly, then remove from the dishes.

25 min

350°F/180°C

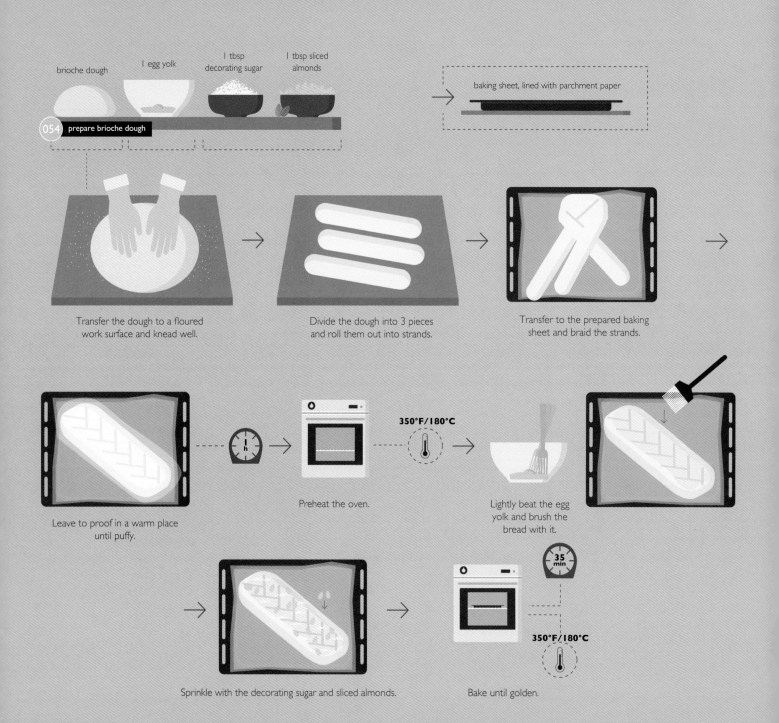

brioche dough | 1 egg yolk | 1 tbsp decorating sugar | 1 tbsp sliced almonds

054 prepare brioche dough

baking sheet, lined with parchment paper

Transfer the dough to a floured work surface and knead well.

Divide the dough into 3 pieces and roll them out into strands.

Transfer to the prepared baking sheet and braid the strands.

Leave to proof in a warm place until puffy.

Preheat the oven.

350°F/180°C

Lightly beat the egg yolk and brush the bread with it.

Sprinkle with the decorating sugar and sliced almonds.

Bake until golden.

35 min

350°F/180°C

## 110 make sheet cake with chiffon cake batter

chiffon cake batter

046 prepare chiffon cake batter

baking sheet, lined with parchment paper

350°F/180°C

Preheat the oven.

Pour the batter onto the prepared baking sheet and and spread it evenly.

Top according to recipe and bake until golden.

35 min

350°F/180°C

Let the cake cool, then cut into squares.

## 111 make apricot sheet cake

30 fresh apricots, pitted and halved

2 tbsp sliced almonds

Top the batter with the apricot halves, cut sides up. Sprinkle with the sliced almonds and bake as directed above.

## 112 make cherry sheet cake

3 cups/1 lb/500 g fresh cherries, pitted

2 tbsp almond slivers

Top the batter with the cherries and almond slivers. Bake as directed above.

## 113 make strawberry-rhubarb sheet cake

1 cup/8 oz/250 g sliced rhubarb

3 tbsp sugar

4 cups/1 lb/250 g hulled and quartered strawberries

Bring the rhubarb, sugar and ½ cup/ 4 fl oz/125 ml water to a boil, then strain through a sieve and let drain.

Top the batter with the rhubarb and strawberries and bake as directed above.

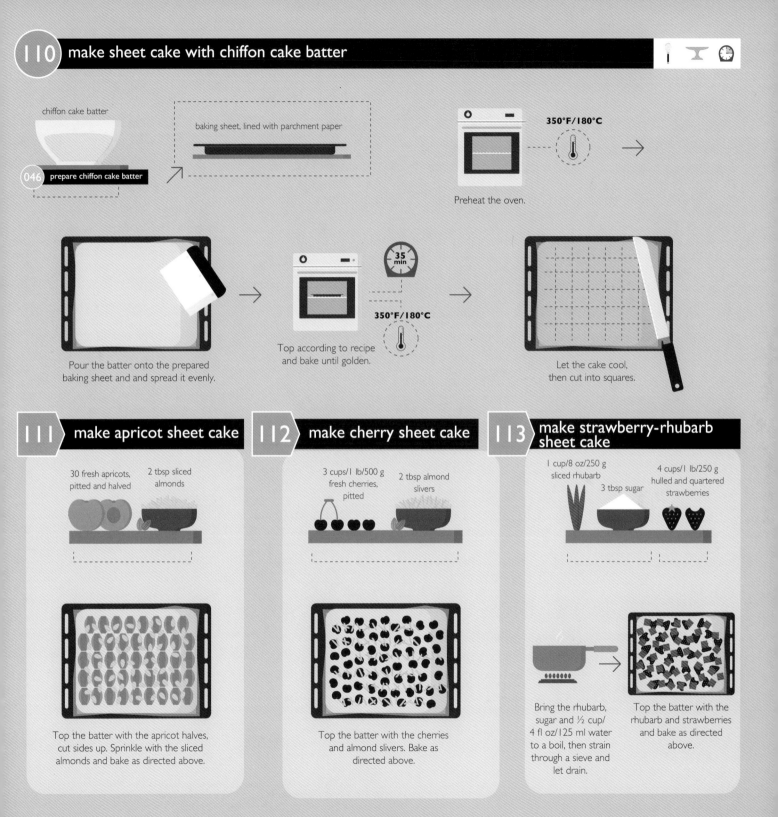

## 114 make sheet cake with yeast dough

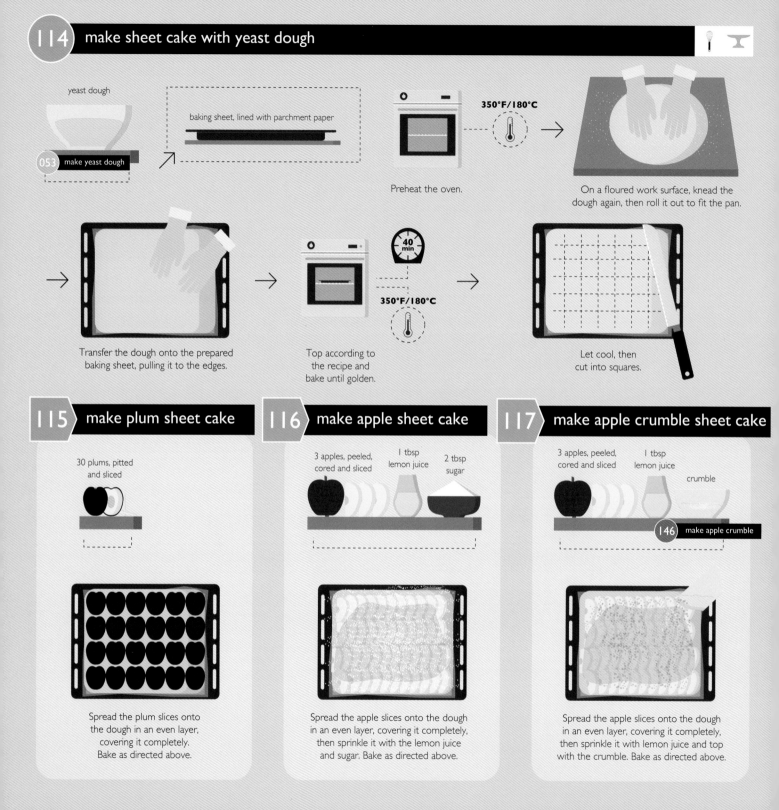

yeast dough

053 make yeast dough

baking sheet, lined with parchment paper

350°F/180°C

Preheat the oven.

On a floured work surface, knead the dough again, then roll it out to fit the pan.

Transfer the dough onto the prepared baking sheet, pulling it to the edges.

40 min

350°F/180°C

Top according to the recipe and bake until golden.

Let cool, then cut into squares.

### 115 make plum sheet cake

30 plums, pitted and sliced

Spread the plum slices onto the dough in an even layer, covering it completely. Bake as directed above.

### 116 make apple sheet cake

3 apples, peeled, cored and sliced

1 tbsp lemon juice

2 tbsp sugar

Spread the apple slices onto the dough in an even layer, covering it completely, then sprinkle it with the lemon juice and sugar. Bake as directed above.

### 117 make apple crumble sheet cake

3 apples, peeled, cored and sliced

1 tbsp lemon juice

crumble

146 make apple crumble

Spread the apple slices onto the dough in an even layer, covering it completely, then sprinkle it with lemon juice and top with the crumble. Bake as directed above.

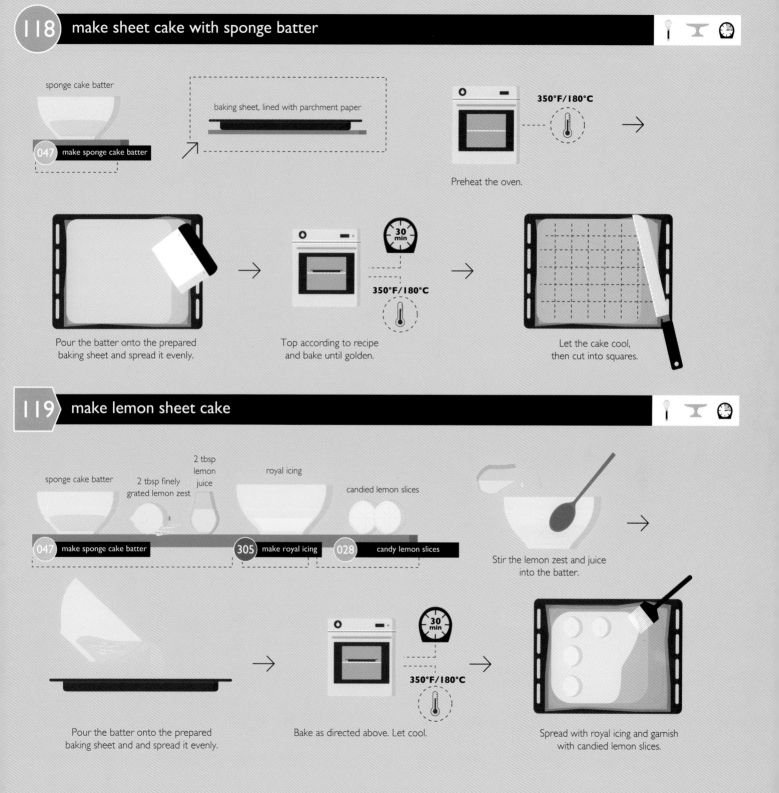

## 118 | make sheet cake with sponge batter

sponge cake batter

**047** make sponge cake batter

baking sheet, lined with parchment paper

350°F/180°C

Preheat the oven.

Pour the batter onto the prepared
baking sheet and spread it evenly.

Top according to recipe
and bake until golden.

30 min
350°F/180°C

Let the cake cool,
then cut into squares.

## 119 | make lemon sheet cake

sponge cake batter

2 tbsp finely
grated lemon zest

2 tbsp
lemon
juice

royal icing

candied lemon slices

**047** make sponge cake batter

**305** make royal icing

**028** candy lemon slices

Stir the lemon zest and juice
into the batter.

Pour the batter onto the prepared
baking sheet and and spread it evenly.

Bake as directed above. Let cool.

30 min
350°F/180°C

Spread with royal icing and garnish
with candied lemon slices.

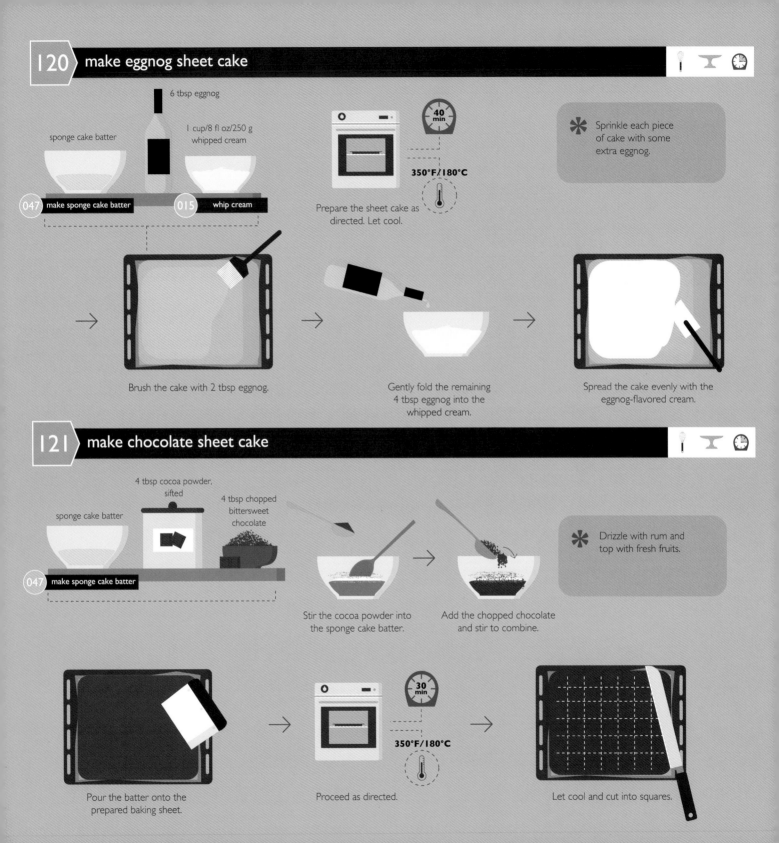

6 tbsp eggnog

sponge cake batter

1 cup/8 fl oz/250 g whipped cream

047 make sponge cake batter

015 whip cream

40 min

350°F/180°C

Prepare the sheet cake as directed. Let cool.

✱ Sprinkle each piece of cake with some extra eggnog.

Brush the cake with 2 tbsp eggnog.

Gently fold the remaining 4 tbsp eggnog into the whipped cream.

Spread the cake evenly with the eggnog-flavored cream.

4 tbsp cocoa powder, sifted

4 tbsp chopped bittersweet chocolate

sponge cake batter

047 make sponge cake batter

Stir the cocoa powder into the sponge cake batter.

Add the chopped chocolate and stir to combine.

✱ Drizzle with rum and top with fresh fruits.

Pour the batter onto the prepared baking sheet.

30 min

350°F/180°C

Proceed as directed.

Let cool and cut into squares.

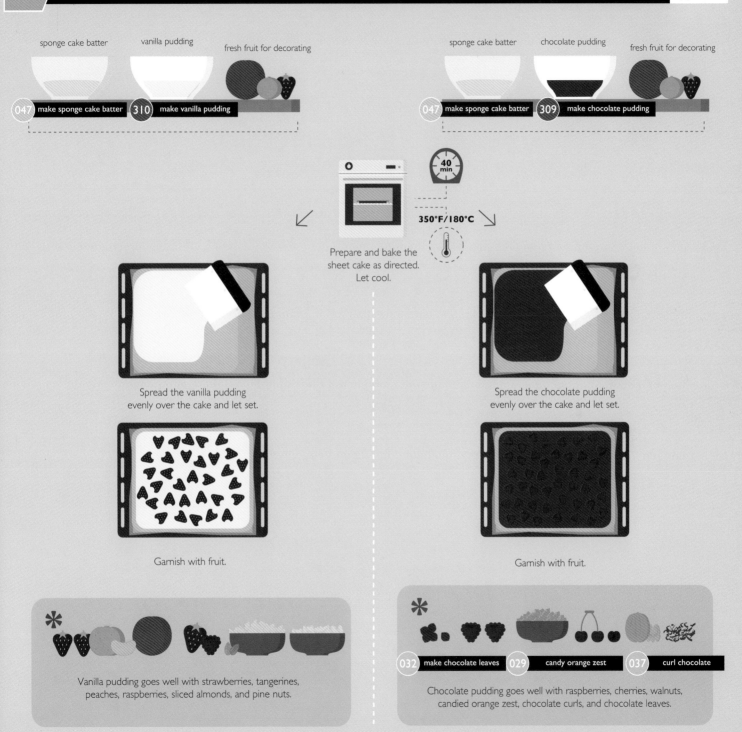

sponge cake batter    vanilla pudding    fresh fruit for decorating

047 make sponge cake batter    310 make vanilla pudding

sponge cake batter    chocolate pudding    fresh fruit for decorating

047 make sponge cake batter    309 make chocolate pudding

40 min

350°F/180°C

Prepare and bake the sheet cake as directed. Let cool.

Spread the vanilla pudding evenly over the cake and let set.

Spread the chocolate pudding evenly over the cake and let set.

Garnish with fruit.

Garnish with fruit.

Vanilla pudding goes well with strawberries, tangerines, peaches, raspberries, sliced almonds, and pine nuts.

032 make chocolate leaves    029 candy orange zest    037 curl chocolate

Chocolate pudding goes well with raspberries, cherries, walnuts, candied orange zest, chocolate curls, and chocolate leaves.

# pies and tarts

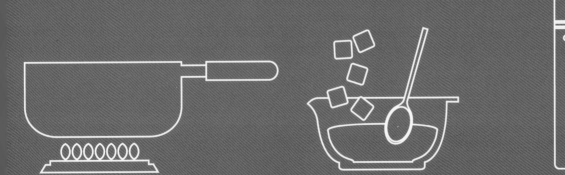

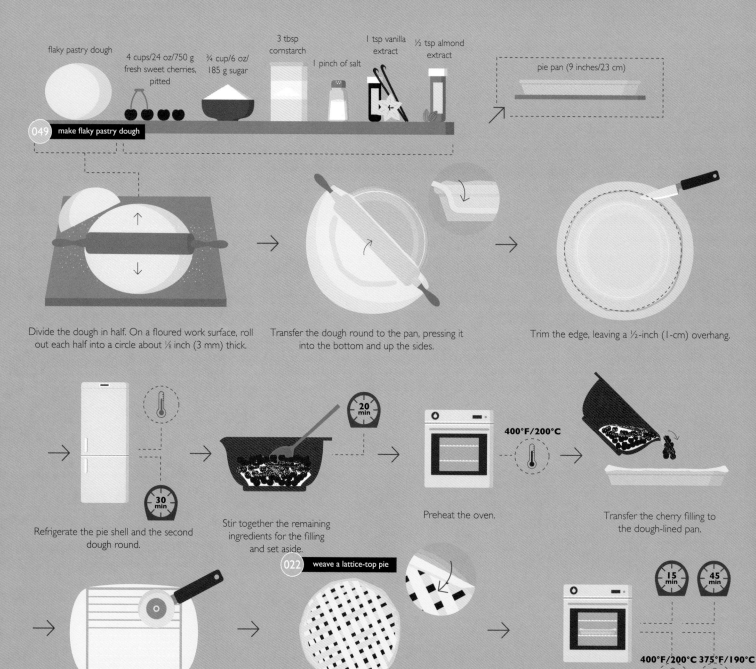

flaky pastry dough

4 cups/24 oz/750 g fresh sweet cherries, pitted

¾ cup/6 oz/ 185 g sugar

3 tbsp cornstarch

1 pinch of salt

1 tsp vanilla extract

½ tsp almond extract

pie pan (9 inches/23 cm)

049 make flaky pastry dough

Divide the dough in half. On a floured work surface, roll out each half into a circle about ⅛ inch (3 mm) thick.

Transfer the dough round to the pan, pressing it into the bottom and up the sides.

Trim the edge, leaving a ½-inch (1-cm) overhang.

30 min

20 min

400°F/200°C

Refrigerate the pie shell and the second dough round.

Stir together the remaining ingredients for the filling and set aside.

Preheat the oven.

Transfer the cherry filling to the dough-lined pan.

022 weave a lattice-top pie

15 min

45 min

Cut the second dough disk into 1-inch (2-cm) inch strips.

Trim the ends of the strips, fold the overhang from the bottom round up and over the edges of the lattice and crimp to seal.

400°F/200°C 375°F/190°C

Bake on the lower rack of the oven. Reduce heat and bake until golden and bubbly.

## 124 > make blueberry pie

8 cups/2 lb/1 kg
blueberries

✱ Make a double-crust pie by topping it with a solid dough round. Cut 4 or 5 holes or slits in the top to allow steam to escape during baking.

Use blueberries instead of the cherries and prepare like cherry pie.

## 125 > make summer berry pie

6 cups/1½ lb/750 g mixed fresh berries (raspberries, red currants, strawberries)

✱ Taste for sweetness. The berry mixture might need more sugar than the cherry pie.

Use summer berries instead of cherries and prepare like cherry pie.

## 126 > make peach pie

5 cups/2 lb/1 kg
pitted and sliced peaches

Use peaches instead of cherries and prepare like cherry pie.

## 127 > make strawberry-rhubarb pie

3 cups/12 oz/375 g
hulled and quartered
strawberries

3 cups/12 oz/375 g sliced rhubarb cut into ½ inch (12 mm) slices

Use rhubarb and strawberries instead of cherries, add an additional ¼ cup/2 oz/60 g sugar to the filling, and prepare like cherry pie.

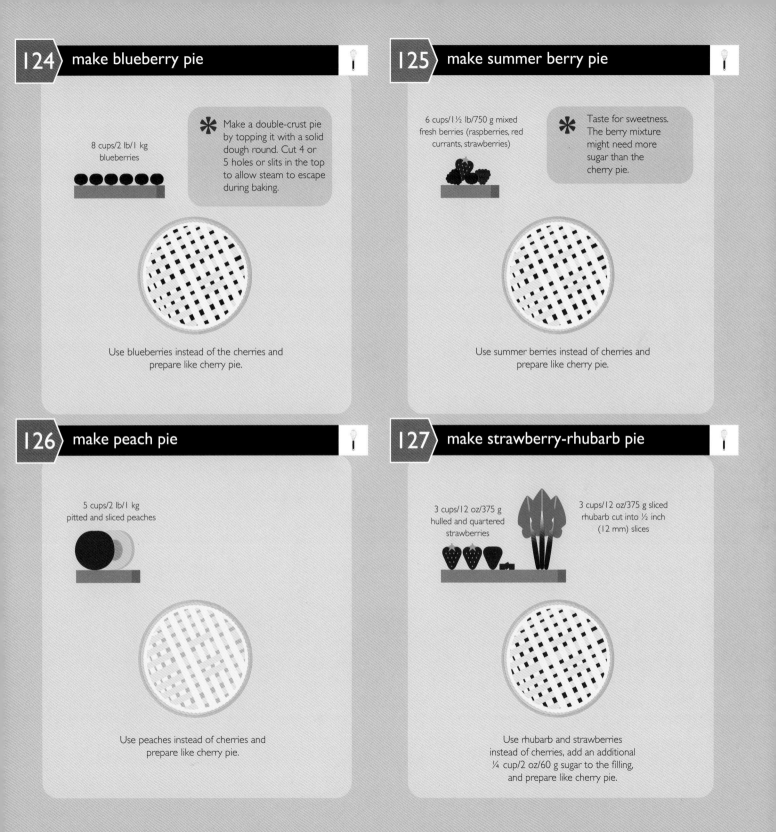

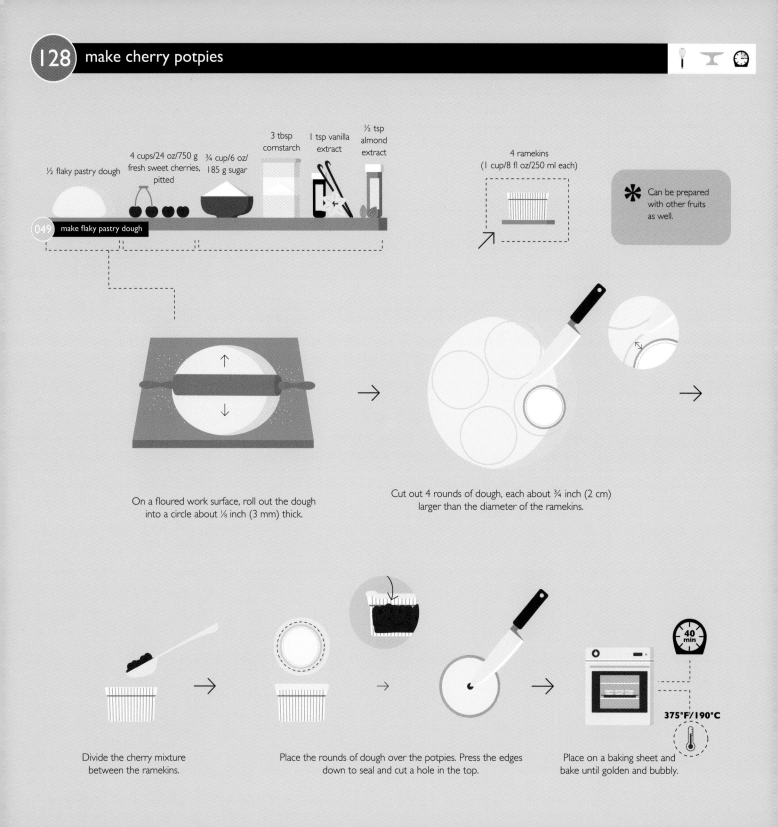

½ flaky pastry dough

4 cups/24 oz/750 g fresh sweet cherries, pitted

¾ cup/6 oz/185 g sugar

3 tbsp cornstarch

1 tsp vanilla extract

½ tsp almond extract

4 ramekins (1 cup/8 fl oz/250 ml each)

049 make flaky pastry dough

✳ Can be prepared with other fruits as well.

On a floured work surface, roll out the dough into a circle about ⅛ inch (3 mm) thick.

Cut out 4 rounds of dough, each about ¾ inch (2 cm) larger than the diameter of the ramekins.

Divide the cherry mixture between the ramekins.

Place the rounds of dough over the potpies. Press the edges down to seal and cut a hole in the top.

Place on a baking sheet and bake until golden and bubbly.

40 min

375°F/190°C

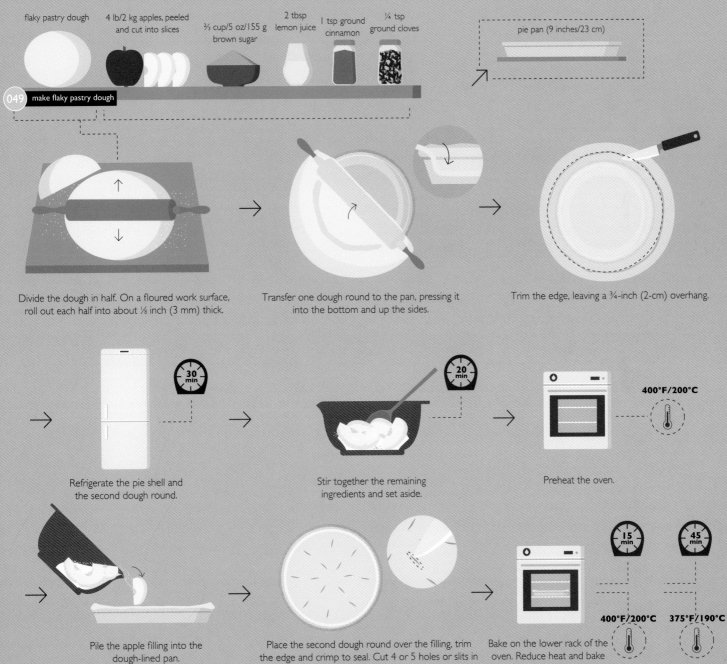

flaky pastry dough

4 lb/2 kg apples, peeled and cut into slices

⅔ cup/5 oz/155 g brown sugar

2 tbsp lemon juice

1 tsp ground cinnamon

¼ tsp ground cloves

pie pan (9 inches/23 cm)

049 make flaky pastry dough

Divide the dough in half. On a floured work surface, roll out each half into about ⅛ inch (3 mm) thick.

Transfer one dough round to the pan, pressing it into the bottom and up the sides.

Trim the edge, leaving a ¾-inch (2-cm) overhang.

Refrigerate the pie shell and the second dough round.

Stir together the remaining ingredients and set aside.

Preheat the oven. 400°F/200°C

Pile the apple filling into the dough-lined pan.

Place the second dough round over the filling, trim the edge and crimp to seal. Cut 4 or 5 holes or slits in the top to allow steam to escape during baking.

Bake on the lower rack of the oven. Reduce heat and bake until golden and bubbly. 400°F/200°C 375°F/190°C

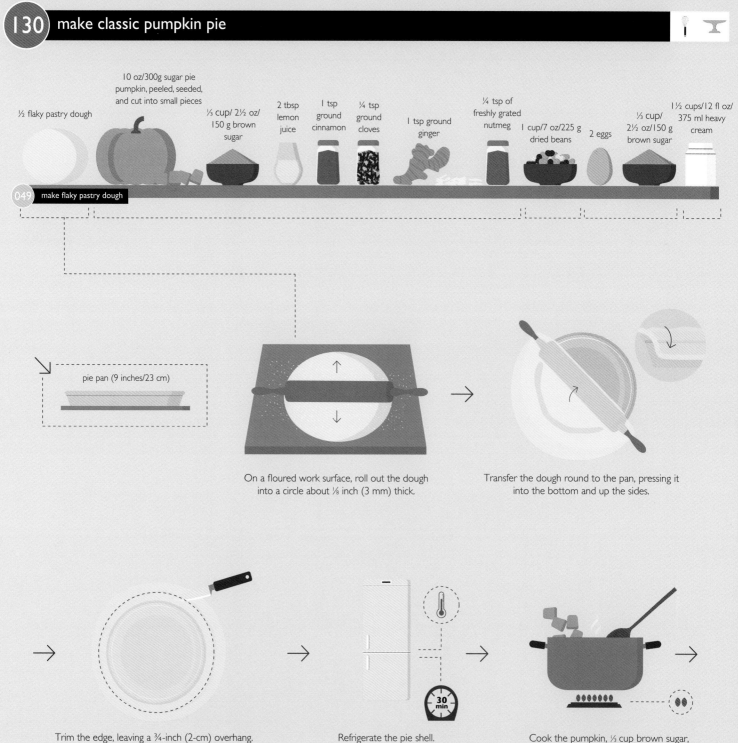

½ flaky pastry dough

10 oz/300g sugar pie pumpkin, peeled, seeded, and cut into small pieces

⅓ cup/ 2½ oz/ 150 g brown sugar

2 tbsp lemon juice

1 tsp ground cinnamon

¼ tsp ground cloves

1 tsp ground ginger

¼ tsp of freshly grated nutmeg

1 cup/7 oz/225 g dried beans

2 eggs

⅓ cup/ 2½ oz/150 g brown sugar

1½ cups/12 fl oz/ 375 ml heavy cream

049 make flaky pastry dough

pie pan (9 inches/23 cm)

On a floured work surface, roll out the dough into a circle about ⅛ inch (3 mm) thick.

Transfer the dough round to the pan, pressing it into the bottom and up the sides.

Trim the edge, leaving a ¾-inch (2-cm) overhang.

Refrigerate the pie shell.

Cook the pumpkin, ⅓ cup brown sugar, the lemon juice, and the spices with 4 tbsp water until the pumpkin is soft.

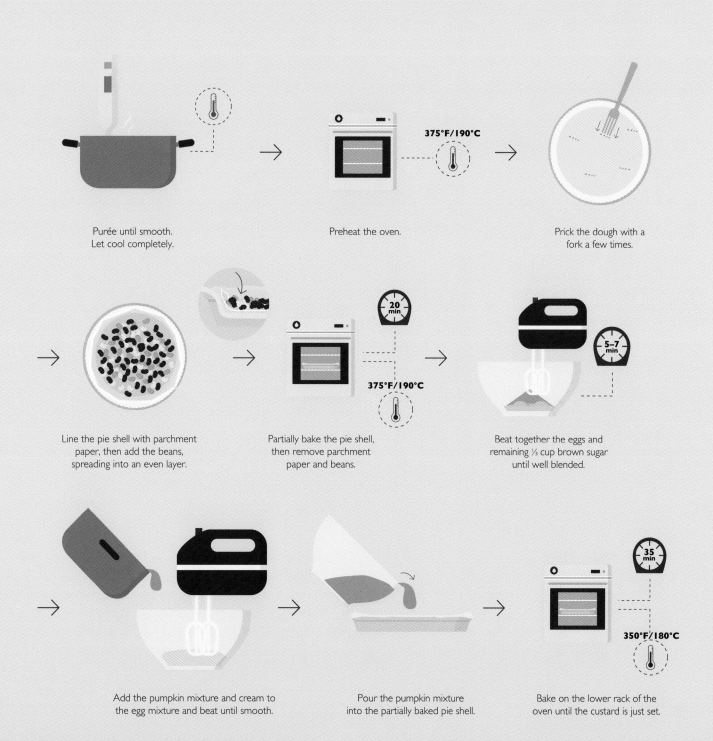

Purée until smooth.
Let cool completely.

Preheat the oven. **375°F/190°C**

Prick the dough with a
fork a few times.

Line the pie shell with parchment
paper, then add the beans,
spreading into an even layer.

Partially bake the pie shell,
then remove parchment
paper and beans.

20 min • **375°F/190°C**

Beat together the eggs and
remaining ⅓ cup brown sugar
until well blended.

5–7 min

Add the pumpkin mixture and cream to
the egg mixture and beat until smooth.

Pour the pumpkin mixture
into the partially baked pie shell.

Bake on the lower rack of the
oven until the custard is just set.

35 min • **350°F/180°C**

½ flaky pastry dough

1 cup/7 oz/225 g dried beans

4 egg yolks

¾ cup/6 oz/185 g sugar

4 tbsp fresh orange juice

3 tbsp finely grated orange zest

3 tbsp cornstarch

4 egg whites

1 pinch of salt

½ cup/4 oz/125 g sugar

049   make flaky pastry dough

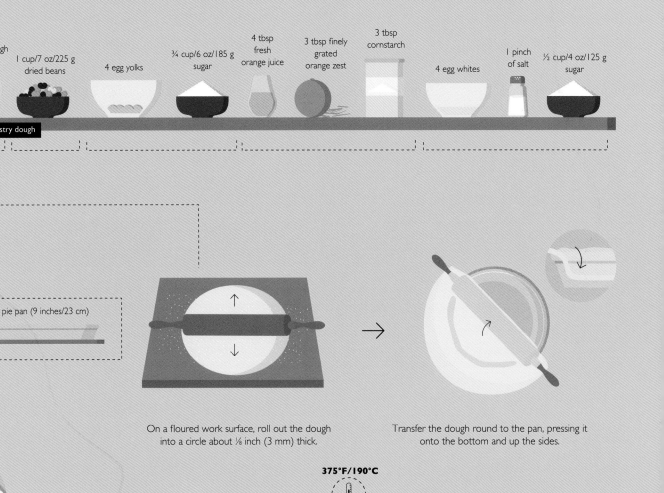

pie pan (9 inches/23 cm)

On a floured work surface, roll out the dough into a circle about ⅛ inch (3 mm) thick.

Transfer the dough round to the pan, pressing it onto the bottom and up the sides.

Trim the edge, leaving a ¾ inch (2 cm) overhang. Prick the dough with a fork a few times.

Refrigerate the pie shell.

30 min

375°F/190°C

Preheat the oven.

Line the pie shell with parchment paper, then add beans, spreading into an even layer.

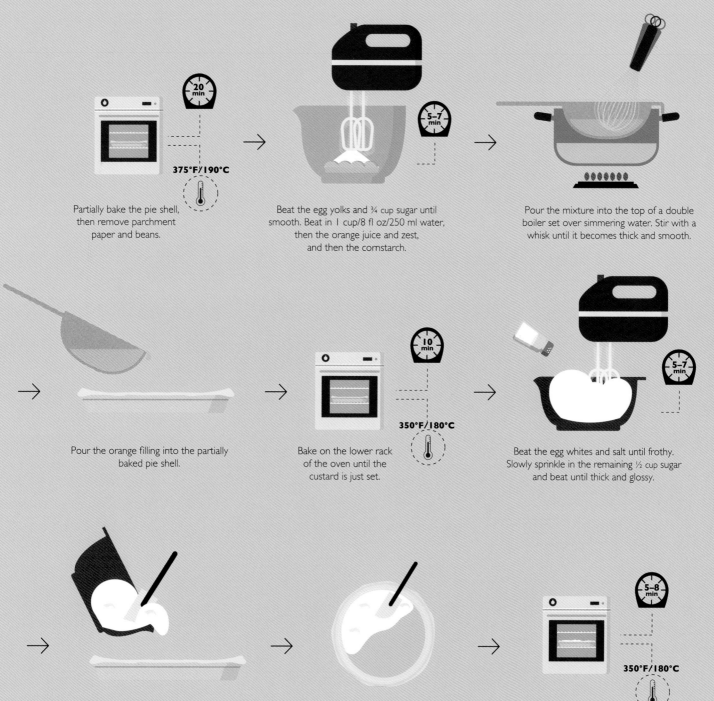

**375°F/190°C**

Partially bake the pie shell, then remove parchment paper and beans.

Beat the egg yolks and ¾ cup sugar until smooth. Beat in 1 cup/8 fl oz/250 ml water, then the orange juice and zest, and then the cornstarch.

Pour the mixture into the top of a double boiler set over simmering water. Stir with a whisk until it becomes thick and smooth.

Pour the orange filling into the partially baked pie shell.

**350°F/180°C**

Bake on the lower rack of the oven until the custard is just set.

Beat the egg whites and salt until frothy. Slowly sprinkle in the remaining ½ cup sugar and beat until thick and glossy.

Remove the pie from the oven and spread the meringue evenly onto the filling.

**350°F/180°C**

Bake until the meringue is golden brown.

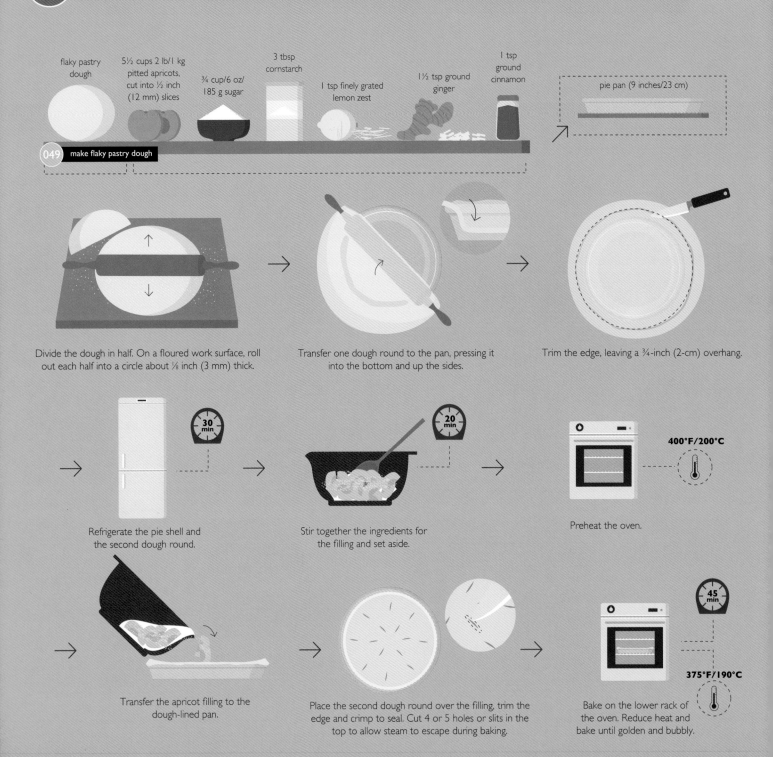

flaky pastry dough

5½ cups 2 lb/1 kg pitted apricots, cut into ½ inch (12 mm) slices

¾ cup/6 oz/ 185 g sugar

3 tbsp cornstarch

1 tsp finely grated lemon zest

1½ tsp ground ginger

1 tsp ground cinnamon

pie pan (9 inches/23 cm)

049 make flaky pastry dough

Divide the dough in half. On a floured work surface, roll out each half into a circle about ⅛ inch (3 mm) thick.

Transfer one dough round to the pan, pressing it into the bottom and up the sides.

Trim the edge, leaving a ¾-inch (2-cm) overhang.

Refrigerate the pie shell and the second dough round.

30 min

Stir together the ingredients for the filling and set aside.

20 min

Preheat the oven.

400°F/200°C

Transfer the apricot filling to the dough-lined pan.

Place the second dough round over the filling, trim the edge and crimp to seal. Cut 4 or 5 holes or slits in the top to allow steam to escape during baking.

Bake on the lower rack of the oven. Reduce heat and bake until golden and bubbly.

45 min

375°F/190°C

tart pan (9½ inches/24 cm)

shortcrust pastry

1 cup/7 oz/225 g dried beans

2 cups/22 oz/ 700 g maple syrup

2 tbsp unsalted butter

2 eggs

¼ cup/2 oz/60 g brown sugar

1 pinch of salt

1 tsp vanilla extract

1½ cups/6 oz/ 185 g chopped pecans

whipped cream

048 make shortcrust pastry

015 whip cream

8 min

Boil the maple syrup until reduced by one-forth. Let cool.

Add the butter and stir until melted. Set aside.

Preheat the oven.

375°F/190°C

On a floured work surface roll out the dough into a circle about ⅛ inch (3 mm) thick.

Line the pan with the dough, pressing it into the bottom and up the sides. Cut off any excess dough at the rim.

Prick the dough with a fork a few times. Line the tart shell with parchment paper, then add the beans, spreading into an even layer.

20 min

375°F/190°C

Partially bake the tart shell, then remove the parchment paper and beans.

Stir together the maple syrup mixture, the eggs, sugar, salt, vanilla, and pecans.

Pour the mixture into the partially baked tart shell.

30 min

350°F/180°C

Bake until the center is firm to the touch.

Let cool completely. Serve with whipped cream.

✳ The tart can be decorated with a white chocolate lace.

033 make chocolate lace

shortcrust pastry

1 cup/7 oz/225 g
dried beans

crème brûlée mixture

2 tbsp brown
sugar

kitchen torch

6 tartlet pans
(4 inches/10 cm),
greased

048   make shortcrust pastry

272   make crème brûlée

375°F/190°C

Preheat the oven.

On a floured work surface roll out the dough
into a circle about ⅛ inch (3 mm) thick.

Cut out 6 rounds of dough, each about 2 inches (5 cm)
larger than the diameter of the pan. You may have to
press together then re-roll the dough to get 6 rounds.

Line the pans with the dough,
cutting off any excess dough
at the rim.

Prick the dough with a
fork a few times.

Line each with parchment paper
and divide the beans among them,
spreading them into an even layer.

15 min

375°F/190°C

Partially bake the tartlet shells,
then remove the parchment
paper and beans. Return to the
oven and bake until golden.

Let cool and carefully
unmold.

Pour the crème brûlée mixture
into the tartlet shells and cover
each with plastic wrap.

Refrigerate
until chilled.

Just before serving, sprinkle the tartlets with the brown
sugar and use a kitchen torch to caramelize the tops.

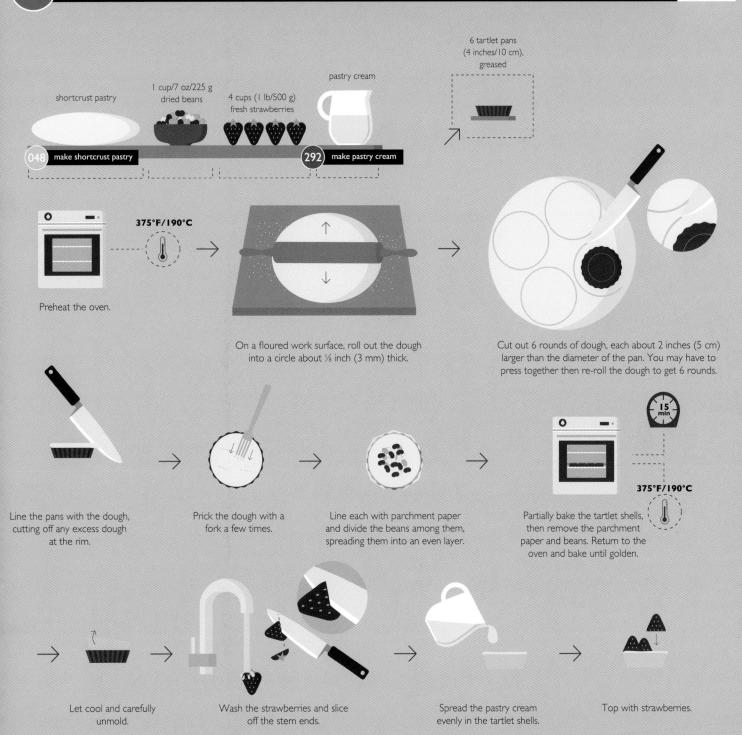

shortcrust pastry

1 cup/7 oz/225 g dried beans

4 cups (1 lb/500 g) fresh strawberries

pastry cream

6 tartlet pans (4 inches/10 cm), greased

048 make shortcrust pastry

292 make pastry cream

375°F/190°C

Preheat the oven.

On a floured work surface, roll out the dough into a circle about ⅛ inch (3 mm) thick.

Cut out 6 rounds of dough, each about 2 inches (5 cm) larger than the diameter of the pan. You may have to press together then re-roll the dough to get 6 rounds.

Line the pans with the dough, cutting off any excess dough at the rim.

Prick the dough with a fork a few times.

Line each with parchment paper and divide the beans among them, spreading them into an even layer.

15 min

375°F/190°C

Partially bake the tartlet shells, then remove the parchment paper and beans. Return to the oven and bake until golden.

Let cool and carefully unmold.

Wash the strawberries and slice off the stem ends.

Spread the pastry cream evenly in the tartlet shells.

Top with strawberries.

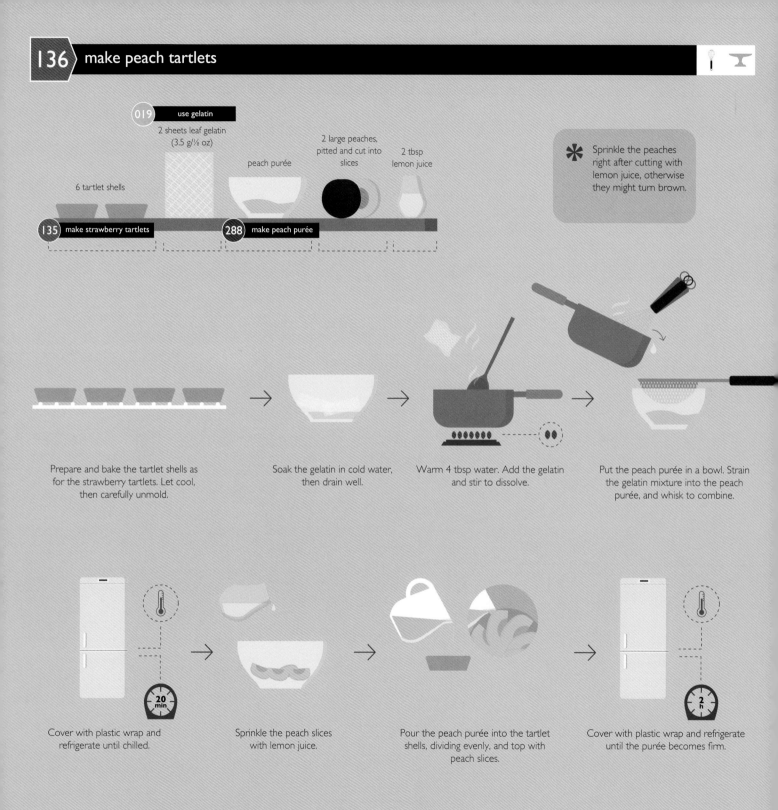

019 use gelatin
2 sheets leaf gelatin
(3.5 g/⅛ oz)

peach purée

2 large peaches,
pitted and cut into
slices

2 tbsp
lemon juice

6 tartlet shells

135 make strawberry tartlets

288 make peach purée

*Sprinkle the peaches
right after cutting with
lemon juice, otherwise
they might turn brown.

Prepare and bake the tartlet shells as
for the strawberry tartlets. Let cool,
then carefully unmold.

Soak the gelatin in cold water,
then drain well.

Warm 4 tbsp water. Add the gelatin
and stir to dissolve.

Put the peach purée in a bowl. Strain
the gelatin mixture into the peach
purée, and whisk to combine.

Cover with plastic wrap and
refrigerate until chilled.

20 min

Sprinkle the peach slices
with lemon juice.

Pour the peach purée into the tartlet
shells, dividing evenly, and top with
peach slices.

Cover with plastic wrap and refrigerate
until the purée becomes firm.

2 h

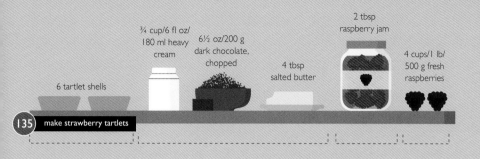

¾ cup/6 fl oz/ 180 ml heavy cream

6½ oz/200 g dark chocolate, chopped

4 tbsp salted butter

2 tbsp raspberry jam

4 cups/1 lb/ 500 g fresh raspberries

6 tartlet shells

135 make strawberry tartlets

Prepare and bake the tartlet shells as for the strawberry tartlets. Let cool, then carefully unmold.

Bring the cream to a simmer.

Put the chocolate into a bowl, then pour the cream over the chocolate and let stand until the chocolate has melted.

Add the butter and stir until smooth.

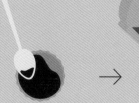

Spread a thin layer of raspberry jam on the bottom of each shell, dividing it evenly.

Fill the tartlet shells with the chocolate cream to just below the edge.

Let stand at room temperature until set.

Top with the whole raspberries.

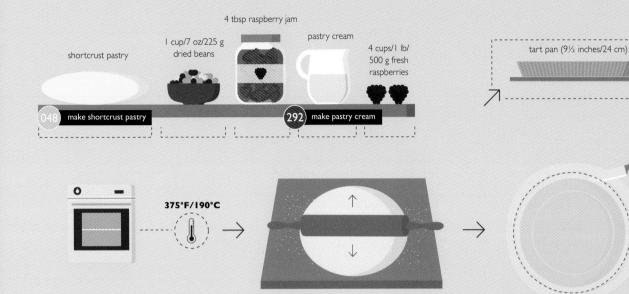

shortcrust pastry

1 cup/7 oz/225 g dried beans

4 tbsp raspberry jam

pastry cream

4 cups/1 lb/ 500 g fresh raspberries

tart pan (9½ inches/24 cm)

048  make shortcrust pastry

292  make pastry cream

**375°F/190°C**

Preheat the oven.

On a floured work surface, roll out the dough into a circle about ⅛ inch (3 mm) thick.

Line the pan with the dough, pressing it into the bottom and up the sides. Cut off any excess dough at the rim.

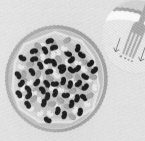

Prick the dough with a fork a few times. Line the tart shell with parchment paper, then add the beans, spreading into an even layer.

**20 min**

**375°F/190°C**

Partially bake the tart shell, then remove the parchment paper and beans.

Let the tart shell cool completely, then carefully unmold.

Spread a thin layer of raspberry jam over the bottom of the shell.

Fill the tart shell with pastry cream to just below the edge.

Cover with plastic wrap and refrigerate until the cream becomes firm.

Top with the raspberries.

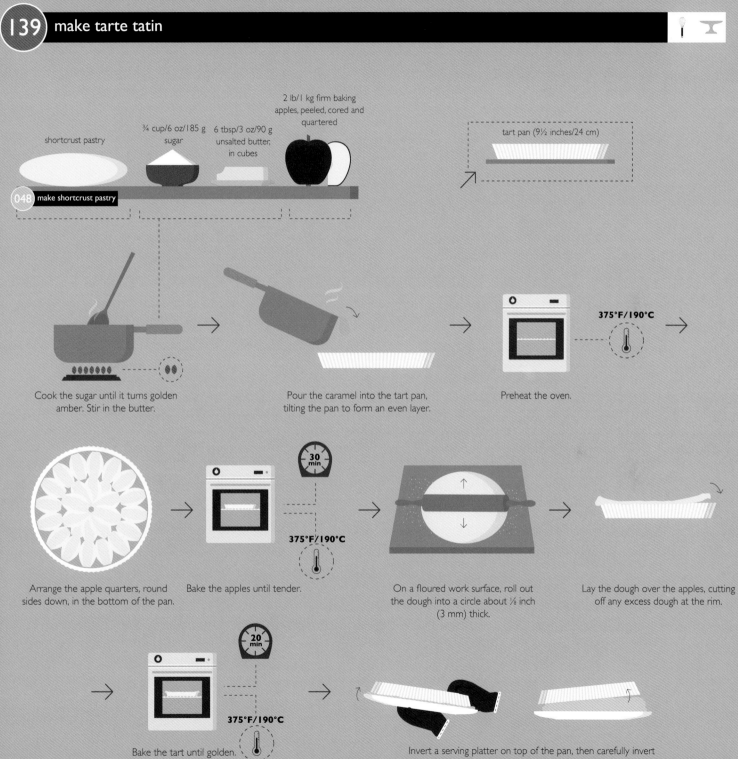

shortcrust pastry

¾ cup/6 oz/185 g sugar

6 tbsp/3 oz/90 g unsalted butter, in cubes

2 lb/1 kg firm baking apples, peeled, cored and quartered

tart pan (9½ inches/24 cm)

048 make shortcrust pastry

Cook the sugar until it turns golden amber. Stir in the butter.

Pour the caramel into the tart pan, tilting the pan to form an even layer.

Preheat the oven.

375°F/190°C

Arrange the apple quarters, round sides down, in the bottom of the pan.

Bake the apples until tender.

30 min

375°F/190°C

On a floured work surface, roll out the dough into a circle about ⅛ inch (3 mm) thick.

Lay the dough over the apples, cutting off any excess dough at the rim.

Bake the tart until golden.

20 min

375°F/190°C

Invert a serving platter on top of the pan, then carefully invert the pan and platter together. Serve warm.

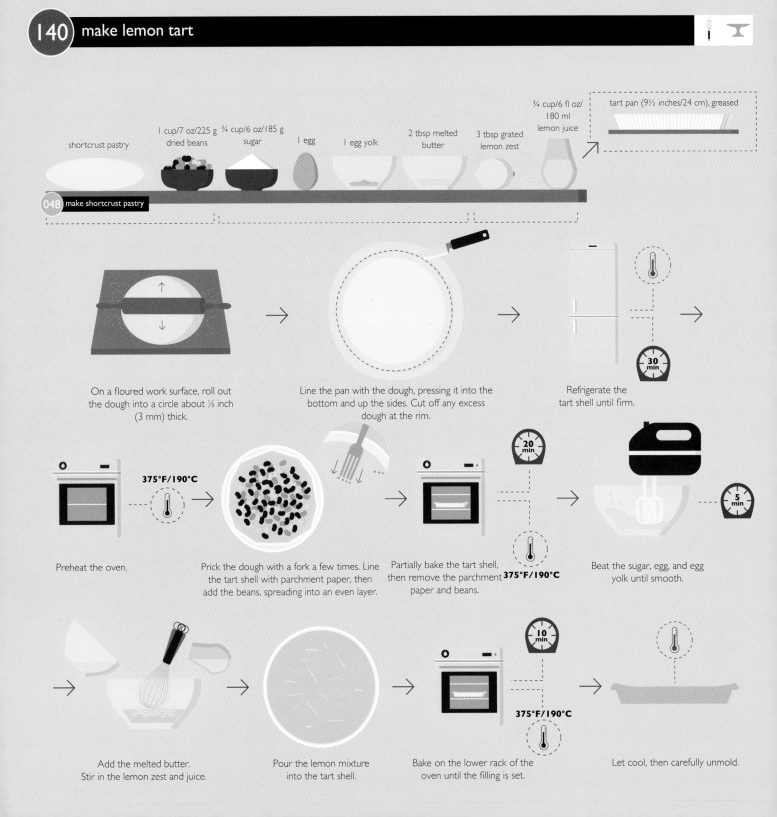

shortcrust pastry

1 cup/7 oz/225 g dried beans

¾ cup/6 oz/185 g sugar

1 egg

1 egg yolk

2 tbsp melted butter

3 tbsp grated lemon zest

¾ cup/6 fl oz/ 180 ml lemon juice

tart pan (9½ inches/24 cm), greased

048 make shortcrust pastry

On a floured work surface, roll out the dough into a circle about ⅛ inch (3 mm) thick.

Line the pan with the dough, pressing it into the bottom and up the sides. Cut off any excess dough at the rim.

Refrigerate the tart shell until firm.

30 min

Preheat the oven.

375°F/190°C

Prick the dough with a fork a few times. Line the tart shell with parchment paper, then add the beans, spreading into an even layer.

20 min

Partially bake the tart shell, then remove the parchment paper and beans. 375°F/190°C

Beat the sugar, egg, and egg yolk until smooth.

5 min

Add the melted butter. Stir in the lemon zest and juice.

Pour the lemon mixture into the tart shell.

10 min

Bake on the lower rack of the oven until the filling is set. 375°F/190°C

Let cool, then carefully unmold.

# make lemon meringue tart

4 egg whites

1 pinch of salt

½ cup/4 oz/ 125 g sugar

Prepare the lemon tart as directed.

5 min

Beat the egg whites and salt until frothy. Slowly add the sugar and beat until thick and glossy.

Spread the meringue evenly over the lemon filling.

5 min

**375°F/190°C**

Bake until the meringue is golden brown.

Let cool, then carefully unmold.

# make lemon meringue tartlets

candied lemon slices

6 tartlet pans (4 inches/10 cm), greased

030    candy lemon zest

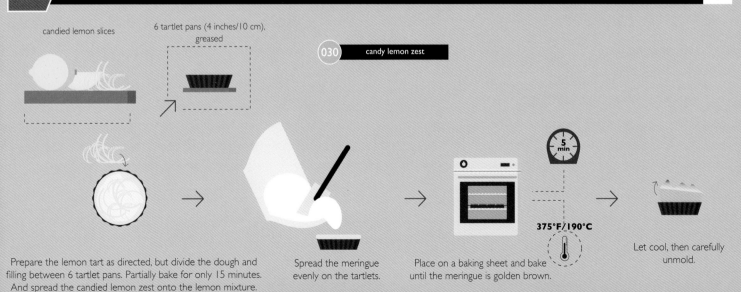

5 min

**375°F/190°C**

Prepare the lemon tart as directed, but divide the dough and filling between 6 tartlet pans. Partially bake for only 15 minutes. And spread the candied lemon zest onto the lemon mixture.

Spread the meringue evenly on the tartlets.

Place on a baking sheet and bake until the meringue is golden brown.

Let cool, then carefully unmold.

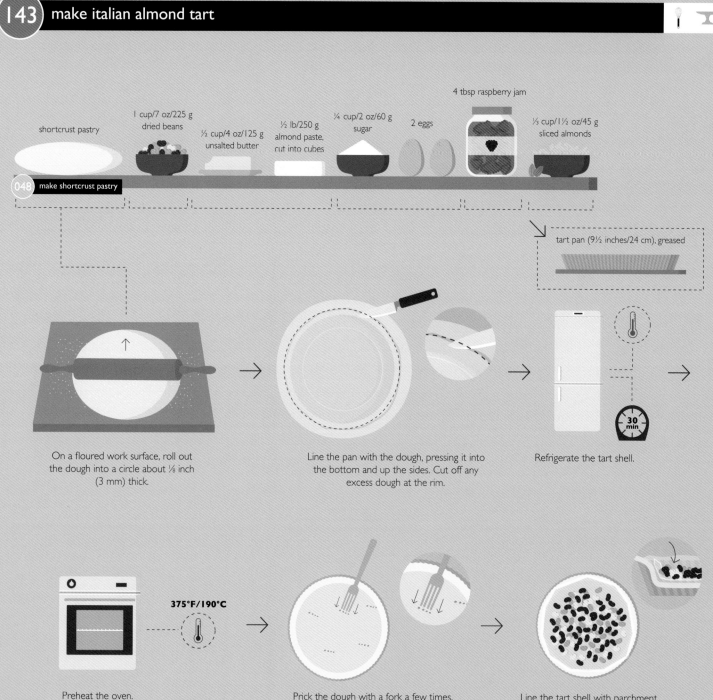

shortcrust pastry

1 cup/7 oz/225 g
dried beans

½ cup/4 oz/125 g
unsalted butter

½ lb/250 g
almond paste,
cut into cubes

¼ cup/2 oz/60 g
sugar

2 eggs

4 tbsp raspberry jam

⅓ cup/1½ oz/45 g
sliced almonds

048 make shortcrust pastry

tart pan (9½ inches/24 cm), greased

On a floured work surface, roll out the dough into a circle about ⅛ inch (3 mm) thick.

Line the pan with the dough, pressing it into the bottom and up the sides. Cut off any excess dough at the rim.

Refrigerate the tart shell.

30 min

Preheat the oven.

375°F/190°C

Prick the dough with a fork a few times.

Line the tart shell with parchment paper, then add the beans, spreading into an even layer.

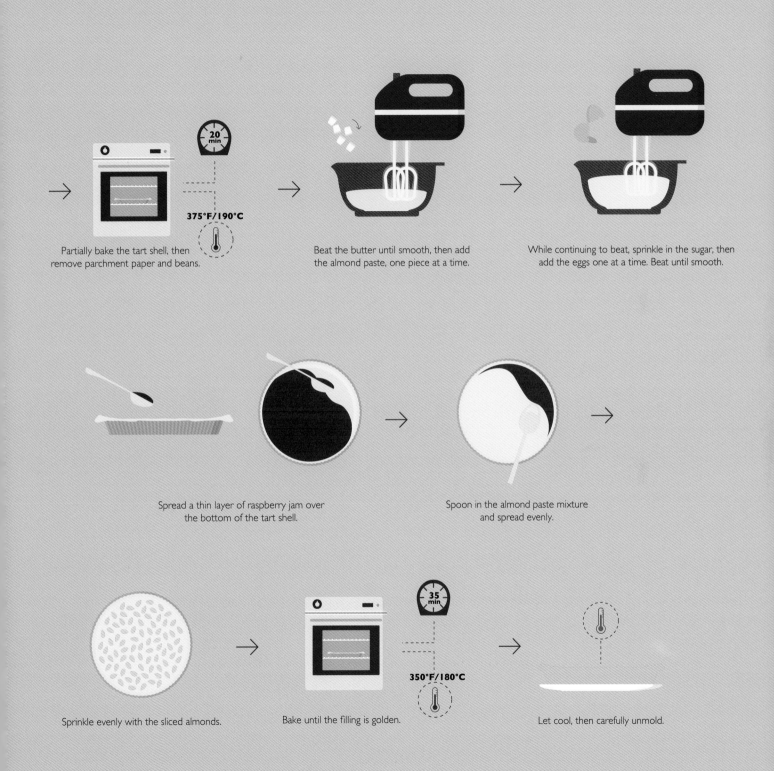

→ **20 min**
**375°F/190°C**
Partially bake the tart shell, then remove parchment paper and beans.

→ Beat the butter until smooth, then add the almond paste, one piece at a time.

→ While continuing to beat, sprinkle in the sugar, then add the eggs one at a time. Beat until smooth.

Spread a thin layer of raspberry jam over the bottom of the tart shell.

→ Spoon in the almond paste mixture and spread evenly.

→ Sprinkle evenly with the sliced almonds.

→ **35 min**
**350°F/180°C**
Bake until the filling is golden.

→ Let cool, then carefully unmold.

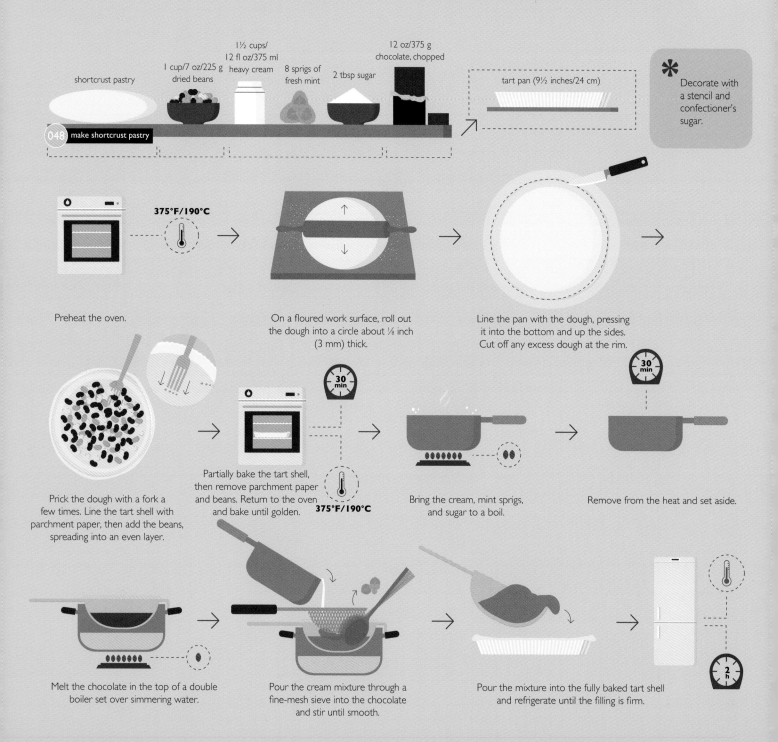

shortcrust pastry

1 cup/7 oz/225 g dried beans

1½ cups/ 12 fl oz/375 ml heavy cream

8 sprigs of fresh mint

2 tbsp sugar

12 oz/375 g chocolate, chopped

tart pan (9½ inches/24 cm)

Decorate with a stencil and confectioner's sugar.

048 make shortcrust pastry

Preheat the oven.

375°F/190°C

On a floured work surface, roll out the dough into a circle about ⅛ inch (3 mm) thick.

Line the pan with the dough, pressing it into the bottom and up the sides. Cut off any excess dough at the rim.

Prick the dough with a fork a few times. Line the tart shell with parchment paper, then add the beans, spreading into an even layer.

Partially bake the tart shell, then remove parchment paper and beans. Return to the oven and bake until golden. 375°F/190°C

30 min

Bring the cream, mint sprigs, and sugar to a boil.

30 min

Remove from the heat and set aside.

Melt the chocolate in the top of a double boiler set over simmering water.

Pour the cream mixture through a fine-mesh sieve into the chocolate and stir until smooth.

Pour the mixture into the fully baked tart shell and refrigerate until the filling is firm.

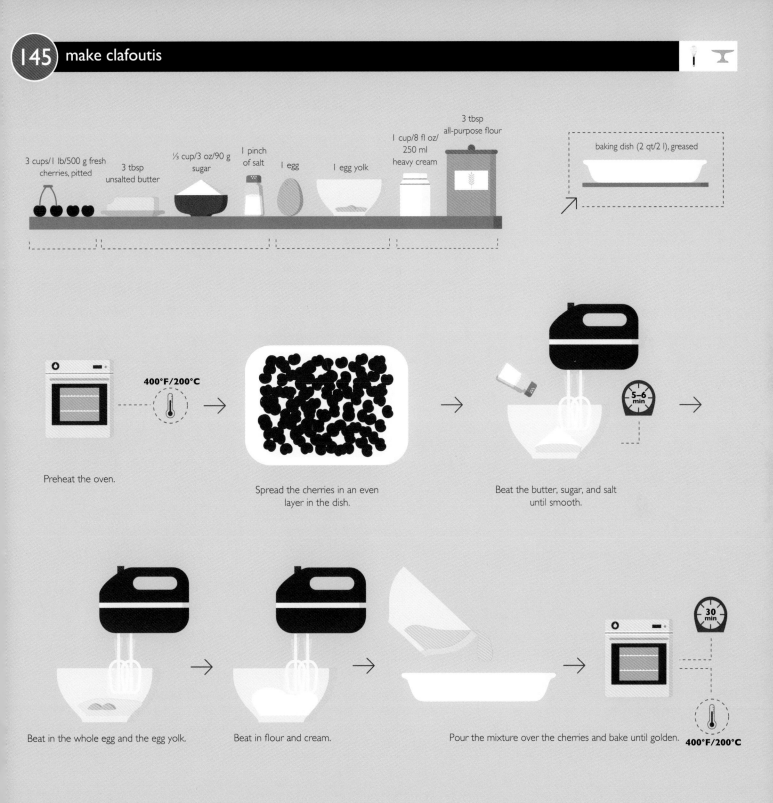

3 cups/1 lb/500 g fresh cherries, pitted

3 tbsp unsalted butter

⅓ cup/3 oz/90 g sugar

1 pinch of salt

1 egg

1 egg yolk

1 cup/8 fl oz/250 ml heavy cream

3 tbsp all-purpose flour

baking dish (2 qt/2 l), greased

Preheat the oven.

400°F/200°C

Spread the cherries in an even layer in the dish.

Beat the butter, sugar, and salt until smooth.

5–6 min

Beat in the whole egg and the egg yolk.

Beat in flour and cream.

Pour the mixture over the cherries and bake until golden.

30 min

400°F/200°C

# 146 make apple crumble

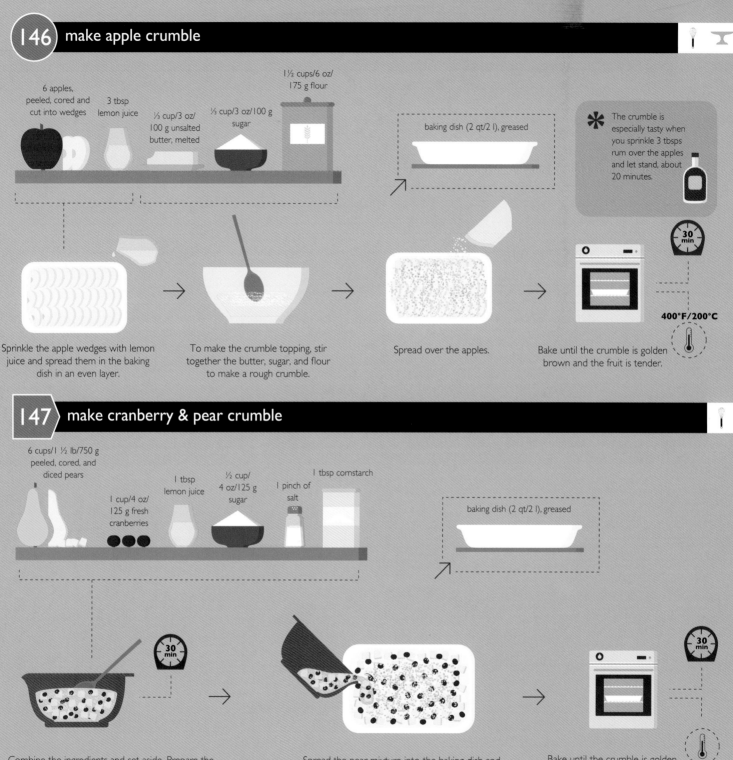

6 apples, peeled, cored and cut into wedges

3 tbsp lemon juice

⅓ cup/3 oz/100 g unsalted butter, melted

½ cup/3 oz/100 g sugar

1½ cups/6 oz/175 g flour

baking dish (2 qt/2 l), greased

*The crumble is especially tasty when you sprinkle 3 tbsps rum over the apples and let stand, about 20 minutes.

30 min

400°F/200°C

Sprinkle the apple wedges with lemon juice and spread them in the baking dish in an even layer.

To make the crumble topping, stir together the butter, sugar, and flour to make a rough crumble.

Spread over the apples.

Bake until the crumble is golden brown and the fruit is tender.

# 147 make cranberry & pear crumble

6 cups/1 ½ lb/750 g peeled, cored, and diced pears

1 cup/4 oz/125 g fresh cranberries

1 tbsp lemon juice

½ cup/4 oz/125 g sugar

1 pinch of salt

1 tbsp cornstarch

baking dish (2 qt/2 l), greased

30 min

30 min

400°F/200°C

Combine the ingredients and set aside. Prepare the crumble topping as directed in the apple crumble recipe.

Spread the pear mixture into the baking dish and top with the crumble topping.

Bake until the crumble is golden brown and the fruit is tender. **400°F/200°C**

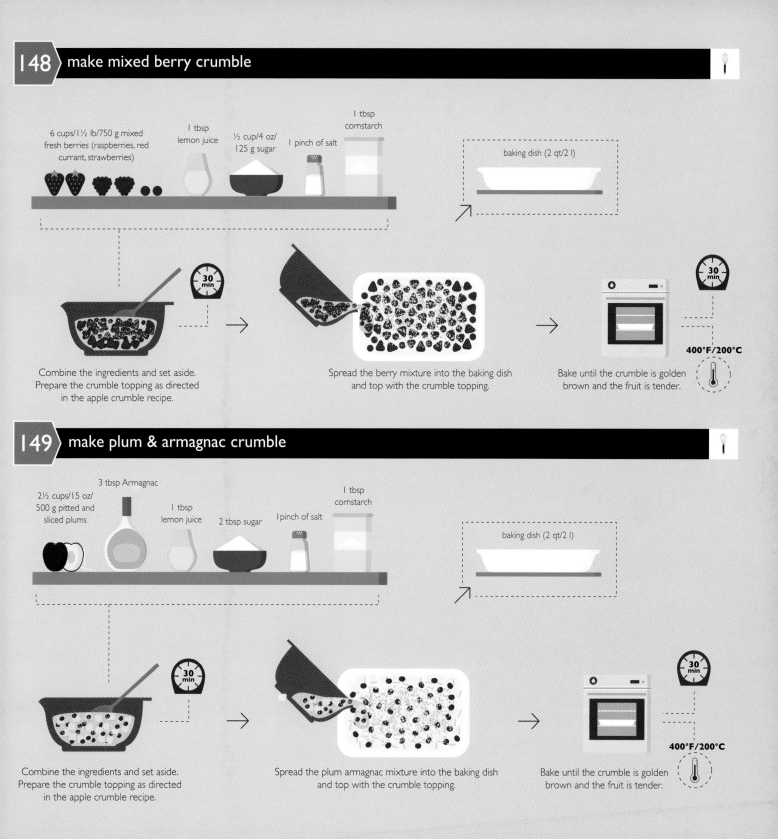

## 148 › make mixed berry crumble

6 cups/1½ lb/750 g mixed fresh berries (raspberries, red currant, strawberries)

1 tbsp lemon juice

½ cup/4 oz/ 125 g sugar

1 pinch of salt

1 tbsp cornstarch

baking dish (2 qt/2 l)

30 min

Combine the ingredients and set aside. Prepare the crumble topping as directed in the apple crumble recipe.

Spread the berry mixture into the baking dish and top with the crumble topping.

30 min

400°F/200°C

Bake until the crumble is golden brown and the fruit is tender.

## 149 › make plum & armagnac crumble

2½ cups/15 oz/ 500 g pitted and sliced plums

3 tbsp Armagnac

1 tbsp lemon juice

2 tbsp sugar

1 pinch of salt

1 tbsp cornstarch

baking dish (2 qt/2 l)

30 min

Combine the ingredients and set aside. Prepare the crumble topping as directed in the apple crumble recipe.

Spread the plum armagnac mixture into the baking dish and top with the crumble topping.

30 min

400°F/200°C

Bake until the crumble is golden brown and the fruit is tender.

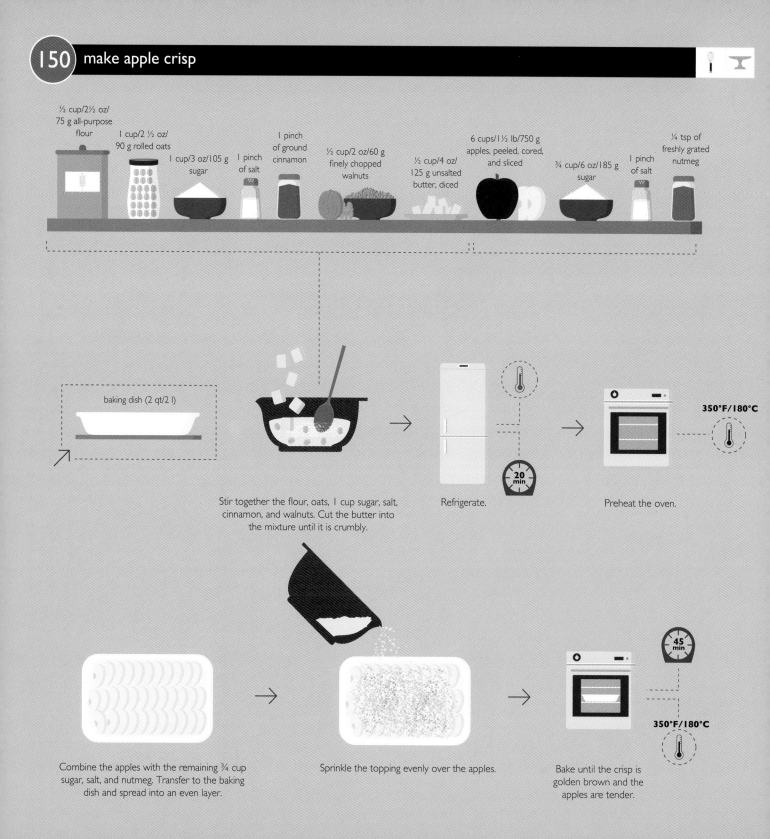

½ cup/2½ oz/ 75 g all-purpose flour

1 cup/2 ½ oz/ 90 g rolled oats

1 cup/3 oz/105 g sugar

1 pinch of salt

1 pinch of ground cinnamon

½ cup/2 oz/60 g finely chopped walnuts

½ cup/4 oz/ 125 g unsalted butter, diced

6 cups/1½ lb/750 g apples, peeled, cored, and sliced

¾ cup/6 oz/185 g sugar

1 pinch of salt

¼ tsp of freshly grated nutmeg

baking dish (2 qt/2 l)

Stir together the flour, oats, 1 cup sugar, salt, cinnamon, and walnuts. Cut the butter into the mixture until it is crumbly.

Refrigerate. 20 min

Preheat the oven. 350°F/180°C

Combine the apples with the remaining ¾ cup sugar, salt, and nutmeg. Transfer to the baking dish and spread into an even layer.

Sprinkle the topping evenly over the apples.

Bake until the crisp is golden brown and the apples are tender. 45 min 350°F/180°C

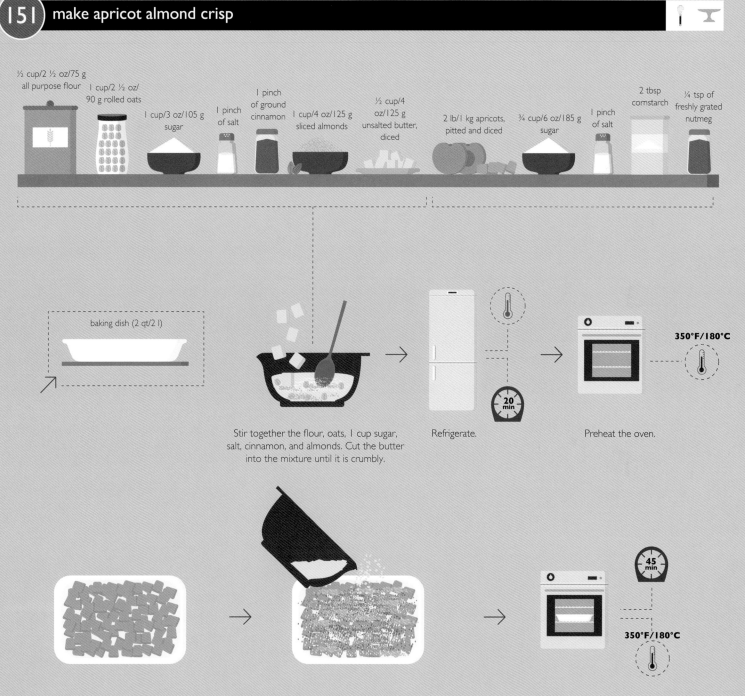

½ cup/2 ½ oz/75 g all purpose flour

1 cup/2 ½ oz/90 g rolled oats

1 cup/3 oz/105 g sugar

1 pinch of salt

1 pinch of ground cinnamon

1 cup/4 oz/125 g sliced almonds

½ cup/4 oz/125 g unsalted butter, diced

2 lb/1 kg apricots, pitted and diced

¾ cup/6 oz/185 g sugar

1 pinch of salt

2 tbsp cornstarch

¼ tsp of freshly grated nutmeg

baking dish (2 qt/2 l)

Stir together the flour, oats, 1 cup sugar, salt, cinnamon, and almonds. Cut the butter into the mixture until it is crumbly.

Refrigerate.

20 min

350°F/180°C

Preheat the oven.

Combine the apricots with the remaining ¾ cup sugar, salt, cornstarch, and nutmeg. Transfer to the baking dish and spread into an even layer.

Sprinkle the topping evenly over the apricots.

45 min

350°F/180°C

Bake until the crisp is golden brown and the apricots are tender.

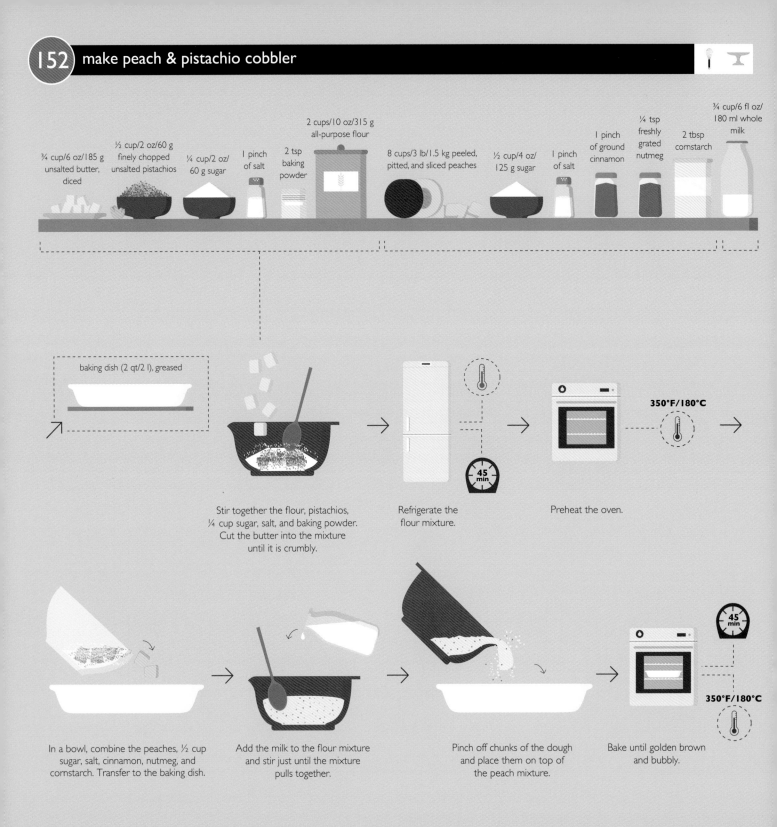

¾ cup/6 oz/185 g unsalted butter, diced

½ cup/2 oz/60 g finely chopped unsalted pistachios

¼ cup/2 oz/60 g sugar

1 pinch of salt

2 tsp baking powder

2 cups/10 oz/315 g all-purpose flour

8 cups/3 lb/1.5 kg peeled, pitted, and sliced peaches

½ cup/4 oz/125 g sugar

1 pinch of salt

1 pinch of ground cinnamon

¼ tsp freshly grated nutmeg

2 tbsp cornstarch

¾ cup/6 fl oz/180 ml whole milk

baking dish (2 qt/2 l), greased

Stir together the flour, pistachios, ¼ cup sugar, salt, and baking powder. Cut the butter into the mixture until it is crumbly.

Refrigerate the flour mixture. 45 min

Preheat the oven. 350°F/180°C

In a bowl, combine the peaches, ½ cup sugar, salt, cinnamon, nutmeg, and cornstarch. Transfer to the baking dish.

Add the milk to the flour mixture and stir just until the mixture pulls together.

Pinch off chunks of the dough and place them on top of the peach mixture.

Bake until golden brown and bubbly. 45 min 350°F/180°C

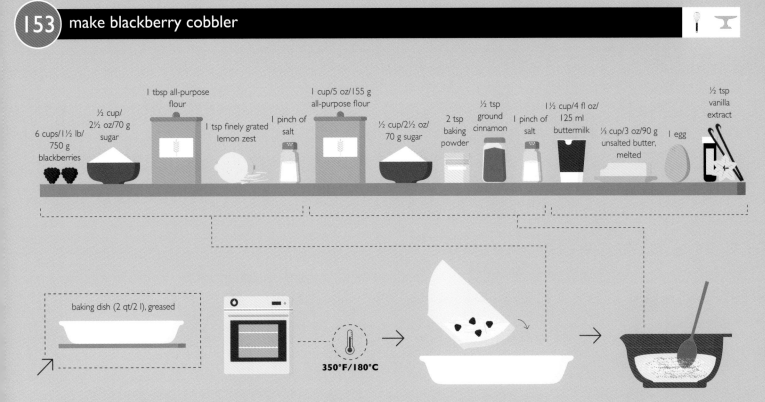

6 cups/1½ lb/ 750 g blackberries

½ cup/ 2½ oz/70 g sugar

1 tbsp all-purpose flour

1 tsp finely grated lemon zest

1 pinch of salt

1 cup/5 oz/155 g all-purpose flour

½ cup/2½ oz/ 70 g sugar

2 tsp baking powder

½ tsp ground cinnamon

1 pinch of salt

1½ cup/4 fl oz/ 125 ml buttermilk

⅓ cup/3 oz/90 g unsalted butter, melted

1 egg

½ tsp vanilla extract

baking dish (2 qt/2 l), greased

350°F/180°C

Preheat the oven.

Combine the blackberries, ½ cup sugar, 1 tbsp flour, lemon zest, and salt. Transfer to the baking dish.

Stir together 1 cup flour, ½ cup sugar, baking powder, cinnamon, and salt.

In another bowl, whisk together the buttermilk, melted butter, egg, and vanilla extract.

Add to the flour mixture to the buttermilk mixture a little at a time and stir just until the mixture forms a soft dough.

Drop heaping spoonfuls of the dough onto the blackberries.

45 min

350°F/180°C

Bake until golden brown and bubbly.

## 154  make cherry cobbler

4 cups/24 oz/750 g
fresh sweet cherries,
pitted

Follow directions for the blackberry
cobbler, using cherries instead of the
blackberries.

## 155  make summer berry cobbler

6 cups/1 ½ lb/750 g mixed
fresh berries (raspberries,
red currants, strawberries)

Follow directions for the blackberry
cobbler, using mixed berries instead
of the blackberries.

## 156  add flavor to cobbler fruits

1 tsp
vanilla
extract

¼ tsp
freshly grated
nutmeg

1 tbsp rum

30
min

Add vanilla extract, nutmeg,
and rum to the fruit mixture
and let rest.

Proceed as directed for the
blackberry cobbler.

## 157  make cobbler with nut topping

2 tbsp chopped
walnuts

2 tbsp sliced
almonds

Sprinkle the cobbler topping
with chopped walnuts and
sliced almonds.

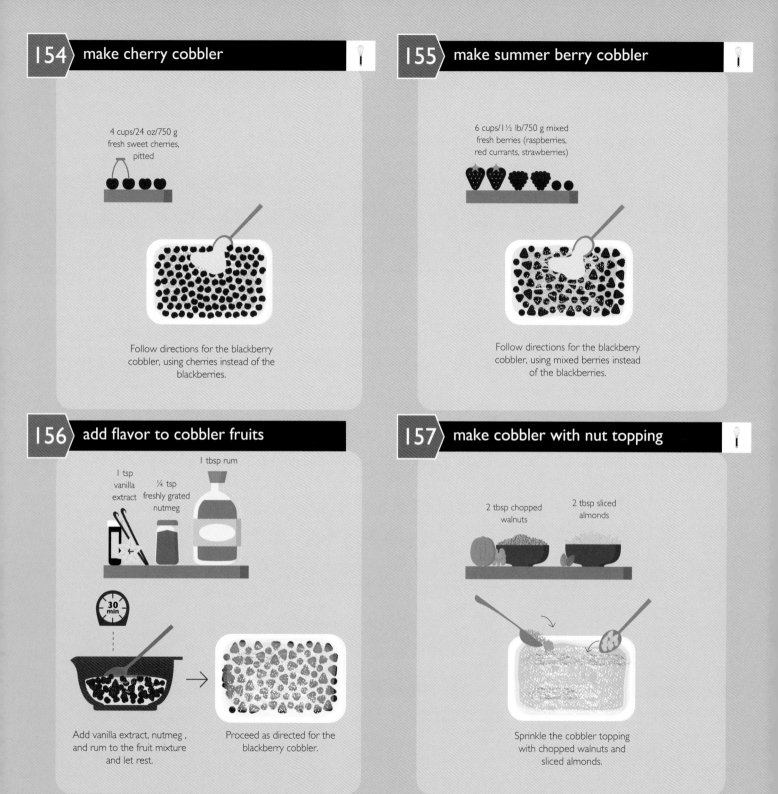

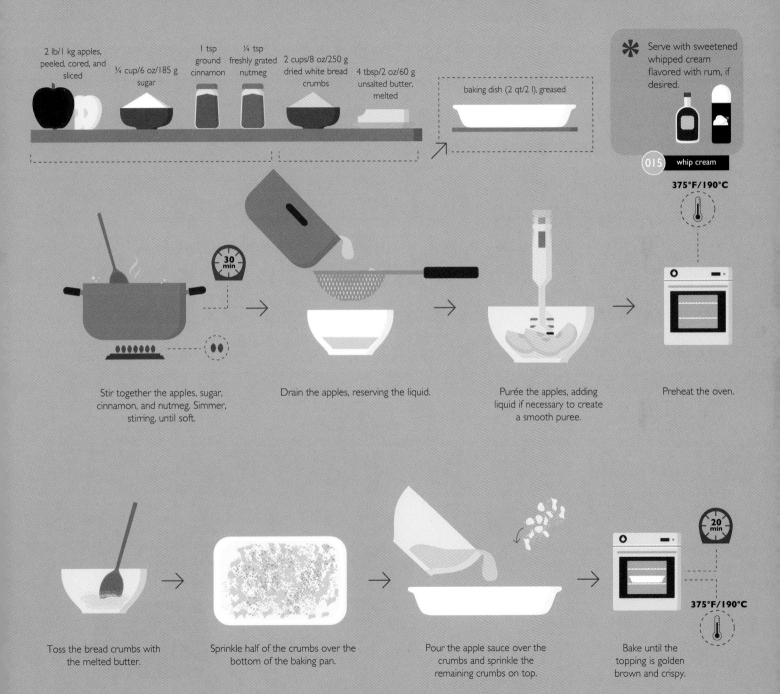

2 lb/1 kg apples, peeled, cored, and sliced

¾ cup/6 oz/185 g sugar

1 tsp ground cinnamon

¼ tsp freshly grated nutmeg

2 cups/8 oz/250 g dried white bread crumbs

4 tbsp/2 oz/60 g unsalted butter, melted

baking dish (2 qt/2 l), greased

Serve with sweetened whipped cream flavored with rum, if desired.

015 whip cream

375°F/190°C

Stir together the apples, sugar, cinnamon, and nutmeg. Simmer, stirring, until soft.

Drain the apples, reserving the liquid.

Purée the apples, adding liquid if necessary to create a smooth puree.

Preheat the oven.

Toss the bread crumbs with the melted butter.

Sprinkle half of the crumbs over the bottom of the baking pan.

Pour the apple sauce over the crumbs and sprinkle the remaining crumbs on top.

Bake until the topping is golden brown and crispy.

375°F/190°C

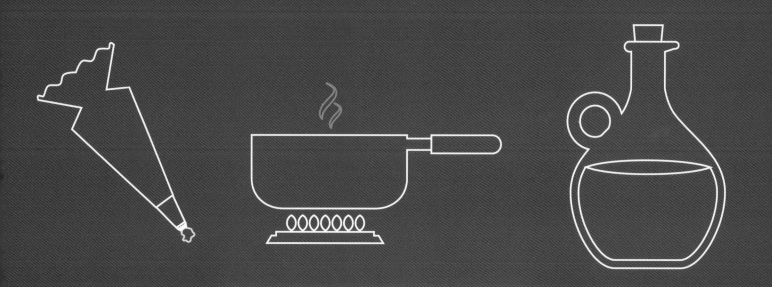

# muffins and cupcakes

1½ cups/7½ oz/ 235 g flour

2 tsp baking powder

1 pinch of ground cinnamon

2 eggs

⅔ cup/5 oz/ 155 g sugar

¼ cup/2 fl oz/ 60 ml oil

1 cup/8 oz/ 250 g yogurt

2 tbsp unsalted butter

12-cup muffin pan, greased

350°F/180°C

Preheat the oven.

Stir together the flour, baking powder, and cinnamon.

3 min

In another bowl, beat the egg and sugar until combined.

Beat in the oil and yogurt.

Stir in the flour mixture.

Spoon the batter evenly into the muffin pan.

Fill the cups three-fourths full.

20 min

Bake until golden.

350°F/180°C

## 160 › make blueberry muffins

1 tsp ground cinnamon

2 cups/8 oz/250 g blueberries

Add blueberries and cinnamon to the flour mixture. Prepare like muffins.

## 161 › make chocolate muffins

3 tbsp cocoa powder

Add cocoa powder to the flour mixture. Prepare like muffins.

## 162 › make chocolate chip muffins

2 cups/12 oz/200 g chocolate chips

Stir chocolate chips into the batter. Prepare like muffins.

## 163 › make zucchini muffins

2 cups/10 oz/300 g shredded zucchini

1 cup/8 oz/250 g crème fraîche

Use crème fraîche instead of yogurt. Add the shredded zucchini to the batter. Prepare like muffins.

## 164 › make lemon-yogurt muffins

3 tbsp lemon juice

2 tbsp finely grated lemon zest

Add lemon juice and zest to the batter. Prepare like muffins.

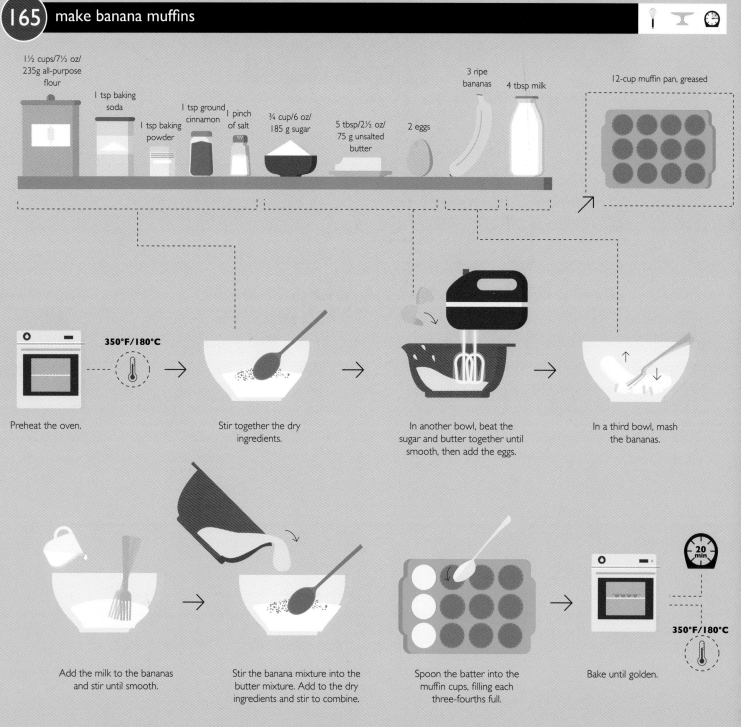

1½ cups/7½ oz/235g all-purpose flour

1 tsp baking soda

1 tsp baking powder

1 tsp ground cinnamon

1 pinch of salt

¾ cup/6 oz/185 g sugar

5 tbsp/2½ oz/75 g unsalted butter

2 eggs

3 ripe bananas

4 tbsp milk

12-cup muffin pan, greased

350°F/180°C

Preheat the oven.

Stir together the dry ingredients.

In another bowl, beat the sugar and butter together until smooth, then add the eggs.

In a third bowl, mash the bananas.

Add the milk to the bananas and stir until smooth.

Stir the banana mixture into the butter mixture. Add to the dry ingredients and stir to combine.

Spoon the batter into the muffin cups, filling each three-fourths full.

Bake until golden.

20 min

350°F/180°C

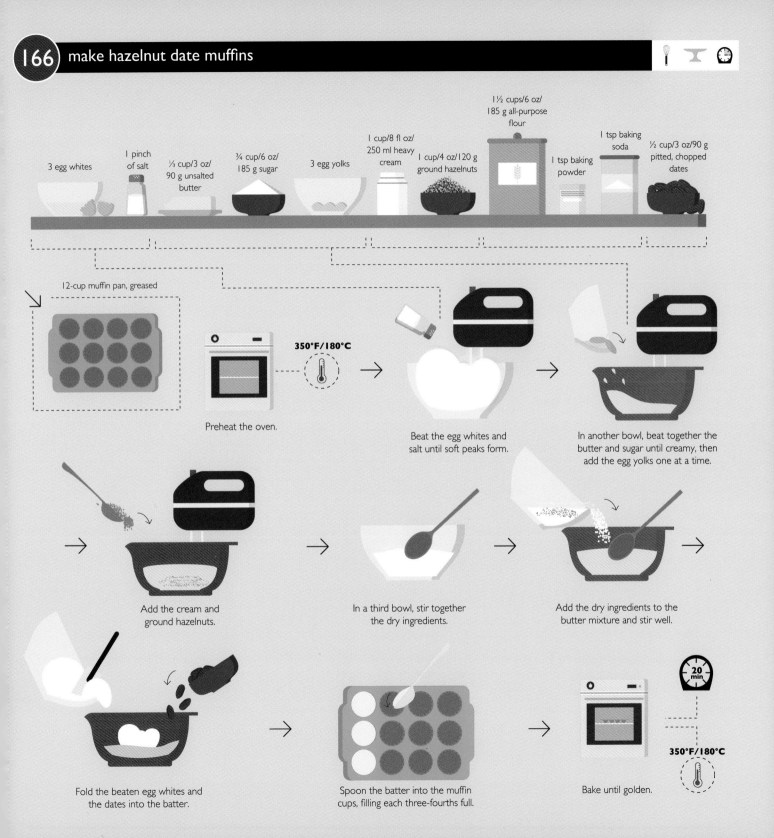

3 egg whites

1 pinch of salt

⅓ cup/3 oz/ 90 g unsalted butter

¾ cup/6 oz/ 185 g sugar

3 egg yolks

1 cup/8 fl oz/ 250 ml heavy cream

1 cup/4 oz/120 g ground hazelnuts

1½ cups/6 oz/ 185 g all-purpose flour

1 tsp baking powder

1 tsp baking soda

½ cup/3 oz/90 g pitted, chopped dates

12-cup muffin pan, greased

350°F/180°C

Preheat the oven.

Beat the egg whites and salt until soft peaks form.

In another bowl, beat together the butter and sugar until creamy, then add the egg yolks one at a time.

Add the cream and ground hazelnuts.

In a third bowl, stir together the dry ingredients.

Add the dry ingredients to the butter mixture and stir well.

Fold the beaten egg whites and the dates into the batter.

Spoon the batter into the muffin cups, filling each three-fourths full.

Bake until golden.

20 min

350°F/180°C

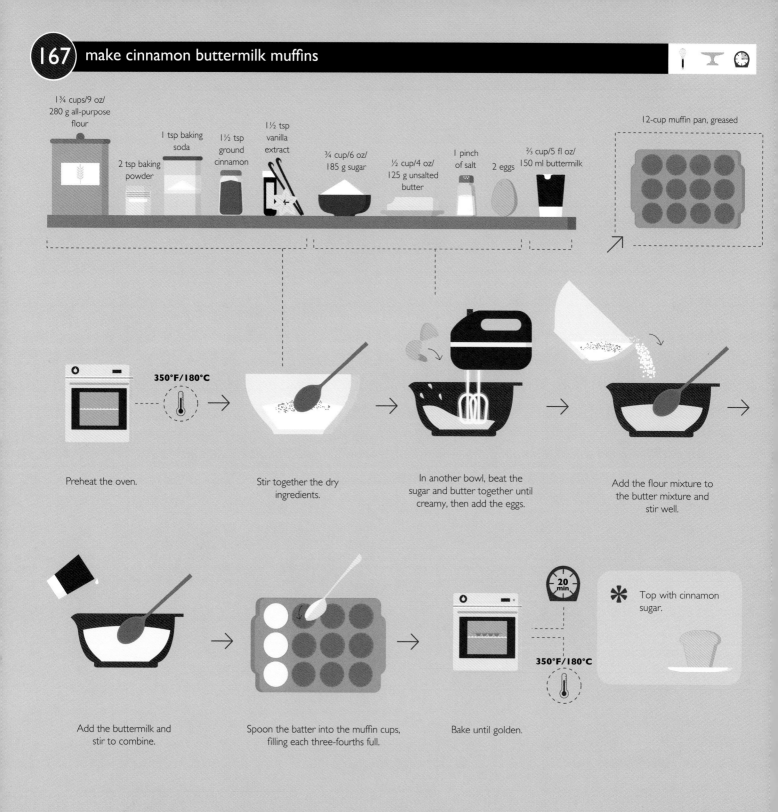

1¾ cups/9 oz/ 280 g all-purpose flour

2 tsp baking powder

1 tsp baking soda

1½ tsp ground cinnamon

1½ tsp vanilla extract

¾ cup/6 oz/ 185 g sugar

½ cup/4 oz/ 125 g unsalted butter

1 pinch of salt

2 eggs

⅔ cup/5 fl oz/ 150 ml buttermilk

12-cup muffin pan, greased

350°F/180°C

Preheat the oven.

Stir together the dry ingredients.

In another bowl, beat the sugar and butter together until creamy, then add the eggs.

Add the flour mixture to the butter mixture and stir well.

Add the buttermilk and stir to combine.

Spoon the batter into the muffin cups, filling each three-fourths full.

Bake until golden.

20 min

350°F/180°C

* Top with cinnamon sugar.

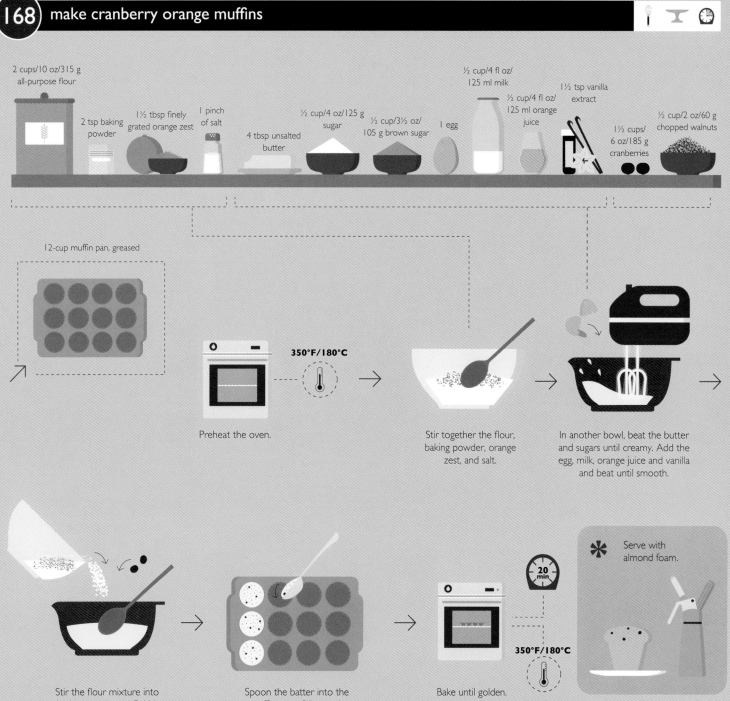

2 cups/10 oz/315 g all-purpose flour

2 tsp baking powder

1½ tbsp finely grated orange zest

1 pinch of salt

4 tbsp unsalted butter

½ cup/4 oz/125 g sugar

½ cup/3½ oz/105 g brown sugar

1 egg

½ cup/4 fl oz/125 ml milk

½ cup/4 fl oz/125 ml orange juice

1½ tsp vanilla extract

1½ cups/6 oz/185 g cranberries

½ cup/2 oz/60 g chopped walnuts

12-cup muffin pan, greased

350°F/180°C

Preheat the oven.

Stir together the flour, baking powder, orange zest, and salt.

In another bowl, beat the butter and sugars until creamy. Add the egg, milk, orange juice and vanilla and beat until smooth.

Stir the flour mixture into the butter mixture. Fold in the cranberries and walnuts.

Spoon the batter into the muffin cups, filling each three-fourths full.

Bake until golden.

20 min

350°F/180°C

Serve with almond foam.

**304** make almond foam

1 cup/8 fl oz/ 250 ml apple juice

6 tbsp/3 oz/ 90 g unsalted butter

12 oz/375 g dried figs, chopped

1 tbsp finely grated orange zest

2 cups/10 oz/ 315 g all-purpose flour

¾ cup/6 oz/185 g brown sugar

1 tbsp baking powder

1 tsp vanilla extract

2 eggs

12- cup muffin pan, greased

**350°F/180°C**

Preheat the oven.

Warm the apple juice and butter until the butter melts.

4–6 min

Add the dried figs and orange zest and set aside.

2 h

Stir together the dry ingredients and make a well in the center.

In another bowl, lightly beat the egg with the vanilla.

Pour the fig mixture and egg mixture into the well.

Stir to combine, but do not overmix.

Spoon the batter into the muffin cups, filling each three-fourths full.

20 min

Bake until golden.

**350°F/180°C**

### 170 make dried plum muffins

2¼ cups/12 oz/375 g finely chopped dried plums

Use dried plums instead of figs.

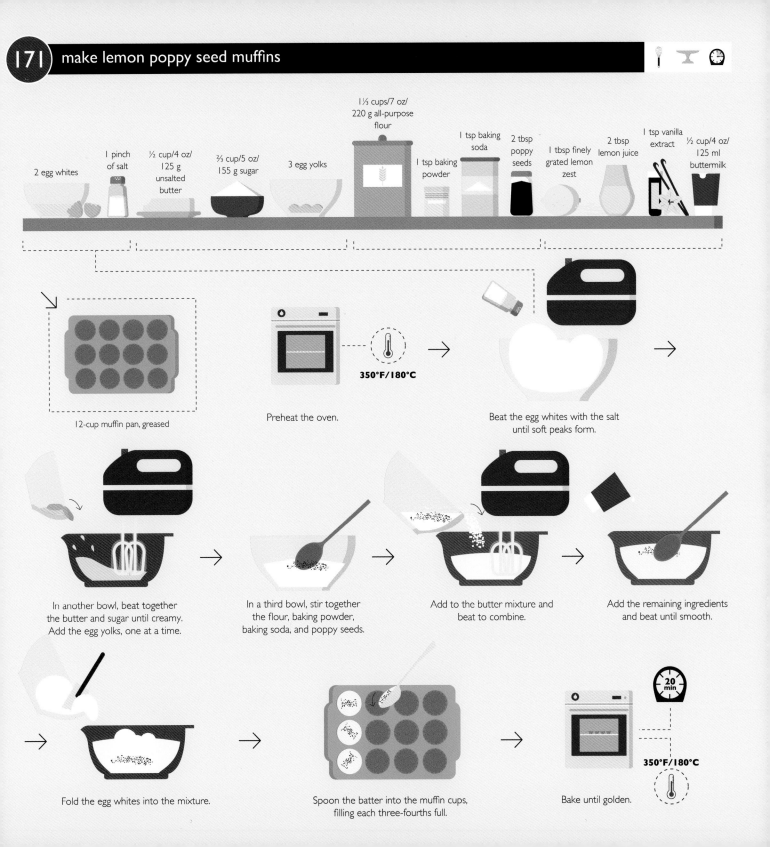

1⅓ cups/7 oz/ 220 g all-purpose flour

2 egg whites

1 pinch of salt

½ cup/4 oz/ 125 g unsalted butter

⅔ cup/5 oz/ 155 g sugar

3 egg yolks

1 tsp baking powder

1 tsp baking soda

2 tbsp poppy seeds

1 tbsp finely grated lemon zest

2 tbsp lemon juice

1 tsp vanilla extract

½ cup/4 oz/ 125 ml buttermilk

12-cup muffin pan, greased

Preheat the oven. **350°F/180°C**

Beat the egg whites with the salt until soft peaks form.

In another bowl, beat together the butter and sugar until creamy. Add the egg yolks, one at a time.

In a third bowl, stir together the flour, baking powder, baking soda, and poppy seeds.

Add to the butter mixture and beat to combine.

Add the remaining ingredients and beat until smooth.

Fold the egg whites into the mixture.

Spoon the batter into the muffin cups, filling each three-fourths full.

Bake until golden. **20 min** **350°F/180°C**

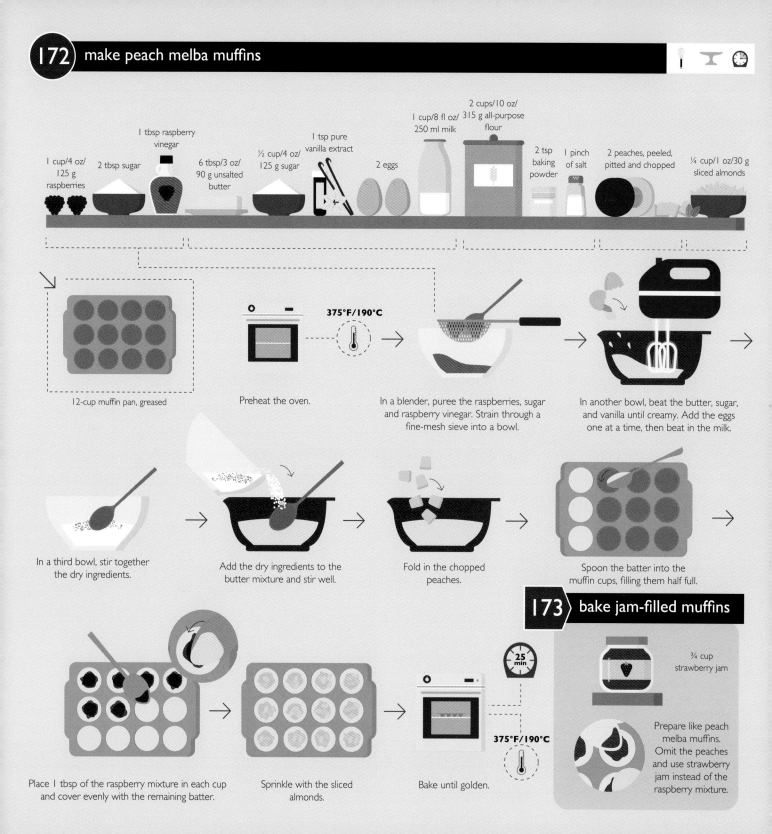

1 cup/4 oz/ 125 g raspberries

2 tbsp sugar

1 tbsp raspberry vinegar

6 tbsp/3 oz/ 90 g unsalted butter

½ cup/4 oz/ 125 g sugar

1 tsp pure vanilla extract

2 eggs

1 cup/8 fl oz/ 250 ml milk

2 cups/10 oz/ 315 g all-purpose flour

2 tsp baking powder

1 pinch of salt

2 peaches, peeled, pitted and chopped

¼ cup/1 oz/30 g sliced almonds

12-cup muffin pan, greased

Preheat the oven.

375°F/190°C

In a blender, puree the raspberries, sugar and raspberry vinegar. Strain through a fine-mesh sieve into a bowl.

In another bowl, beat the butter, sugar, and vanilla until creamy. Add the eggs one at a time, then beat in the milk.

In a third bowl, stir together the dry ingredients.

Add the dry ingredients to the butter mixture and stir well.

Fold in the chopped peaches.

Spoon the batter into the muffin cups, filling them half full.

Place 1 tbsp of the raspberry mixture in each cup and cover evenly with the remaining batter.

Sprinkle with the sliced almonds.

Bake until golden.

25 min

375°F/190°C

173 bake jam-filled muffins

¾ cup strawberry jam

Prepare like peach melba muffins. Omit the peaches and use strawberry jam instead of the raspberry mixture.

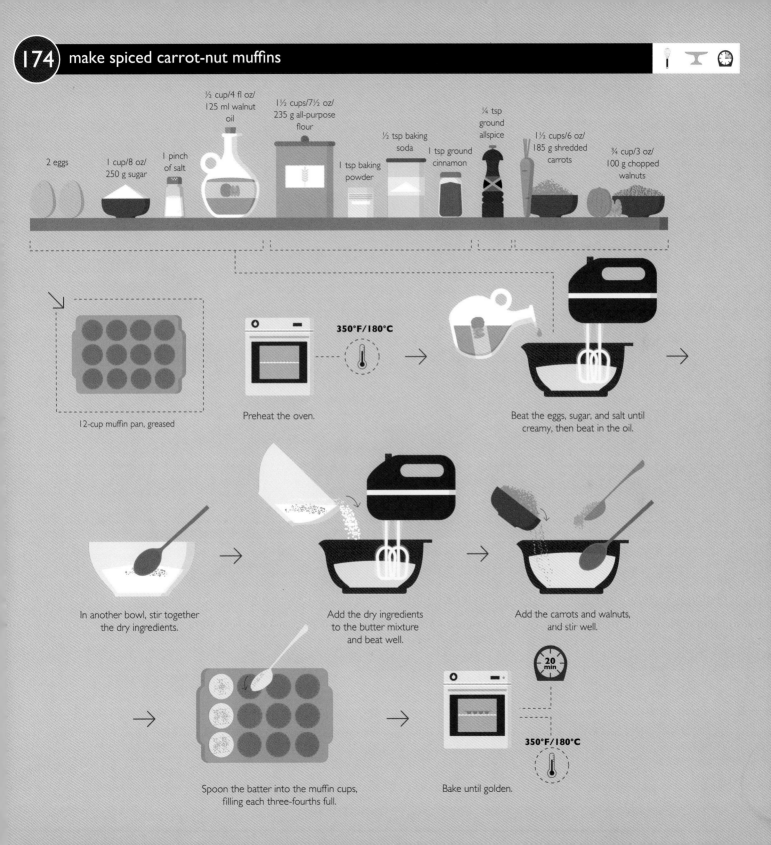

2 eggs

1 cup/8 oz/ 250 g sugar

1 pinch of salt

½ cup/4 fl oz/ 125 ml walnut oil

1½ cups/7½ oz/ 235 g all-purpose flour

1 tsp baking powder

½ tsp baking soda

1 tsp ground cinnamon

¼ tsp ground allspice

1½ cups/6 oz/ 185 g shredded carrots

¾ cup/3 oz/ 100 g chopped walnuts

350°F/180°C

12-cup muffin pan, greased

Preheat the oven.

Beat the eggs, sugar, and salt until creamy, then beat in the oil.

In another bowl, stir together the dry ingredients.

Add the dry ingredients to the butter mixture and beat well.

Add the carrots and walnuts, and stir well.

Spoon the batter into the muffin cups, filling each three-fourths full.

Bake until golden.

20 min

350°F/180°C

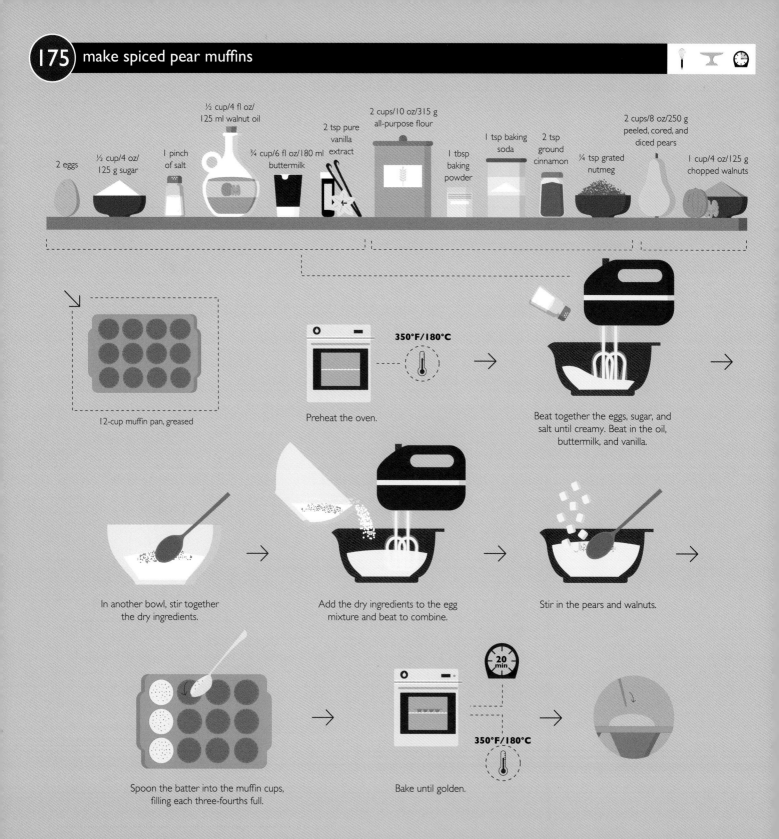

2 eggs

½ cup/4 oz/125 g sugar

1 pinch of salt

½ cup/4 fl oz/125 ml walnut oil

¾ cup/6 fl oz/180 ml buttermilk

2 tsp pure vanilla extract

2 cups/10 oz/315 g all-purpose flour

1 tbsp baking powder

1 tsp baking soda

2 tsp ground cinnamon

¼ tsp grated nutmeg

2 cups/8 oz/250 g peeled, cored, and diced pears

1 cup/4 oz/125 g chopped walnuts

12-cup muffin pan, greased

Preheat the oven.

350°F/180°C

Beat together the eggs, sugar, and salt until creamy. Beat in the oil, buttermilk, and vanilla.

In another bowl, stir together the dry ingredients.

Add the dry ingredients to the egg mixture and beat to combine.

Stir in the pears and walnuts.

Spoon the batter into the muffin cups, filling each three-fourths full.

Bake until golden.

20 min

350°F/180°C

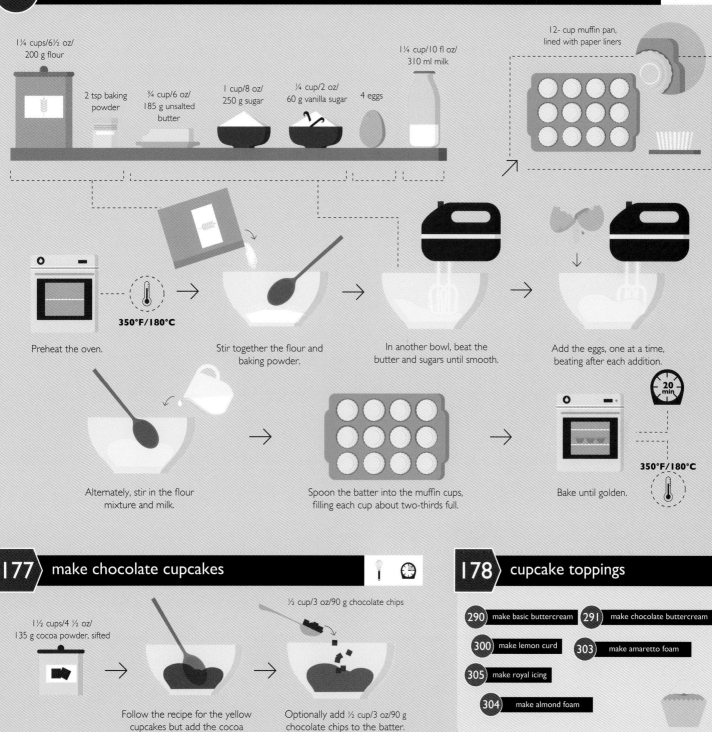

1¼ cups/6½ oz/ 200 g flour

2 tsp baking powder

¾ cup/6 oz/ 185 g unsalted butter

1 cup/8 oz/ 250 g sugar

¼ cup/2 oz/ 60 g vanilla sugar

4 eggs

1¼ cup/10 fl oz/ 310 ml milk

12- cup muffin pan, lined with paper liners

**350°F/180°C**

Preheat the oven.

Stir together the flour and baking powder.

In another bowl, beat the butter and sugars until smooth.

Add the eggs, one at a time, beating after each addition.

Alternately, stir in the flour mixture and milk.

Spoon the batter into the muffin cups, filling each cup about two-thirds full.

Bake until golden.

**20 min**

**350°F/180°C**

1½ cups/4 ½ oz/ 135 g cocoa powder, sifted

½ cup/3 oz/90 g chocolate chips

Follow the recipe for the yellow cupcakes but add the cocoa powder to the flour mixture.

Optionally add ½ cup/3 oz/90 g chocolate chips to the batter. Bake like yellow cupcakes.

**290** make basic buttercream
**291** make chocolate buttercream
**300** make lemon curd
**303** make amaretto foam
**305** make royal icing
**304** make almond foam

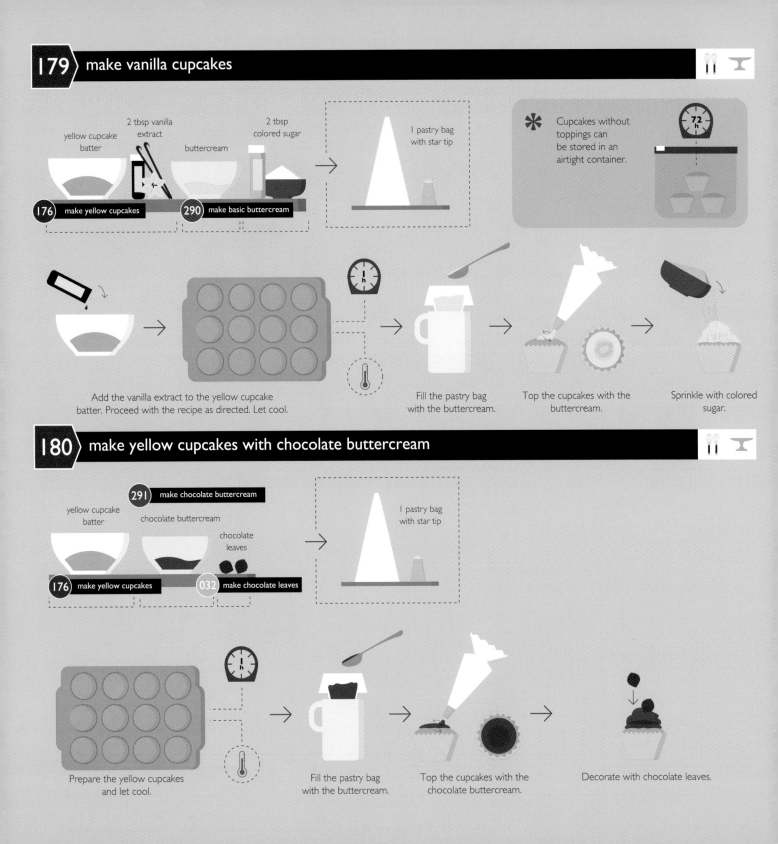

## 179 make vanilla cupcakes

yellow cupcake batter

2 tbsp vanilla extract

buttercream

2 tbsp colored sugar

I pastry bag with star tip

176 make yellow cupcakes

290 make basic buttercream

Cupcakes without toppings can be stored in an airtight container.

72 h

Add the vanilla extract to the yellow cupcake batter. Proceed with the recipe as directed. Let cool.

Fill the pastry bag with the buttercream.

Top the cupcakes with the buttercream.

Sprinkle with colored sugar.

## 180 make yellow cupcakes with chocolate buttercream

291 make chocolate buttercream

yellow cupcake batter

chocolate buttercream

chocolate leaves

176 make yellow cupcakes

032 make chocolate leaves

I pastry bag with star tip

Prepare the yellow cupcakes and let cool.

Fill the pastry bag with the buttercream.

Top the cupcakes with the chocolate buttercream.

Decorate with chocolate leaves.

## 181 ⬡ make chocolate orange cupcakes

¼ cup/2 fl oz/60 ml
Grand Marnier

chocolate cupcake
batter

3 tbsp finely grated
orange zest

027  candy orange slices

chocolate
buttercream

candied orange slices

I pastry bag
with star tip

177 make chocolate cupcakes

291 make chocolate buttercream

Add the Grand Marnier and orange zest to the chocolate cupcake batter.
Proceed with the recipe as directed. Let cool.

Fill the pastry bag with the buttercream.
Top the cupcakes with the chocolate buttercream.

Decorate with
candied orange slices.

## 182 ⬡ make coconut cupcakes with lemon curd

yellow cupcake
batter

1½ cups/6 oz/180 g
shredded coconut

lemon curd

I cup/8 fl oz/250 g
whipped cream

176 make yellow cupcakes

300 make lemon curd

015  whip cream

Add the shredded coconut to the yellow cupcake
batter. Proceed with the recipe as directed.

Let cool.

Using a spoon, hollow out the
center of each cupcake.

Fill with lemon curd.

Top with whipped cream and sprinkle
with additional shredded coconut.

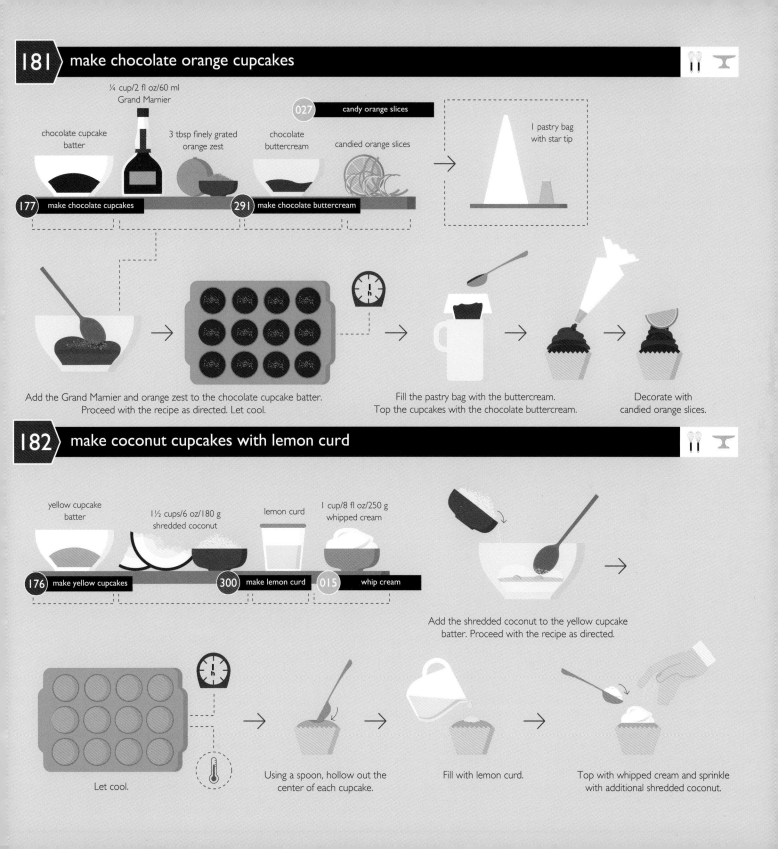

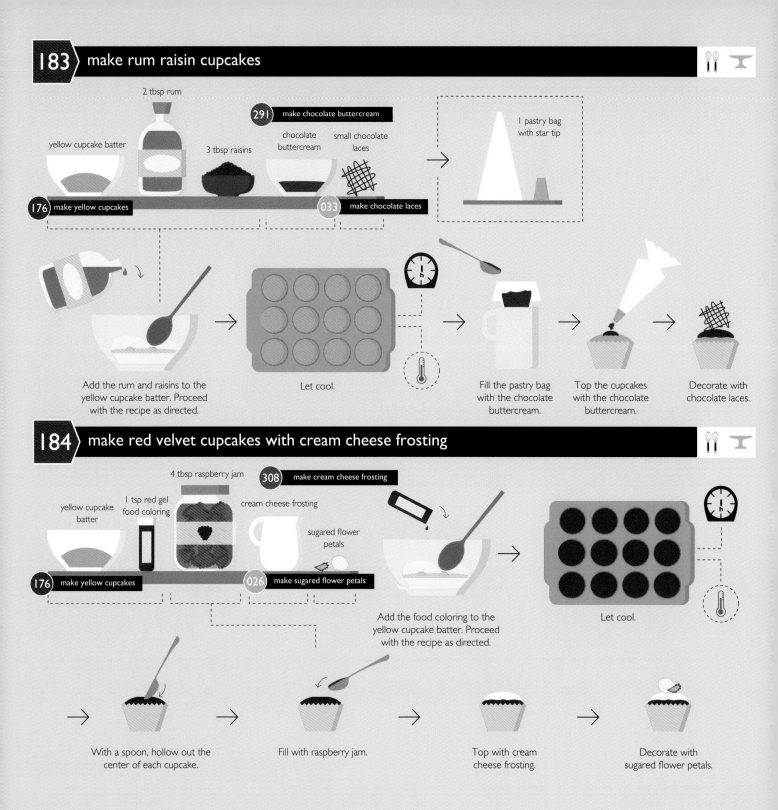

## 183 make rum raisin cupcakes

2 tbsp rum

291 make chocolate buttercream

yellow cupcake batter

3 tbsp raisins

chocolate buttercream

small chocolate laces

1 pastry bag with star tip

176 make yellow cupcakes

033 make chocolate laces

Add the rum and raisins to the yellow cupcake batter. Proceed with the recipe as directed.

Let cool.

Fill the pastry bag with the chocolate buttercream.

Top the cupcakes with the chocolate buttercream.

Decorate with chocolate laces.

## 184 make red velvet cupcakes with cream cheese frosting

4 tbsp raspberry jam

308 make cream cheese frosting

yellow cupcake batter

1 tsp red gel food coloring

cream cheese frosting

sugared flower petals

176 make yellow cupcakes

026 make sugared flower petals

Add the food coloring to the yellow cupcake batter. Proceed with the recipe as directed.

Let cool.

With a spoon, hollow out the center of each cupcake.

Fill with raspberry jam.

Top with cream cheese frosting.

Decorate with sugared flower petals.

## 185 make ice cream cupcakes

chocolate cupcake batter

1 pt/14 oz/440 ml vanilla ice cream

chocolate curls

177 make chocolate cupcakes

037 curl chocolate

✳ Decorate the cupcakes with fresh fruit, like raspberries, blueberries, or small strawberries.

Bake the chocolate cupcakes and let cool.

Slice off the top off the cupcakes.

Top with a scoop of ice cream, then decorate with chocolate curls.

## 186 make chai and honey cupcakes

yellow cupcake batter

⅔ cup/5 fl oz/ 160 ml water

3 chai-spice tea bags

¼ cup honey, plus 2 tbsp

1½ cups/ 12 fl oz/375 ml heavy cream

176 make yellow cupcakes

Bring the water to a boil.

Steep the tea bags in the boiling water.

Remove the tea bags and add the tea and ¼ cup honey to the batter. Proceed with the recipe as directed. Let cool.

Beat the cream and 2 tbsp honey until stiff peaks form.

Decorate the cupcakes with the honey cream.

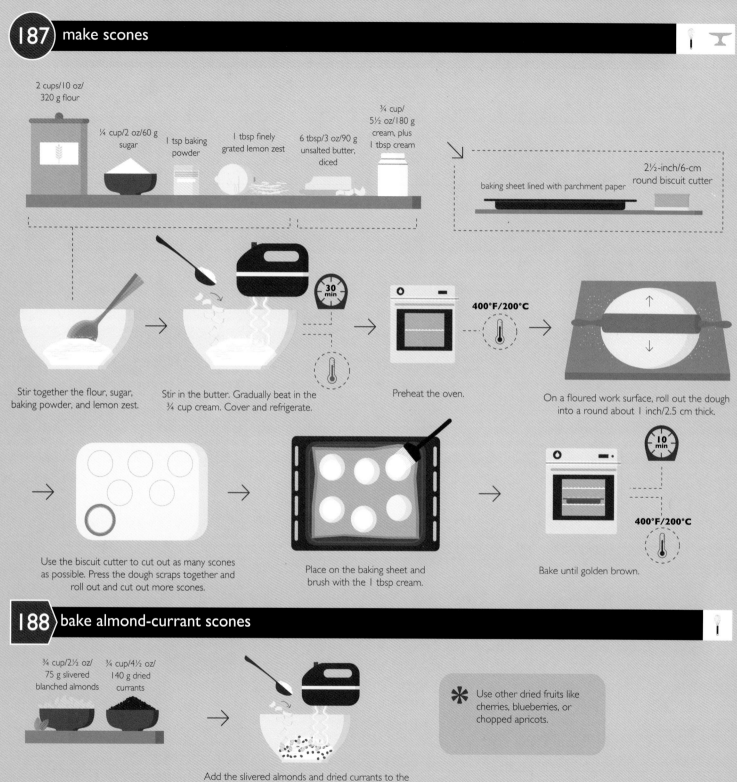

2 cups/10 oz/ 320 g flour

¼ cup/2 oz/60 g sugar

1 tsp baking powder

1 tbsp finely grated lemon zest

6 tbsp/3 oz/90 g unsalted butter, diced

¾ cup/ 5½ oz/180 g cream, plus 1 tbsp cream

baking sheet lined with parchment paper

2½-inch/6-cm round biscuit cutter

30 min

400°F/200°C

Stir together the flour, sugar, baking powder, and lemon zest.

Stir in the butter. Gradually beat in the ¾ cup cream. Cover and refrigerate.

Preheat the oven.

On a floured work surface, roll out the dough into a round about 1 inch/2.5 cm thick.

10 min

400°F/200°C

Use the biscuit cutter to cut out as many scones as possible. Press the dough scraps together and roll out and cut out more scones.

Place on the baking sheet and brush with the 1 tbsp cream.

Bake until golden brown.

# 188 bake almond-currant scones

¾ cup/2½ oz/ 75 g slivered blanched almonds

¾ cup/4½ oz/ 140 g dried currants

✳ Use other dried fruits like cherries, blueberries, or chopped apricots.

Add the slivered almonds and dried currants to the mixture along with the butter. Proceed as directed.

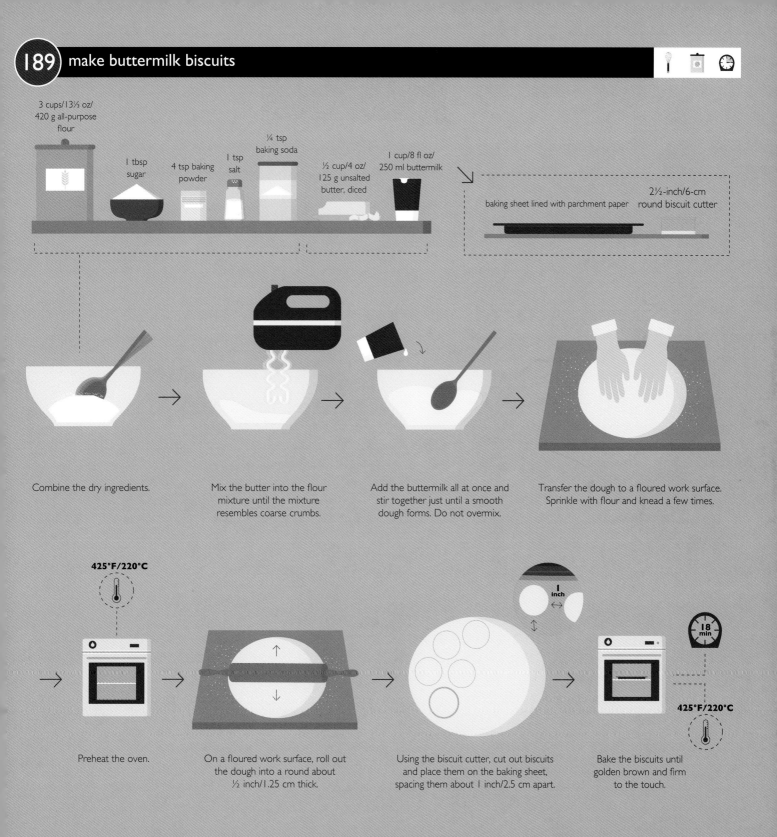

3 cups/13⅓ oz/ 420 g all-purpose flour

1 tbsp sugar

4 tsp baking powder

1 tsp salt

¼ tsp baking soda

½ cup/4 oz/ 125 g unsalted butter, diced

1 cup/8 fl oz/ 250 ml buttermilk

baking sheet lined with parchment paper

2½-inch/6-cm round biscuit cutter

Combine the dry ingredients.

Mix the butter into the flour mixture until the mixture resembles coarse crumbs.

Add the buttermilk all at once and stir together just until a smooth dough forms. Do not overmix.

Transfer the dough to a floured work surface. Sprinkle with flour and knead a few times.

425°F/220°C

1 inch

18 min

425°F/220°C

Preheat the oven.

On a floured work surface, roll out the dough into a round about ½ inch/1.25 cm thick.

Using the biscuit cutter, cut out biscuits and place them on the baking sheet, spacing them about 1 inch/2.5 cm apart.

Bake the biscuits until golden brown and firm to the touch.

cookies
and
bars

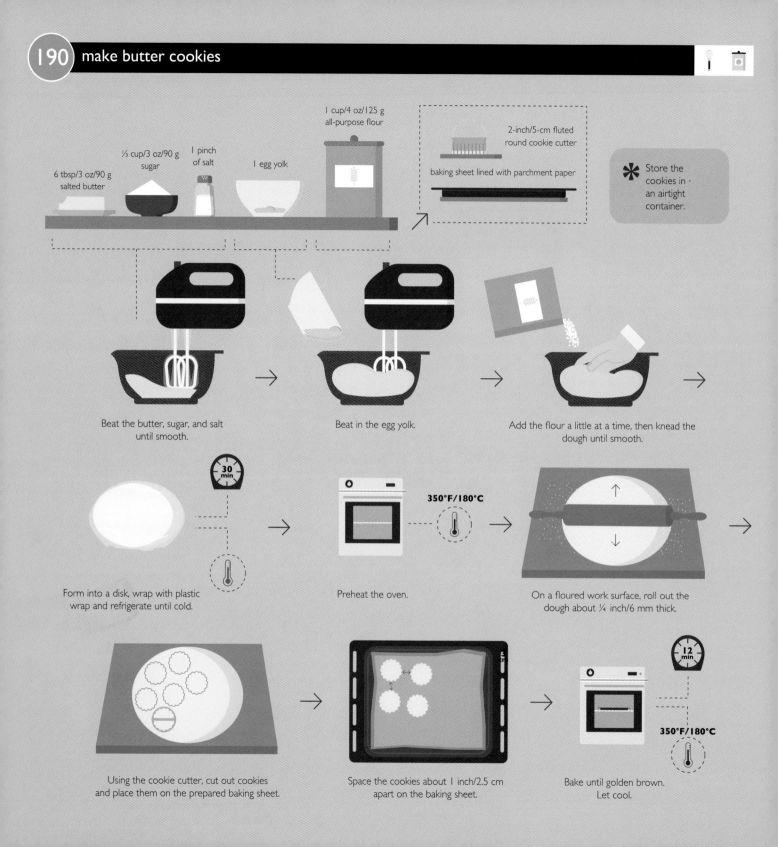

1 cup/4 oz/125 g
all-purpose flour

⅓ cup/3 oz/90 g
sugar

1 pinch
of salt

1 egg yolk

6 tbsp/3 oz/90 g
salted butter

2-inch/5-cm fluted
round cookie cutter

baking sheet lined with parchment paper

Store the cookies in an airtight container.

Beat the butter, sugar, and salt until smooth.

Beat in the egg yolk.

Add the flour a little at a time, then knead the dough until smooth.

30 min

Form into a disk, wrap with plastic wrap and refrigerate until cold.

Preheat the oven.

350°F/180°C

On a floured work surface, roll out the dough about ¼ inch/6 mm thick.

Using the cookie cutter, cut out cookies and place them on the prepared baking sheet.

Space the cookies about 1 inch/2.5 cm apart on the baking sheet.

12 min

350°F/180°C

Bake until golden brown. Let cool.

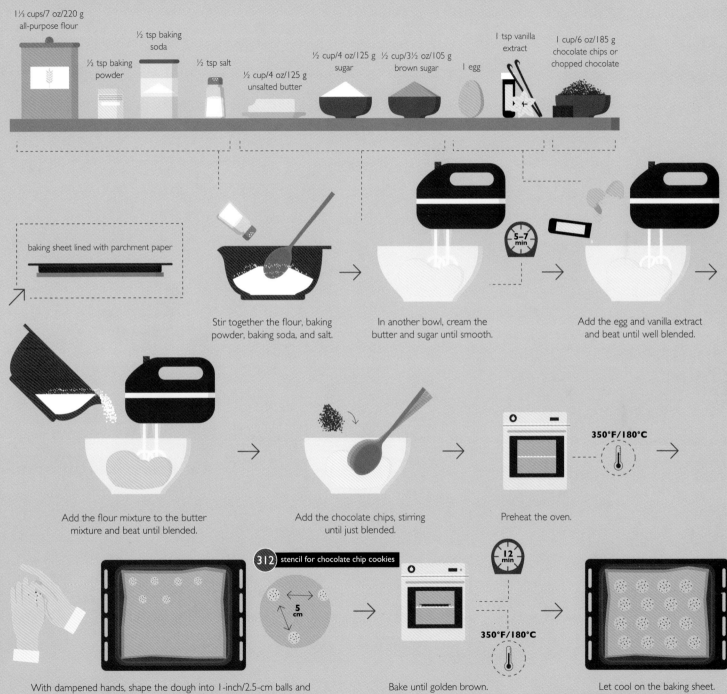

1⅓ cups/7 oz/220 g all-purpose flour

½ tsp baking powder

½ tsp baking soda

½ tsp salt

½ cup/4 oz/125 g unsalted butter

½ cup/4 oz/125 g sugar

½ cup/3½ oz/105 g brown sugar

1 egg

1 tsp vanilla extract

1 cup/6 oz/185 g chocolate chips or chopped chocolate

baking sheet lined with parchment paper

5–7 min

Stir together the flour, baking powder, baking soda, and salt.

In another bowl, cream the butter and sugar until smooth.

Add the egg and vanilla extract and beat until well blended.

Add the flour mixture to the butter mixture and beat until blended.

Add the chocolate chips, stirring until just blended.

350°F/180°C

Preheat the oven.

312 stencil for chocolate chip cookies

5 cm

12 min

350°F/180°C

With dampened hands, shape the dough into 1-inch/2.5-cm balls and place on the baking sheet, spacing the cookies about 2 inches/5 cm apart.

Bake until golden brown.

Let cool on the baking sheet.

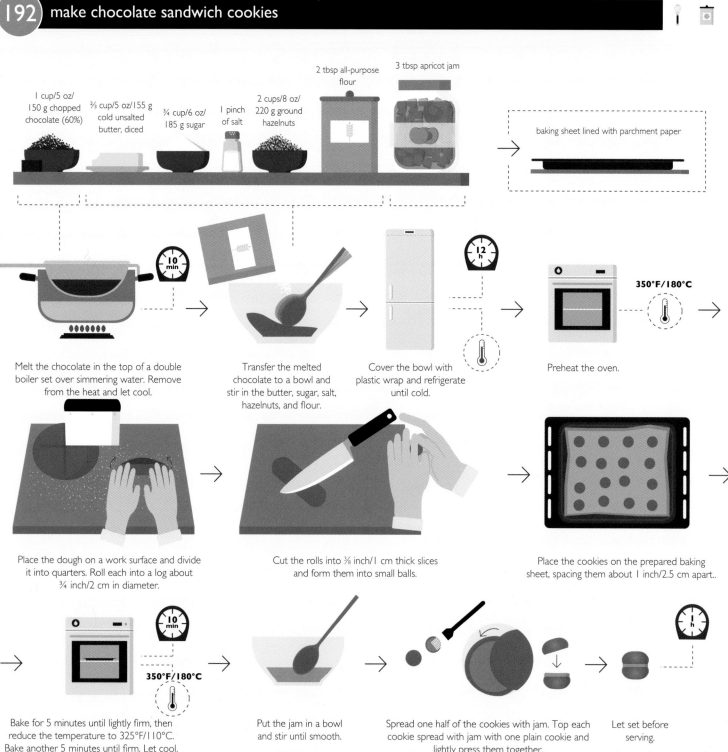

1 cup/5 oz/ 150 g chopped chocolate (60%)

⅔ cup/5 oz/155 g cold unsalted butter, diced

¾ cup/6 oz/ 185 g sugar

1 pinch of salt

2 cups/8 oz/ 220 g ground hazelnuts

2 tbsp all-purpose flour

3 tbsp apricot jam

baking sheet lined with parchment paper

350°F/180°C

Melt the chocolate in the top of a double boiler set over simmering water. Remove from the heat and let cool.

Transfer the melted chocolate to a bowl and stir in the butter, sugar, salt, hazelnuts, and flour.

Cover the bowl with plastic wrap and refrigerate until cold.

Preheat the oven.

Place the dough on a work surface and divide it into quarters. Roll each into a log about ¾ inch/2 cm in diameter.

Cut the rolls into ⅜ inch/1 cm thick slices and form them into small balls.

Place the cookies on the prepared baking sheet, spacing them about 1 inch/2.5 cm apart..

350°F/180°C

Bake for 5 minutes until lightly firm, then reduce the temperature to 325°F/110°C. Bake another 5 minutes until firm. Let cool.

Put the jam in a bowl and stir until smooth.

Spread one half of the cookies with jam. Top each cookie spread with jam with one plain cookie and lightly press them together.

Let set before serving.

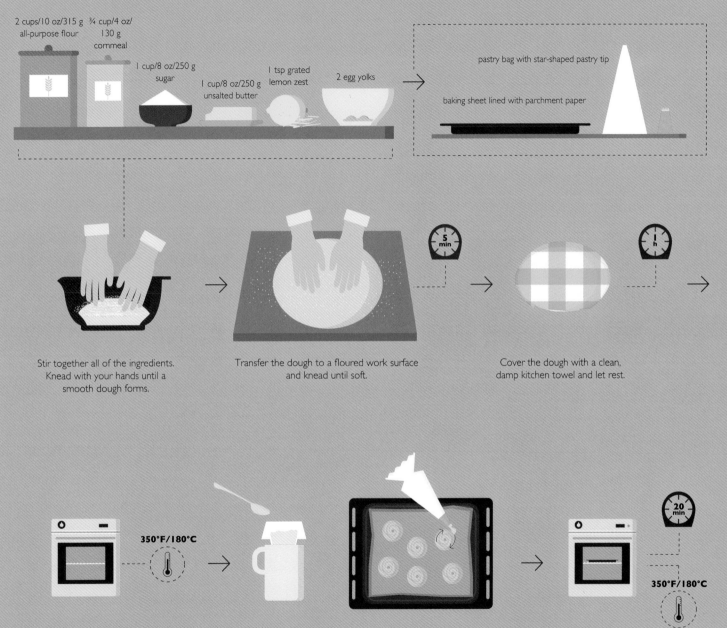

2 cups/10 oz/315 g all-purpose flour

¾ cup/4 oz/130 g cornmeal

1 cup/8 oz/250 g sugar

1 cup/8 oz/250 g unsalted butter

1 tsp grated lemon zest

2 egg yolks

pastry bag with star-shaped pastry tip

baking sheet lined with parchment paper

Stir together all of the ingredients. Knead with your hands until a smooth dough forms.

5 min

Transfer the dough to a floured work surface and knead until soft.

Cover the dough with a clean, damp kitchen towel and let rest.

350°F/180°C

Preheat the oven.

Transfer the dough to a pastry bag fitted with a star-shaped pastry tip and pipe rounds 2 inches/5 cm in diameter onto the baking sheet, spacing them about 2 inches/5 cm apart.

20 min

350°F/180°C

Bake until golden brown. Let cool.

1 cup/3½ oz/
110 g blanched
almonds, ground

1 cup/8 oz/240 g
unsalted butter, cut
into small pieces

⅓ cup/3 oz/80 g
sugar

1 pinch
of salt

seeds of 1 vanilla
bean

1¾ cups/
9 oz/280 g
all-purpose flour

1 cup/4 oz/125 g
confectioners'
sugar, sifted

2 tbsp
vanilla sugar

baking sheet lined with parchment paper

**020** work with vanilla beans

**021** make your own vanilla sugar

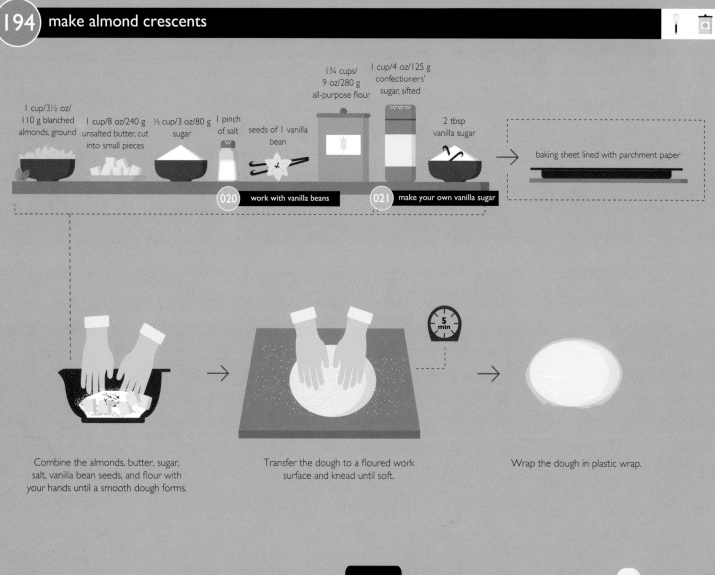

Combine the almonds, butter, sugar,
salt, vanilla bean seeds, and flour with
your hands until a smooth dough forms.

Transfer the dough to a floured work
surface and knead until soft.

Wrap the dough in plastic wrap.

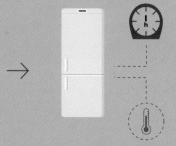

Refrigerate until cold.

Place the dough on a work surface and divide it into
quarters. Roll each into a log about ¾ inch/2 cm in diameter.

Cut the rolls into 2-inch/5-cm wide
pieces.

 →   Bend the logs into crescents and place them on the prepared baking sheet. → 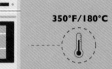 Preheat the oven.

Roll each slice into a small log, tapering the ends.

**350°F/180°C**

→ 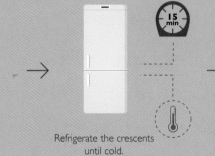 Refrigerate the crescents until cold. → 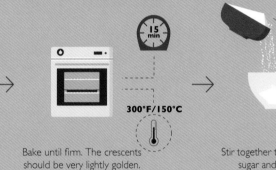 Bake until firm. The crescents should be very lightly golden. → Stir together the confectioners' sugar and vanilla sugar. →

**300°F/150°C**

 Turn the hot crescents carefully in the sugar mixture to coat them evenly. →

✽ Store these for up to 2 weeks in an airtight cookie jar. The crescents will remain soft and tender.

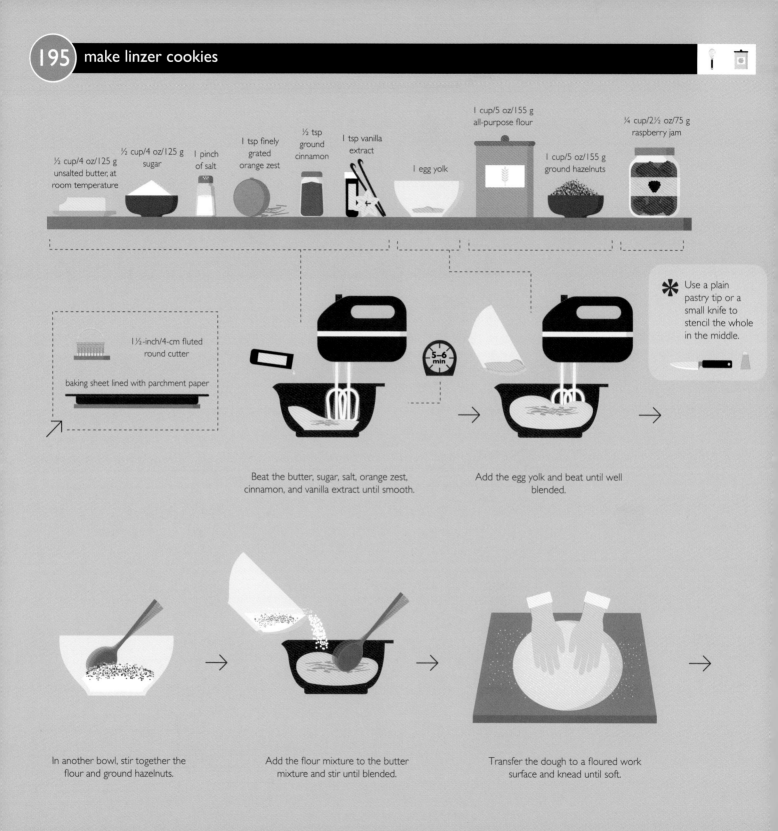

½ cup/4 oz/125 g unsalted butter, at room temperature

½ cup/4 oz/125 g sugar

1 pinch of salt

1 tsp finely grated orange zest

½ tsp ground cinnamon

1 tsp vanilla extract

1 egg yolk

1 cup/5 oz/155 g all-purpose flour

1 cup/5 oz/155 g ground hazelnuts

¼ cup/2½ oz/75 g raspberry jam

1½-inch/4-cm fluted round cutter

baking sheet lined with parchment paper

5–6 min

Use a plain pastry tip or a small knife to stencil the whole in the middle.

Beat the butter, sugar, salt, orange zest, cinnamon, and vanilla extract until smooth.

Add the egg yolk and beat until well blended.

In another bowl, stir together the flour and ground hazelnuts.

Add the flour mixture to the butter mixture and stir until blended.

Transfer the dough to a floured work surface and knead until soft.

**350°F/180°C**

Wrap the dough in plastic
wrap and refrigerate.

Preheat the oven.

Divide the dough into two equal portions, roll
out one dough half.

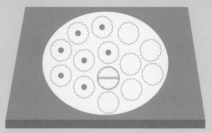

Cut out cookies, using the cookie cutter.
Using a plain pastry tip or a small knife,
cut a hole in the center of half of the cookies.

Transfer the cookies to the
prepared baking sheet.

Bake until golden. Repeat
until the dough is used up.

**12 min**

**350°F/180°C**

Stir the jam until smooth.

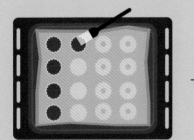

Spread the cookies without a hole
generously with jam.

Top each cookie spread with jam with
a cookie top and lightly press them
together.

Let set before serving.

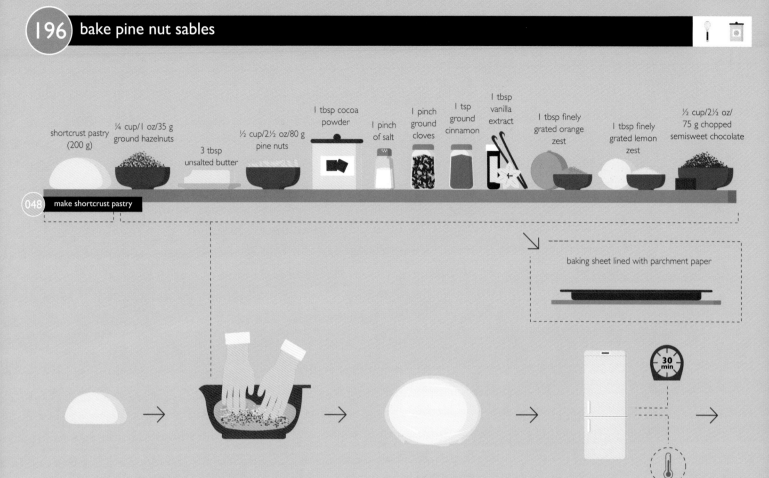

shortcrust pastry (200 g)

¼ cup/1 oz/35 g ground hazelnuts

3 tbsp unsalted butter

½ cup/2½ oz/80 g pine nuts

1 tbsp cocoa powder

1 pinch of salt

1 pinch ground cloves

1 tsp ground cinnamon

1 tbsp vanilla extract

1 tbsp finely grated orange zest

1 tbsp finely grated lemon zest

½ cup/2½ oz/ 75 g chopped semisweet chocolate

048 make shortcrust pastry

baking sheet lined with parchment paper

Place the dough into a bowl and add all of the remaining ingredients. Knead the dough and ingredients until combined and smooth.

Wrap the dough in plastic wrap and refrigerate.

350°F/180°C

Preheat the oven.

Divide the dough in half. Roll each half into a log about 1½ inches/4 cm diameter.

Cut the rolls into slices about ¼ inch/6 mm thick thick, transfer to the prepared baking sheet, and bake until golden.

8–10 min

350°F/180°C

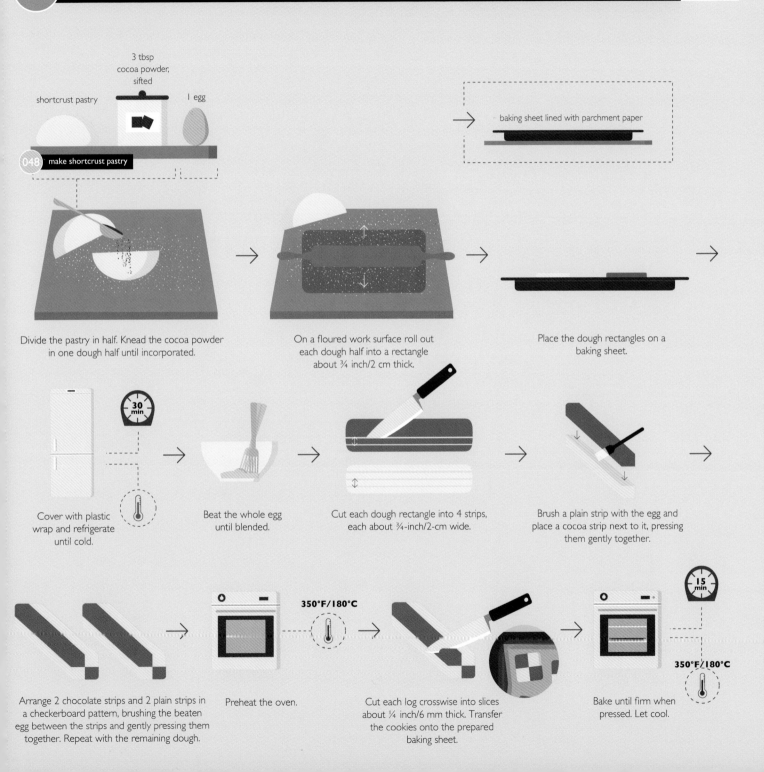

shortcrust pastry

3 tbsp cocoa powder, sifted

1 egg

048 make shortcrust pastry

baking sheet lined with parchment paper

Divide the pastry in half. Knead the cocoa powder in one dough half until incorporated.

On a floured work surface roll out each dough half into a rectangle about ¾ inch/2 cm thick.

Place the dough rectangles on a baking sheet.

30 min

Cover with plastic wrap and refrigerate until cold.

Beat the whole egg until blended.

Cut each dough rectangle into 4 strips, each about ¾-inch/2-cm wide.

Brush a plain strip with the egg and place a cocoa strip next to it, pressing them gently together.

Arrange 2 chocolate strips and 2 plain strips in a checkerboard pattern, brushing the beaten egg between the strips and gently pressing them together. Repeat with the remaining dough.

Preheat the oven.

350°F/180°C

Cut each log crosswise into slices about ¼ inch/6 mm thick. Transfer the cookies onto the prepared baking sheet.

15 min

350°F/180°C

Bake until firm when pressed. Let cool.

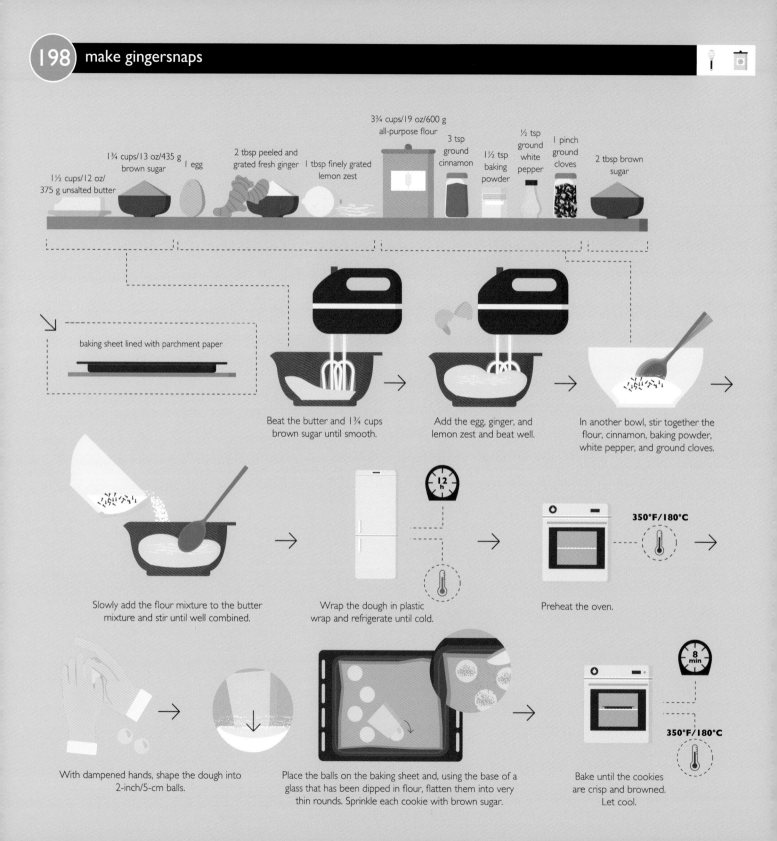

3¾ cups/19 oz/600 g
all-purpose flour

1¾ cups/13 oz/435 g
brown sugar    1 egg

3 tsp
ground
cinnamon

½ tsp
ground
white
pepper

1 pinch
ground
cloves

2 tbsp peeled and
grated fresh ginger

1 tbsp finely grated
lemon zest

1½ tsp
baking
powder

2 tbsp brown
sugar

1½ cups/12 oz/
375 g unsalted butter

baking sheet lined with parchment paper

Beat the butter and 1¾ cups
brown sugar until smooth.

Add the egg, ginger, and
lemon zest and beat well.

In another bowl, stir together the
flour, cinnamon, baking powder,
white pepper, and ground cloves.

Slowly add the flour mixture to the butter
mixture and stir until well combined.

12 h

Wrap the dough in plastic
wrap and refrigerate until cold.

350°F/180°C

Preheat the oven.

With dampened hands, shape the dough into
2-inch/5-cm balls.

Place the balls on the baking sheet and, using the base of a
glass that has been dipped in flour, flatten them into very
thin rounds. Sprinkle each cookie with brown sugar.

8 min

350°F/180°C

Bake until the cookies
are crisp and browned.
Let cool.

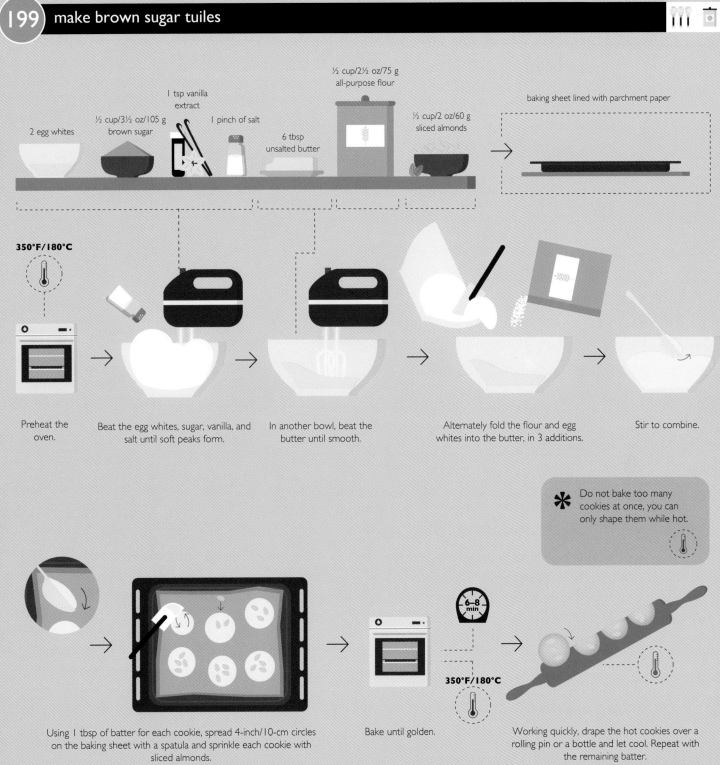

½ cup/2½ oz/75 g
all-purpose flour

baking sheet lined with parchment paper

1 tsp vanilla
extract

½ cup/3½ oz/105 g
brown sugar

1 pinch of salt

½ cup/2 oz/60 g
sliced almonds

2 egg whites

6 tbsp
unsalted butter

350°F/180°C

Preheat the
oven.

Beat the egg whites, sugar, vanilla, and
salt until soft peaks form.

In another bowl, beat the
butter until smooth.

Alternately fold the flour and egg
whites into the butter, in 3 additions.

Stir to combine.

* Do not bake too many
cookies at once, you can
only shape them while hot.

Using 1 tbsp of batter for each cookie, spread 4-inch/10-cm circles
on the baking sheet with a spatula and sprinkle each cookie with
sliced almonds.

Bake until golden.

6–8
min

350°F/180°C

Working quickly, drape the hot cookies over a
rolling pin or a bottle and let cool. Repeat with
the remaining batter.

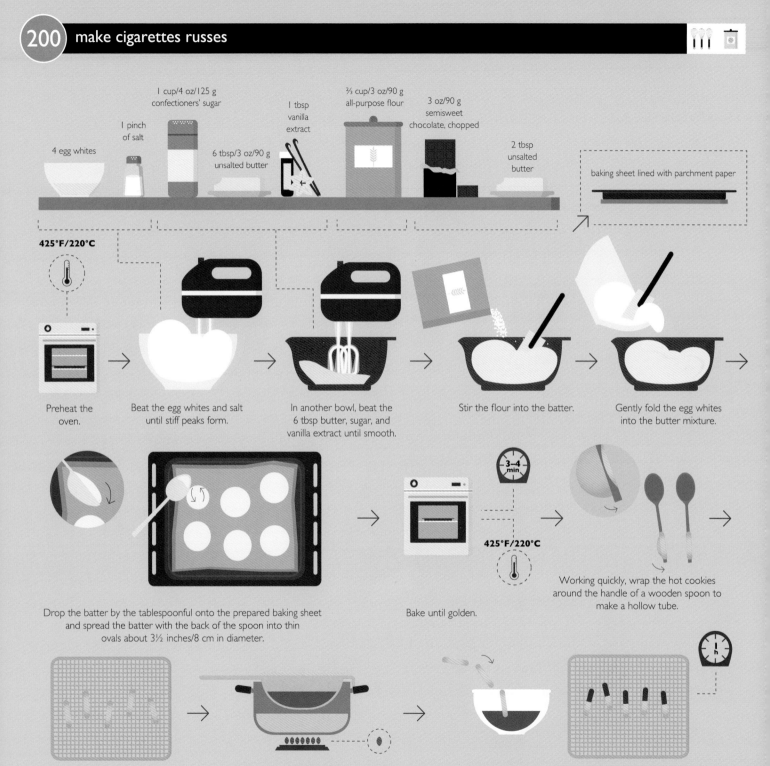

4 egg whites

I pinch of salt

1 cup/4 oz/125 g confectioners' sugar

6 tbsp/3 oz/90 g unsalted butter

I tbsp vanilla extract

⅔ cup/3 oz/90 g all-purpose flour

3 oz/90 g semisweet chocolate, chopped

2 tbsp unsalted butter

baking sheet lined with parchment paper

425°F/220°C

Preheat the oven.

Beat the egg whites and salt until stiff peaks form.

In another bowl, beat the 6 tbsp butter, sugar, and vanilla extract until smooth.

Stir the flour into the batter.

Gently fold the egg whites into the butter mixture.

Drop the batter by the tablespoonful onto the prepared baking sheet and spread the batter with the back of the spoon into thin ovals about 3½ inches/8 cm in diameter.

3–4 min

425°F/220°C

Bake until golden.

Working quickly, wrap the hot cookies around the handle of a wooden spoon to make a hollow tube.

Let cool on a wire rack. Repeat with the remaining batter.

Melt the chocolate and 2 tbsp butter in the top of a double boiler set over simmering water.

Dip one end of the cigarettes into the chocolate and let set on the wire rack.

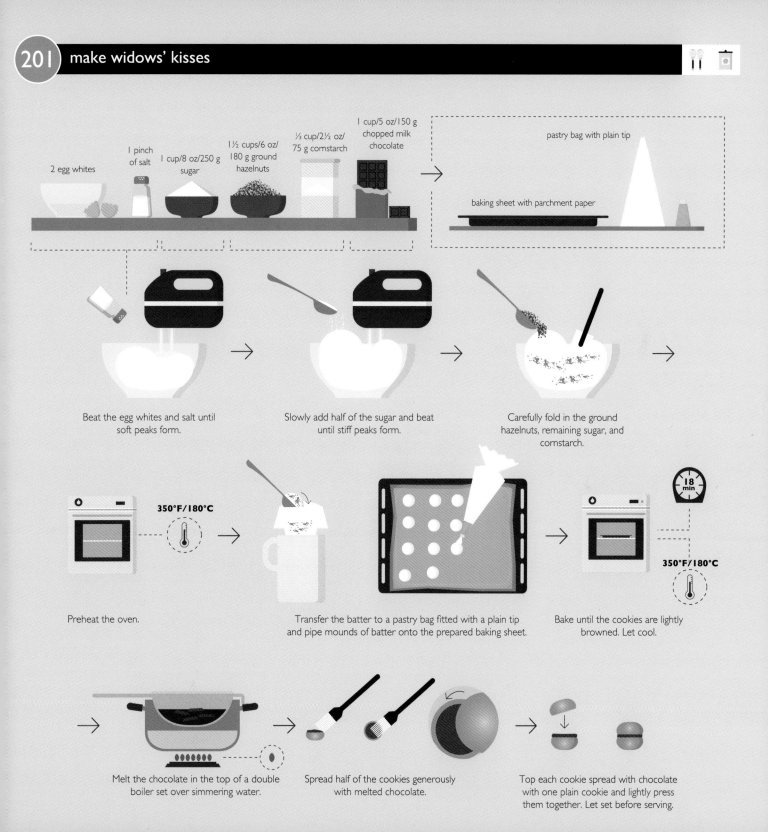

2 egg whites

1 pinch of salt

1 cup/8 oz/250 g sugar

1½ cups/6 oz/180 g ground hazelnuts

⅓ cup/2½ oz/75 g cornstarch

1 cup/5 oz/150 g chopped milk chocolate

pastry bag with plain tip

baking sheet with parchment paper

Beat the egg whites and salt until soft peaks form.

Slowly add half of the sugar and beat until stiff peaks form.

Carefully fold in the ground hazelnuts, remaining sugar, and cornstarch.

Preheat the oven.

350°F/180°C

Transfer the batter to a pastry bag fitted with a plain tip and pipe mounds of batter onto the prepared baking sheet.

Bake until the cookies are lightly browned. Let cool.

18 min

350°F/180°C

Melt the chocolate in the top of a double boiler set over simmering water.

Spread half of the cookies generously with melted chocolate.

Top each cookie spread with chocolate with one plain cookie and lightly press them together. Let set before serving.

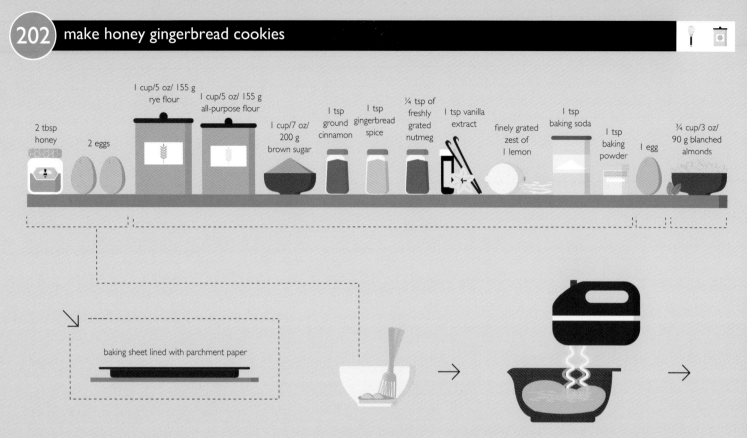

2 tbsp honey

2 eggs

1 cup/5 oz/ 155 g rye flour

1 cup/5 oz/ 155 g all-purpose flour

1 cup/7 oz/ 200 g brown sugar

1 tsp ground cinnamon

1 tsp gingerbread spice

¼ tsp of freshly grated nutmeg

1 tsp vanilla extract

finely grated zest of 1 lemon

1 tsp baking soda

1 tsp baking powder

1 egg

¾ cup/3 oz/ 90 g blanched almonds

baking sheet lined with parchment paper

Whisk the honey and 2 eggs until smooth.

Beat together the flours, sugar, spices, vanilla, lemon zest, baking soda, and baking powder. Beat in the egg mixture until well combined and a firm dough forms.

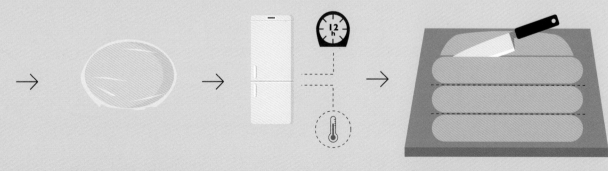

Wrap the dough with plastic wrap and refrigerate until cold.

Place the dough on a work surface and divide it into quarters. Roll each into a log about ¾ inch/2 cm in diameter.

Cut the logs into ⅓ inch/1 cm thick slices.

Transfer them to the prepared baking sheet.

Preheat the oven.

**350°F/180°C**

Whisk the remaining whole egg. Brush the gingerbread cookies with it.

Decorate each cookie with one almond.

Bake until golden brown. Let cool.

15 min

**350°F/180°C**

---

**203** ❯ prepare gingerbread men

---

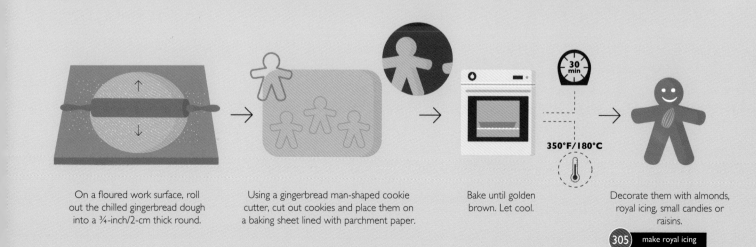

On a floured work surface, roll out the chilled gingerbread dough into a ¾-inch/2-cm thick round.

Using a gingerbread man-shaped cookie cutter, cut out cookies and place them on a baking sheet lined with parchment paper.

Bake until golden brown. Let cool.

30 min

**350°F/180°C**

Decorate them with almonds, royal icing, small candies or raisins.

**305** make royal icing

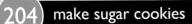

shortcrust pastry    I egg yolk

048 make shortcrust pastry

baking sheet lined with parchment paper    cookie cutters

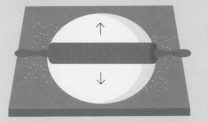

On a floured work surface, roll out the dough into a round about ¼ inch/5 mm thick.

Using the cookie cutters, cut out as many cookies as possible.

Transfer the cookies to the prepared baking sheet.

Knead together the dough scraps.

Roll out the remaining dough and cut out cookies. Repeat until the dough is used up.

350°F/180°C

Preheat the oven.

10 min

Whisk the egg yolk. Brush the cookies with egg yolk and let dry.

14 min

350°F/180°C

Bake until golden.

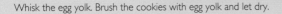

## decorate cookies with almonds

3 tbsp blanched whole almonds

Before baking and after you brush with egg yolk, decorate each cookie with almonds, gently pressing them into the dough.

## decorate cookies with cinnamon sugar

2 tbsp confectioners' sugar, sifted

1 tsp ground cinnamon

Stir together the sugar and cinnamon.

Sprinkle the cookies with the cinnamon sugar before baking.

## decorate cookies with sprinkles

1 cup/4 oz/125 g confectioners' sugar

2 tbsp colored sprinkles

gel food coloring

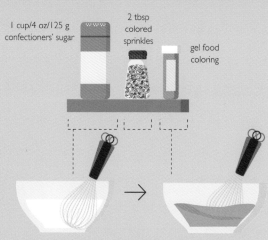

Whisk together the confectioners' sugar and 3 tbsp warm water, stirring until the sugar dissolves. If desired, add a few drops of food coloring.

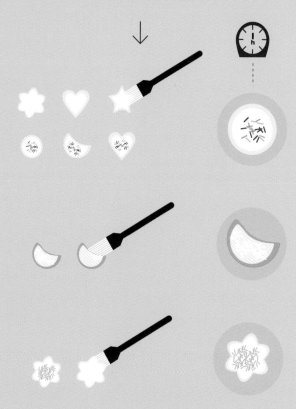

Brush the cookies with the icing, decorate with the sprinkles, and let dry.

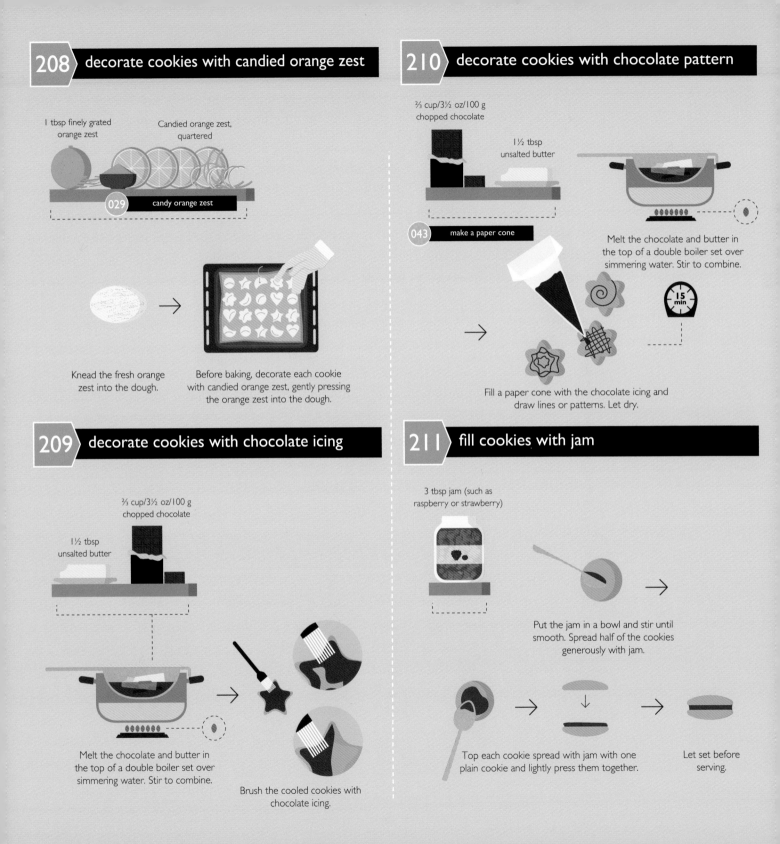

## 208 › decorate cookies with candied orange zest

1 tbsp finely grated orange zest

Candied orange zest, quartered

**029** candy orange zest

Knead the fresh orange zest into the dough.

Before baking, decorate each cookie with candied orange zest, gently pressing the orange zest into the dough.

## 209 › decorate cookies with chocolate icing

⅔ cup/3½ oz/100 g chopped chocolate

1½ tbsp unsalted butter

Melt the chocolate and butter in the top of a double boiler set over simmering water. Stir to combine.

Brush the cooled cookies with chocolate icing.

## 210 › decorate cookies with chocolate pattern

⅔ cup/3½ oz/100 g chopped chocolate

1½ tbsp unsalted butter

**043** make a paper cone

Melt the chocolate and butter in the top of a double boiler set over simmering water. Stir to combine.

15 min

Fill a paper cone with the chocolate icing and draw lines or patterns. Let dry.

## 211 › fill cookies with jam

3 tbsp jam (such as raspberry or strawberry)

Put the jam in a bowl and stir until smooth. Spread half of the cookies generously with jam.

Top each cookie spread with jam with one plain cookie and lightly press them together.

Let set before serving.

043 make a paper cone

305 prepare royal icing
306 color royal icing

love

EAT
ME!

EAT

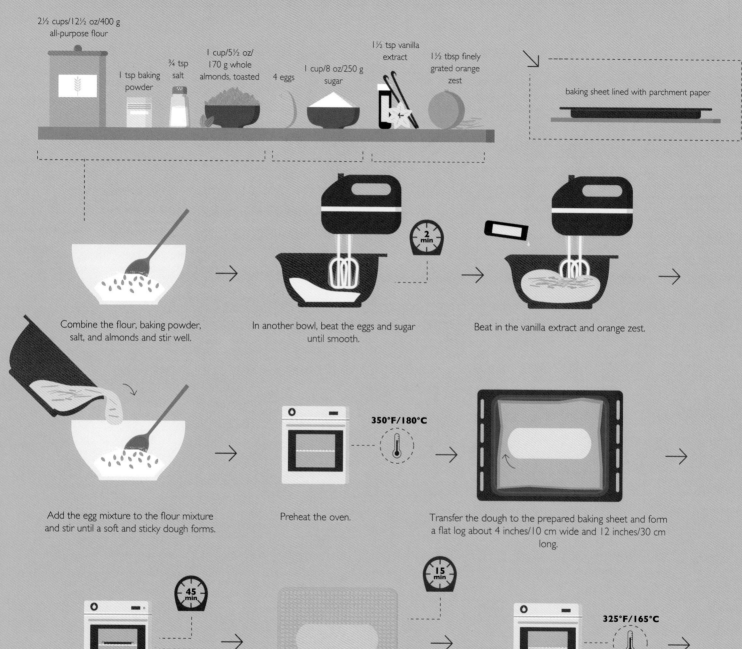

2½ cups/12½ oz/400 g all-purpose flour

1 tsp baking powder

¾ tsp salt

1 cup/5½ oz/170 g whole almonds, toasted

4 eggs

1 cup/8 oz/250 g sugar

1½ tsp vanilla extract

1½ tbsp finely grated orange zest

baking sheet lined with parchment paper

Combine the flour, baking powder, salt, and almonds and stir well.

In another bowl, beat the eggs and sugar until smooth.

2 min

Beat in the vanilla extract and orange zest.

Add the egg mixture to the flour mixture and stir until a soft and sticky dough forms.

Preheat the oven.

350°F/180°C

Transfer the dough to the prepared baking sheet and form a flat log about 4 inches/10 cm wide and 12 inches/30 cm long.

45 min

350°F/180°C

Bake until lightly brown.

15 min

Transfer the baked log to a wire rack to cool.

325°F/165°C

Reduce the oven temperature.

On a work surface, using a long serrated knife, cut the log diagonally into ½-inch/12-mm thick slices. Transfer the slices to a baking sheet lined with parchment paper.

Bake the biscotti, turning them once after 15 minutes. Let cool.

30 min

325°F/165°C

*
The biscotti can be stored in an airtight container for up to two weeks.

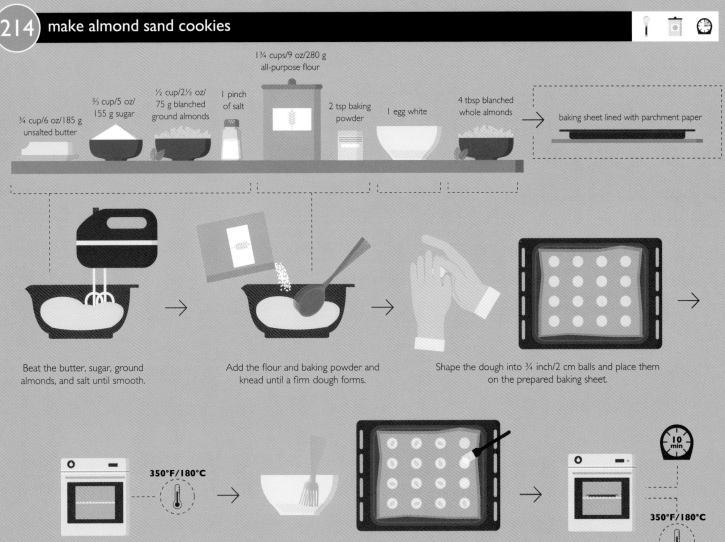

¾ cup/6 oz/185 g unsalted butter

⅔ cup/5 oz/155 g sugar

½ cup/2½ oz/75 g blanched ground almonds

1 pinch of salt

1¾ cups/9 oz/280 g all-purpose flour

2 tsp baking powder

1 egg white

4 tbsp blanched whole almonds

baking sheet lined with parchment paper

Beat the butter, sugar, ground almonds, and salt until smooth.

Add the flour and baking powder and knead until a firm dough forms.

Shape the dough into ¾ inch/2 cm balls and place them on the prepared baking sheet.

350°F/180°C

Preheat the oven.

Beat the egg white and lightly brush the cookies with it. Decorate each cookie with one whole almond.

Bake until golden.

10 min

350°F/180°C

½ cup/4 oz/125 g
unsalted butter

½ cup/4 oz/125 g
sugar

¼ tsp salt

2 eggs

2 tbsp
vanilla
extract

3 tbsp
anise seeds,
crushed

1¾ cups/9 oz/280 g
all-purpose flour

1 tbsp
baking
powder

I egg white

baking sheet lined with parchment paper

Beat the butter, sugar, and salt until smooth, then add the eggs one at a time, beating after each addition.

Beat in the vanilla, anise, flour, and baking powder.

350°F/180°C

Preheat the oven.

Transfer the dough to a floured work surface, divide it in half, and shape into logs about 12 inches/30 cm long and 1½ inches/4 cm in diameter.

Place the logs on the prepared baking sheet. Whisk the egg white. Brush the logs with the egg white.

25 min

350°F/180°C

Bake until lightly brown.

15 min

Transfer the baked logs to a wire rack to cool.

On a floured work surface, using a long serrated knife, cut the log diagonally into ½ inch/12 mm thick slices. Transfer the slices to a baking sheet lined with parchment paper.

10 min

350°F/180°C

Bake the biscotti until golden, turning them once after 5 minutes.

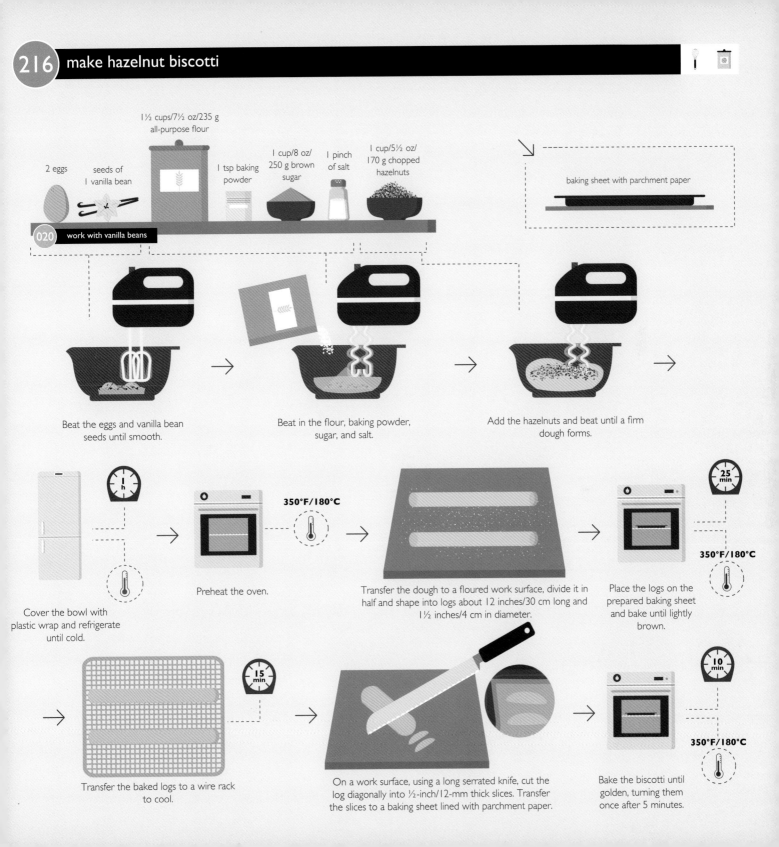

1½ cups/7½ oz/235 g all-purpose flour

2 eggs

seeds of 1 vanilla bean

1 tsp baking powder

1 cup/8 oz/250 g brown sugar

1 pinch of salt

1 cup/5½ oz/170 g chopped hazelnuts

baking sheet with parchment paper

020 work with vanilla beans

Beat the eggs and vanilla bean seeds until smooth.

Beat in the flour, baking powder, sugar, and salt.

Add the hazelnuts and beat until a firm dough forms.

Cover the bowl with plastic wrap and refrigerate until cold.

1 h

Preheat the oven. 350°F/180°C

Transfer the dough to a floured work surface, divide it in half and shape into logs about 12 inches/30 cm long and 1½ inches/4 cm in diameter.

Place the logs on the prepared baking sheet and bake until lightly brown. 25 min — 350°F/180°C

Transfer the baked logs to a wire rack to cool. 15 min

On a work surface, using a long serrated knife, cut the log diagonally into ½-inch/12-mm thick slices. Transfer the slices to a baking sheet lined with parchment paper.

Bake the biscotti until golden, turning them once after 5 minutes. 10 min — 350°F/180°C

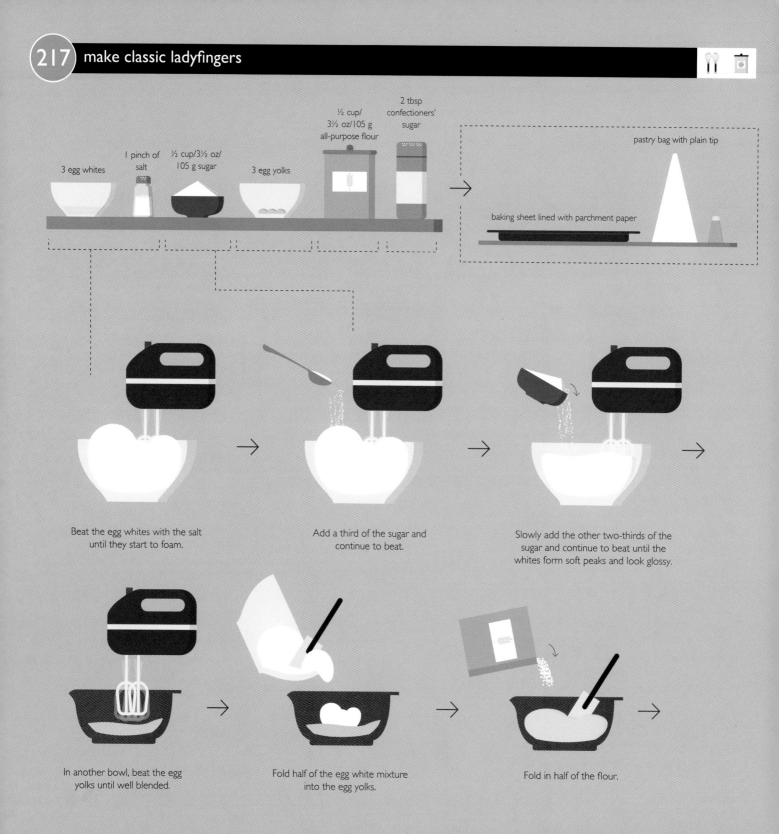

3 egg whites

1 pinch of salt

½ cup/3½ oz/ 105 g sugar

3 egg yolks

½ cup/ 3½ oz/105 g all-purpose flour

2 tbsp confectioners' sugar

pastry bag with plain tip

baking sheet lined with parchment paper

Beat the egg whites with the salt until they start to foam.

Add a third of the sugar and continue to beat.

Slowly add the other two-thirds of the sugar and continue to beat until the whites form soft peaks and look glossy.

In another bowl, beat the egg yolks until well blended.

Fold half of the egg white mixture into the egg yolks.

Fold in half of the flour.

Repeat with the remaining egg whites and flour.

Spoon the batter into a pastry bag fitted with a plain tip.

Pipe 3.5 inch/7.5 cm long and ¾ inch/2 cm wide strips onto the parchment paper, spacing them a bit apart.

Preheat the oven.

**400°F/200°C**

Dust with confectioners' sugar and let dry.

10 min

12 min

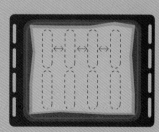

**400°F/200°C**

Bake until puffed and lightly browned.

Turn off the oven. Prop open the oven door with a wooden spoon and let cool.

✳ **Create a stencil**
On the parchment paper draw strips, 3½ inches/7.5 cm long and ¾ inch/ 2 cm wide, spacing them ¾ inch/2 cm apart. Turn the parchment paper before piping strips.

## 218 > make chocolate ladyfingers

2 tbsp cocoa powder, sifted

½ cup/3½ oz/105 g sugar

pastry bag with plain tip

baking sheet lined with parchment paper

Stir together the cocoa powder and sugar.

Proceed as directed with the classic ladyfinger recipe, using the cocoa-sugar in place of the plain sugar.

12 min

400°F/200°C

Bake as directed until puffed and lightly browned.

## 219 > make rothschild ladyfingers

2 tbsp ground hazlenuts

⅔ cup/3½ oz/ 100 g chopped chocolate

Proceed as directed with the classic ladyfingers recipe. Before baking, sprinkle the ladyfingers with ground hazelnuts.

12 min

400°F/200°C

Bake as directed until puffed and lightly browned.

Melt the chocolate in the top of a double boiler set over simmering water.

Brush the underside of the baked ladyfingers' with the melted chocolate.

Let cool, chocolate side up on a wire rack.

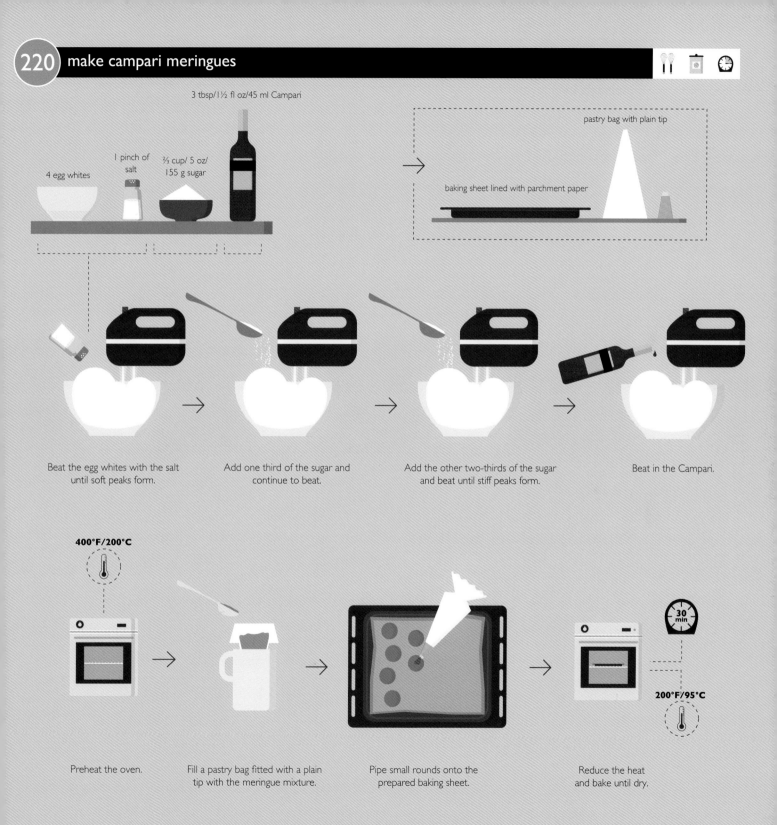

3 tbsp/1½ fl oz/45 ml Campari

pastry bag with plain tip

baking sheet lined with parchment paper

4 egg whites

1 pinch of salt

⅔ cup/ 5 oz/ 155 g sugar

Beat the egg whites with the salt until soft peaks form.

Add one third of the sugar and continue to beat.

Add the other two-thirds of the sugar and beat until stiff peaks form.

Beat in the Campari.

400°F/200°C

Preheat the oven.

Fill a pastry bag fitted with a plain tip with the meringue mixture.

Pipe small rounds onto the prepared baking sheet.

30 min

200°F/95°C

Reduce the heat and bake until dry.

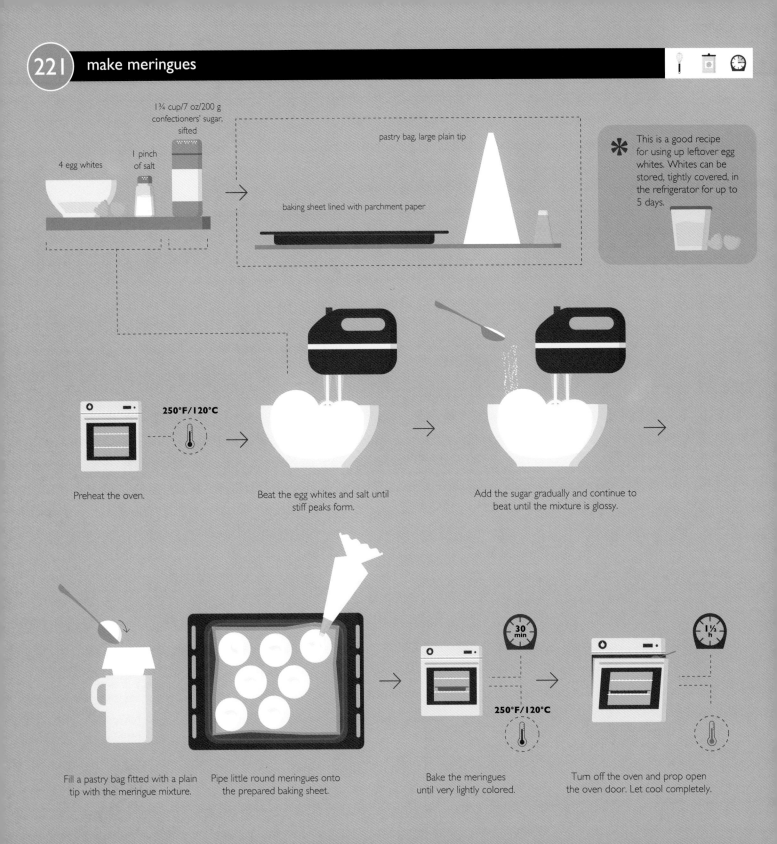

1¾ cup/7 oz/200 g confectioners' sugar, sifted

4 egg whites

I pinch of salt

pastry bag, large plain tip

baking sheet lined with parchment paper

This is a good recipe for using up leftover egg whites. Whites can be stored, tightly covered, in the refrigerator for up to 5 days.

250°F/120°C

Preheat the oven.

Beat the egg whites and salt until stiff peaks form.

Add the sugar gradually and continue to beat until the mixture is glossy.

Fill a pastry bag fitted with a plain tip with the meringue mixture.

Pipe little round meringues onto the prepared baking sheet.

30 min

250°F/120°C

Bake the meringues until very lightly colored.

1½ h

Turn off the oven and prop open the oven door. Let cool completely.

# make raspberry meringues

½ cup/2 oz/60 g
raspberries

**303** make amaretto foam

Serve with amaretto foam.

Purée the raspberries.

Pass the purée through a fine-mesh sieve into the meringue mixture.

Beat to combine. Proceed as directed to bake the meringues.

# make hazelnut meringues

1 ¼ cups/6½ oz/200 g toasted, skinned, and finely chopped hazelnuts

**298** make fruit sauce

Serve with fruit sauce.

**30 min**

250°F/120°C

Reserve 1 tbsp chopped hazelnuts. Fold the remaining hazelnuts into the meringue mixture.

Sprinkle a few of the reserved nuts on top of each meringue.

Proceed as directed to bake the meringue.

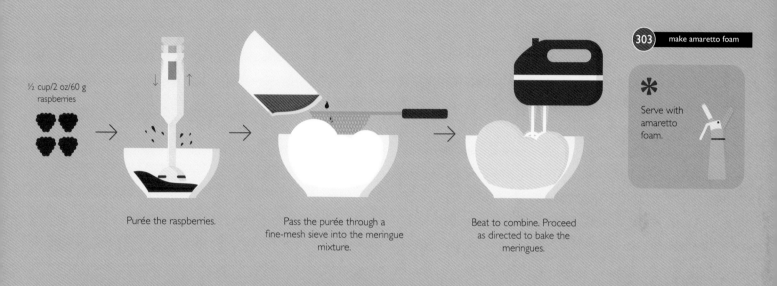

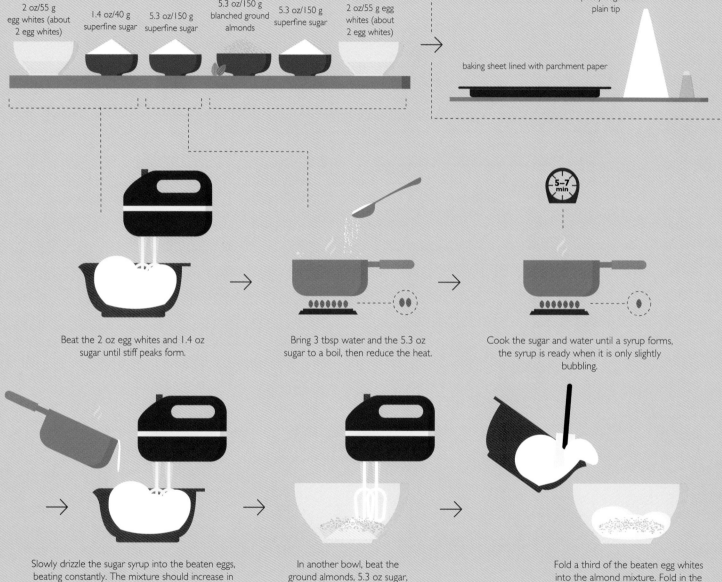

2 oz/55 g egg whites (about 2 egg whites)

1.4 oz/40 g superfine sugar

5.3 oz/150 g superfine sugar

5.3 oz/150 g blanched ground almonds

5.3 oz/150 g superfine sugar

2 oz/55 g egg whites (about 2 egg whites)

2 pastry bags with plain tip

baking sheet lined with parchment paper

Beat the 2 oz egg whites and 1.4 oz sugar until stiff peaks form.

Bring 3 tbsp water and the 5.3 oz sugar to a boil, then reduce the heat.

Cook the sugar and water until a syrup forms, the syrup is ready when it is only slightly bubbling.

5–7 min

Slowly drizzle the sugar syrup into the beaten eggs, beating constantly. The mixture should increase in volume and become shiny.

In another bowl, beat the ground almonds, 5.3 oz sugar, and 2 oz egg whites.

Fold a third of the beaten egg whites into the almond mixture. Fold in the remaining egg whites.

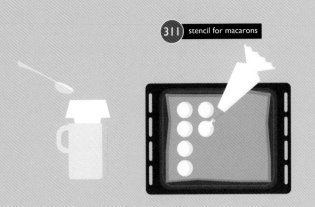

311 stencil for macarons

Fill a pastry bag fitted with a plain tip with the mixture. Pipe 1½ inch/4 cm rounds onto the prepared baking sheet.

✳ Macarons are best within 24 hours after filling.

**30 min**

Let the macarons dry before baking.

**400°F/200°C**

Preheat the oven.

**18 min**

**300°F/150°C**

Reduce the heat and bake until puffed. The macarons should not take on any color.

Turn the oven off. Prop open the oven door with a wooden spoon and let cool.

FILLING MACARONS

Fill a pastry bag fitted with a small plain tip with filling, such as lemon curd or buttercream. Pipe a thin ⅛ inch/3 mm thick layer on half of the macarons.

Top with an unfilled macaron and press together gently.

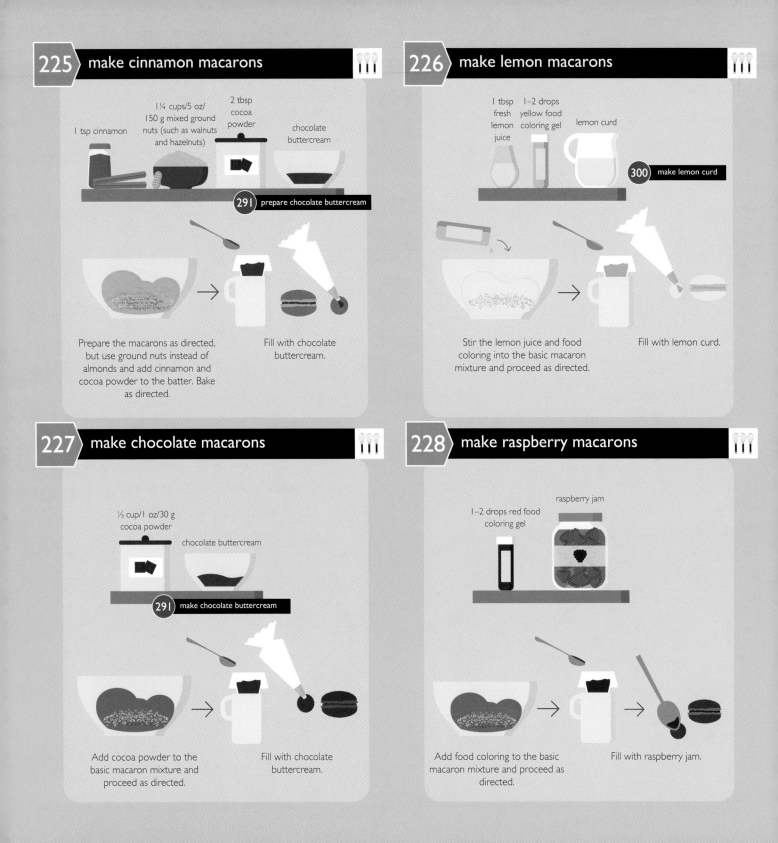

## 225 | make cinnamon macarons

1 tsp cinnamon

1¼ cups/5 oz/ 150 g mixed ground nuts (such as walnuts and hazelnuts)

2 tbsp cocoa powder

chocolate buttercream

**291 | prepare chocolate buttercream**

Prepare the macarons as directed, but use ground nuts instead of almonds and add cinnamon and cocoa powder to the batter. Bake as directed.

Fill with chocolate buttercream.

## 226 | make lemon macarons

1 tbsp fresh lemon juice

1–2 drops yellow food coloring gel

lemon curd

**300 | make lemon curd**

Stir the lemon juice and food coloring into the basic macaron mixture and proceed as directed.

Fill with lemon curd.

## 227 | make chocolate macarons

⅓ cup/1 oz/30 g cocoa powder

chocolate buttercream

**291 | make chocolate buttercream**

Add cocoa powder to the basic macaron mixture and proceed as directed.

Fill with chocolate buttercream.

## 228 | make raspberry macarons

1–2 drops red food coloring gel

raspberry jam

Add food coloring to the basic macaron mixture and proceed as directed.

Fill with raspberry jam.

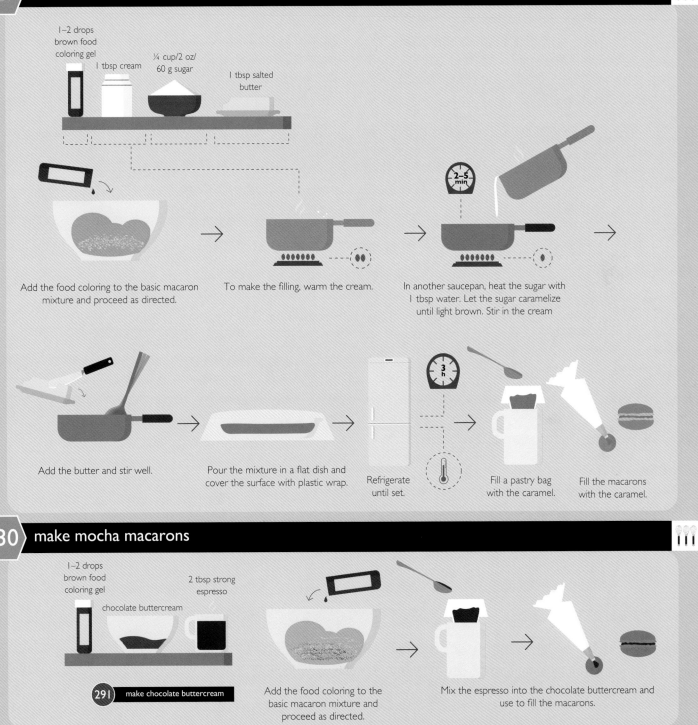

1–2 drops brown food coloring gel

I tbsp cream

¼ cup/2 oz/ 60 g sugar

I tbsp salted butter

Add the food coloring to the basic macaron mixture and proceed as directed.

To make the filling, warm the cream.

2–5 min

In another saucepan, heat the sugar with I tbsp water. Let the sugar caramelize until light brown. Stir in the cream

Add the butter and stir well.

Pour the mixture in a flat dish and cover the surface with plastic wrap.

3 h

Refrigerate until set.

Fill a pastry bag with the caramel.

Fill the macarons with the caramel.

1–2 drops brown food coloring gel

2 tbsp strong espresso

chocolate buttercream

**291** make chocolate buttercream

Add the food coloring to the basic macaron mixture and proceed as directed.

Mix the espresso into the chocolate buttercream and use to fill the macarons.

madeleine mold with 12 molds, greased and floured

2 eggs

1 egg yolk

½ cup/4 oz/125 g sugar

½ cup/4 oz/125 g butter

seeds of 1 vanilla bean

¾ cup/4 oz/125 g all-purpose flour

1 pinch of baking powder

1 pinch of salt

020 work with vanilla beans

Beat the eggs, egg yolk, and sugar until smooth.

Melt the butter.

Beat the vanilla seeds, flour, baking powder and salt into the egg mixture.

Add the melted butter, beating constantly.

Cover and let rest in a cool place.

Preheat the oven.

400°F/200°C

Pour the batter into the madeleine molds. dividing it evenly.

Bake for 3–4 minutes, then reduce the oven temperature.

320°F/160°C

Immediately invert the pan onto a wire rack and let cool.

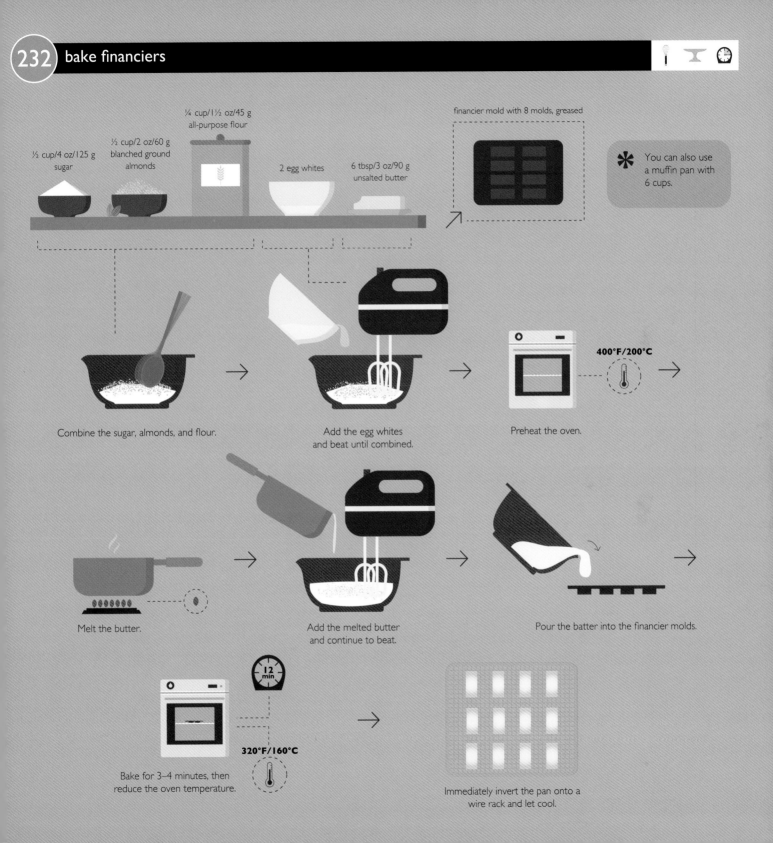

½ cup/4 oz/125 g
sugar

½ cup/2 oz/60 g
blanched ground
almonds

¼ cup/1½ oz/45 g
all-purpose flour

2 egg whites

6 tbsp/3 oz/90 g
unsalted butter

financier mold with 8 molds, greased

✳ You can also use a muffin pan with 6 cups.

Combine the sugar, almonds, and flour.

Add the egg whites and beat until combined.

Preheat the oven.

400°F/200°C

Melt the butter.

Add the melted butter and continue to beat.

Pour the batter into the financier molds.

Bake for 3–4 minutes, then reduce the oven temperature.

12 min

320°F/160°C

Immediately invert the pan onto a wire rack and let cool.

6½ oz/200 g semisweet chocolate, chopped

½ cup/4 oz/125 g unsalted butter

2 eggs

¾ cup/6½ oz/200 g sugar

1 tbsp vanilla sugar

1 cup/4 oz/130 g flour

1 tsp baking powder

3 tbsp chopped walnuts

**021** make your own vanilla sugar

✳ Do not overbake, the brownies should be moist inside.

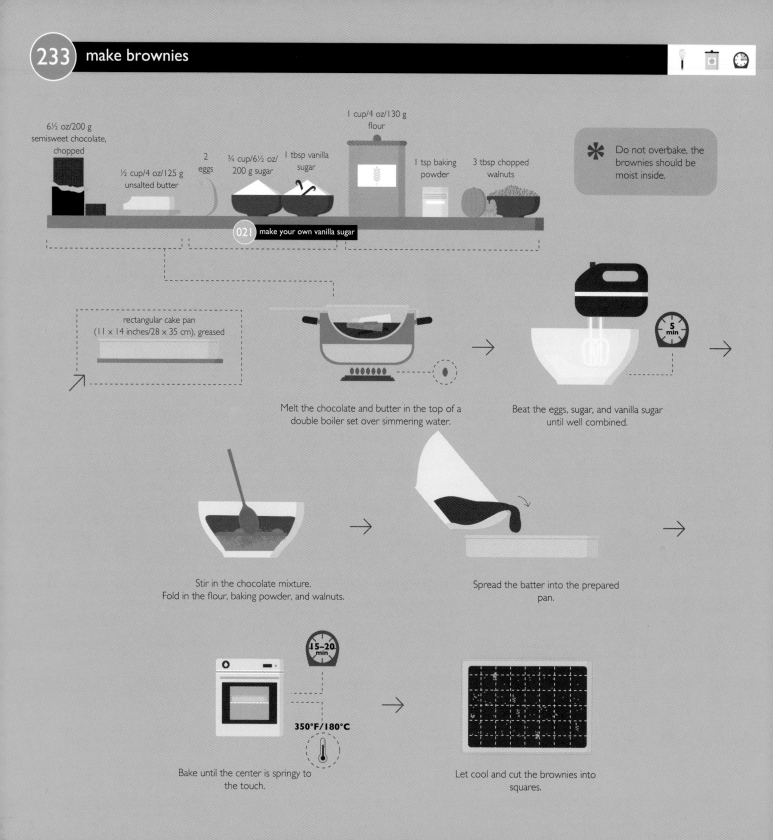

rectangular cake pan (11 × 14 inches/28 × 35 cm), greased

Melt the chocolate and butter in the top of a double boiler set over simmering water.

5 min

Beat the eggs, sugar, and vanilla sugar until well combined.

Stir in the chocolate mixture. Fold in the flour, baking powder, and walnuts.

Spread the batter into the prepared pan.

15–20 min

350°F/180°C

Bake until the center is springy to the touch.

Let cool and cut the brownies into squares.

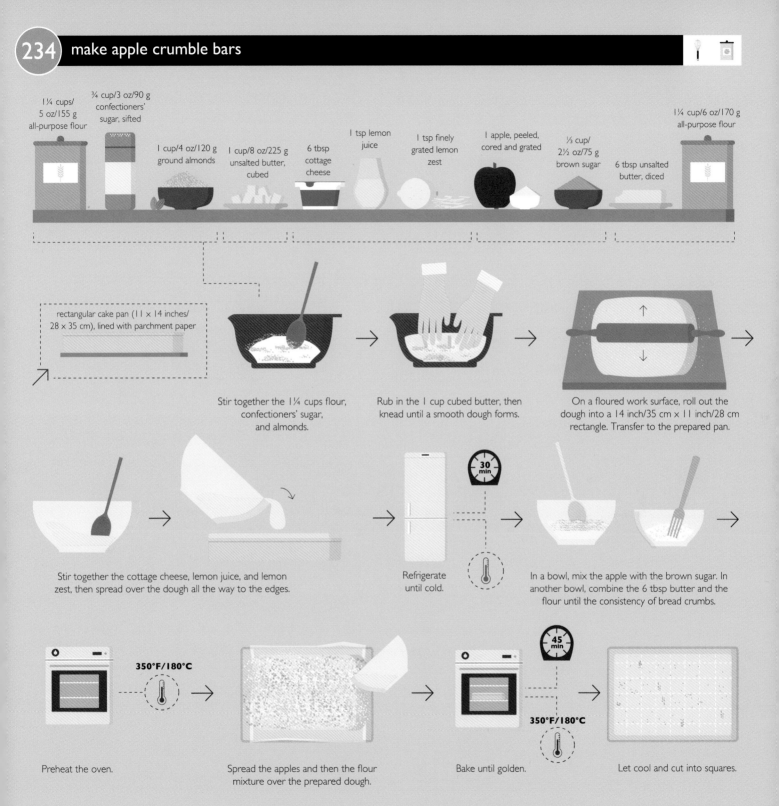

1¼ cups/
5 oz/155 g
all-purpose flour

¾ cup/3 oz/90 g
confectioners'
sugar, sifted

1 cup/4 oz/120 g
ground almonds

1 cup/8 oz/225 g
unsalted butter,
cubed

6 tbsp
cottage
cheese

1 tsp lemon
juice

1 tsp finely
grated lemon
zest

1 apple, peeled,
cored and grated

⅓ cup/
2½ oz/75 g
brown sugar

6 tbsp unsalted
butter, diced

1¼ cup/6 oz/170 g
all-purpose flour

rectangular cake pan (11 x 14 inches/
28 x 35 cm), lined with parchment paper

Stir together the 1¼ cups flour,
confectioners' sugar,
and almonds.

Rub in the 1 cup cubed butter, then
knead until a smooth dough forms.

On a floured work surface, roll out the
dough into a 14 inch/35 cm x 11 inch/28 cm
rectangle. Transfer to the prepared pan.

Stir together the cottage cheese, lemon juice, and lemon
zest, then spread over the dough all the way to the edges.

30 min

Refrigerate
until cold.

In a bowl, mix the apple with the brown sugar. In
another bowl, combine the 6 tbsp butter and the
flour until the consistency of bread crumbs.

350°F/180°C

Preheat the oven.

Spread the apples and then the flour
mixture over the prepared dough.

45 min

350°F/180°C

Bake until golden.

Let cool and cut into squares.

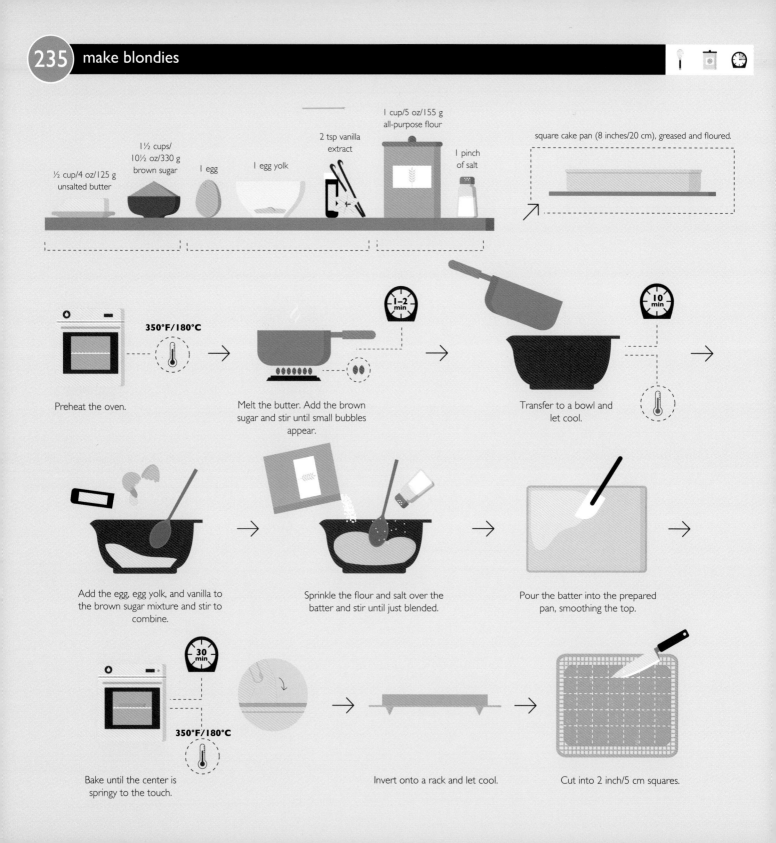

½ cup/4 oz/125 g unsalted butter

1½ cups/ 10½ oz/330 g brown sugar

1 egg

1 egg yolk

2 tsp vanilla extract

1 cup/5 oz/155 g all-purpose flour

1 pinch of salt

square cake pan (8 inches/20 cm), greased and floured.

**350°F/180°C**

Preheat the oven.

Melt the butter. Add the brown sugar and stir until small bubbles appear.

Transfer to a bowl and let cool.

Add the egg, egg yolk, and vanilla to the brown sugar mixture and stir to combine.

Sprinkle the flour and salt over the batter and stir until just blended.

Pour the batter into the prepared pan, smoothing the top.

**350°F/180°C**

Bake until the center is springy to the touch.

Invert onto a rack and let cool.

Cut into 2 inch/5 cm squares.

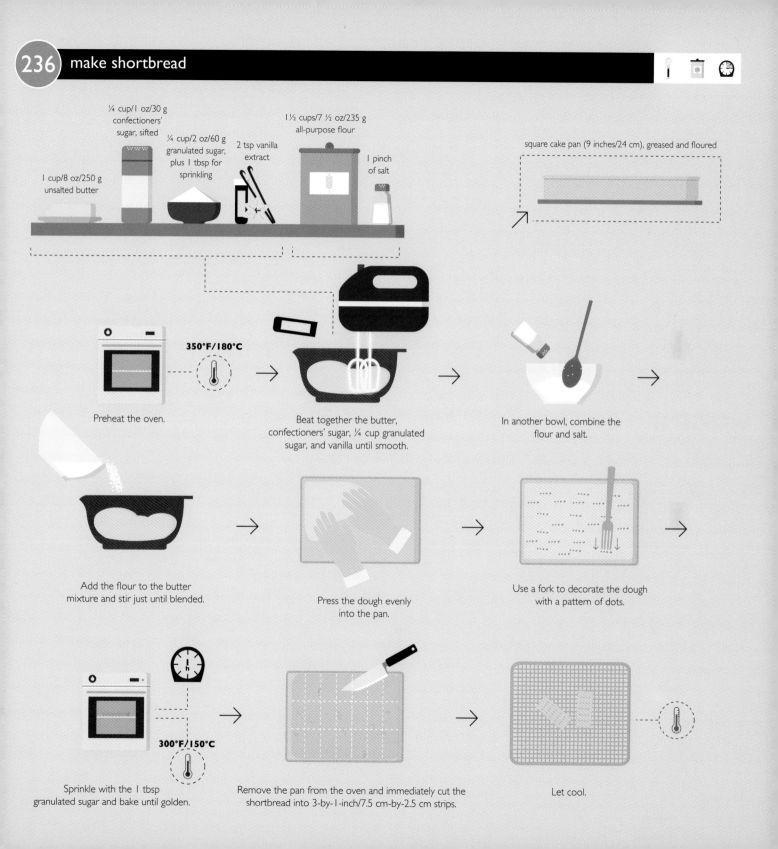

¼ cup/1 oz/30 g confectioners' sugar, sifted

¼ cup/2 oz/60 g granulated sugar, plus 1 tbsp for sprinkling

2 tsp vanilla extract

1½ cups/7 ½ oz/235 g all-purpose flour

1 pinch of salt

1 cup/8 oz/250 g unsalted butter

square cake pan (9 inches/24 cm), greased and floured

350°F/180°C

Preheat the oven.

Beat together the butter, confectioners' sugar, ¼ cup granulated sugar, and vanilla until smooth.

In another bowl, combine the flour and salt.

Add the flour to the butter mixture and stir just until blended.

Press the dough evenly into the pan.

Use a fork to decorate the dough with a pattern of dots.

300°F/150°C

Sprinkle with the 1 tbsp granulated sugar and bake until golden.

Remove the pan from the oven and immediately cut the shortbread into 3-by-1-inch/7.5 cm-by-2.5 cm strips.

Let cool.

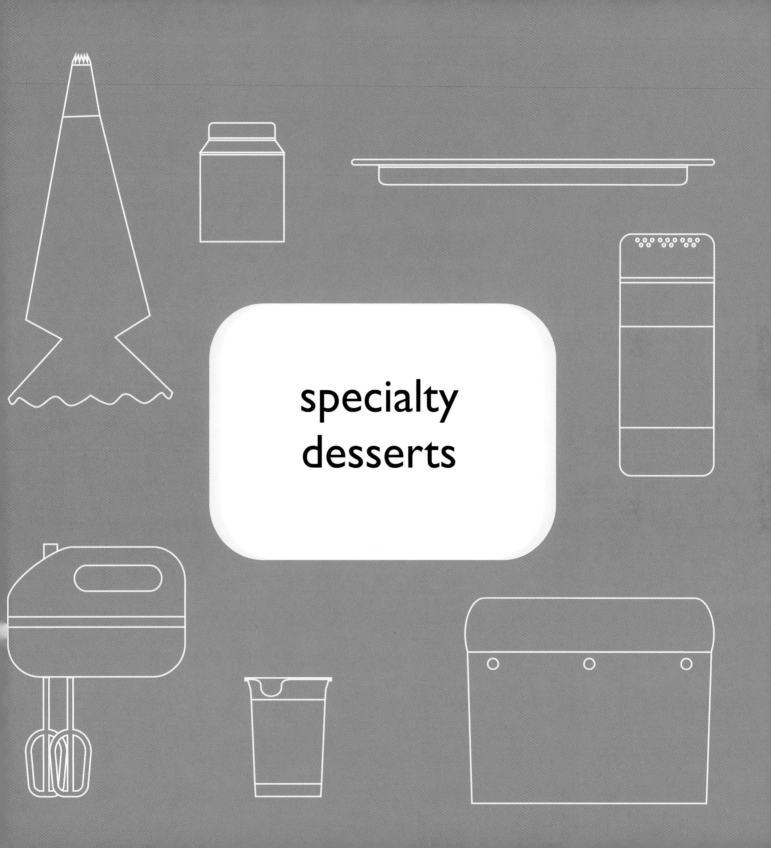

specialty
desserts

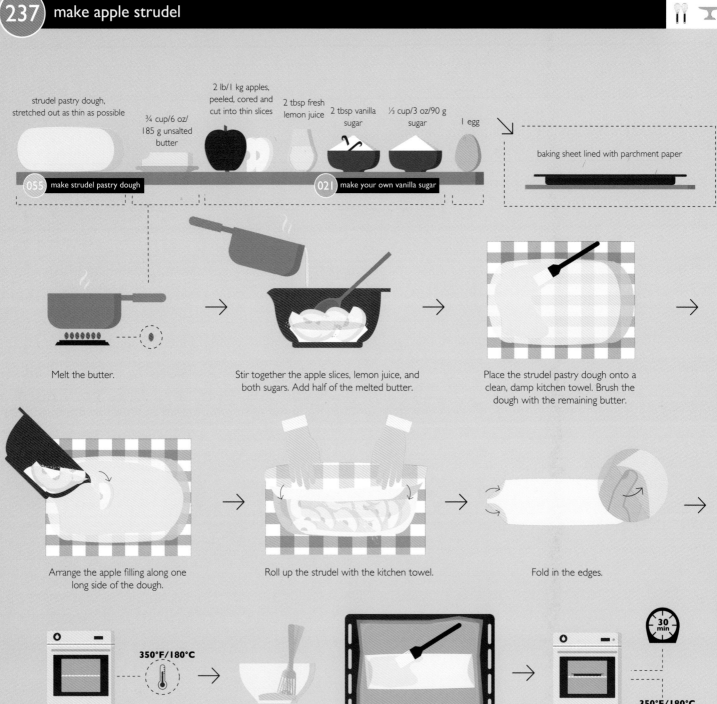

strudel pastry dough, stretched out as thin as possible

¾ cup/6 oz/185 g unsalted butter

2 lb/1 kg apples, peeled, cored and cut into thin slices

2 tbsp fresh lemon juice

2 tbsp vanilla sugar

⅓ cup/3 oz/90 g sugar

1 egg

baking sheet lined with parchment paper

055 | make strudel pastry dough

021 | make your own vanilla sugar

Melt the butter.

Stir together the apple slices, lemon juice, and both sugars. Add half of the melted butter.

Place the strudel pastry dough onto a clean, damp kitchen towel. Brush the dough with the remaining butter.

Arrange the apple filling along one long side of the dough.

Roll up the strudel with the kitchen towel.

Fold in the edges.

Preheat the oven.

350°F/180°C

Whisk the egg.

Transfer the strudel to the baking sheet, seam side down, and brush with the beaten egg.

Bake until golden brown and the apples are tender.

350°F/180°C

30 min

## 238 make apricot-almond strudel

2 lb/1 kg apricots, pitted and cut into slices

1 tsp vanilla extract

1 tbsp fresh lemon juice

½ cup/2 oz/60 g dried bread crumbs

½ cup/2 oz/60 g ground almonds

Brush the dough with melted butter as directed in the apple strudel recipe.

Mix all of the ingredients for the filling and proceed as directed for the apple strudel.

## 239 make pear-walnut strudel

2 lb/1 kg pears, peeled, cored and cut into slices

1 tsp vanilla extract

1 tbsp rum

1 tbsp fresh lemon juice

½ cup/2 oz/60 g dried bread crumbs

½ cup/2 oz/60 g ground walnuts

Brush the dough with melted butter as directed in the apple strudel recipe.

Mix all of the ingredients for the filling and proceed as directed for the apple strudel.

## 240 make plum-hazelnut strudel

2 lb/1 kg plums, pitted and cut into slices

1 tsp vanilla extract

1 tbsp rum

1 tbsp fresh lemon juice

½ cup/2 oz/60 g dried bread crumbs

½ cup/2 oz/60 g ground hazelnuts

Brush the dough with melted butter as directed in the apple strudel recipe.

Mix all of the ingredients for the filling and proceed as directed for the apple strudel.

## 241 make dried fruit strudel

2 lb/1 kg mixed dried fruit, chopped

2 tbsp fresh lemon juice

1 cup/4 oz/125 g dried bread crumbs

1 tbsp sugar

Brush the dough with melted butter as directed in the apple strudel recipe. Warm the dried fruit with the lemon juice and ½ cup/4 fl oz/125 g water.

Remove from the heat and set aside.

Stir together the bread crumbs and sugar. Add the dried fruit mixture. Proceed as directed for the apple strudel.

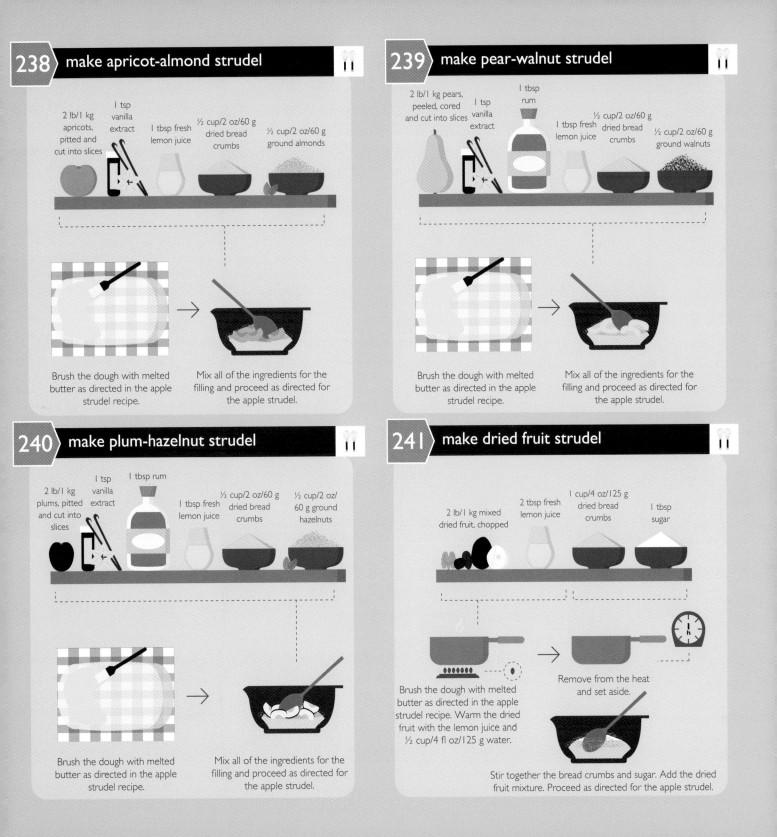

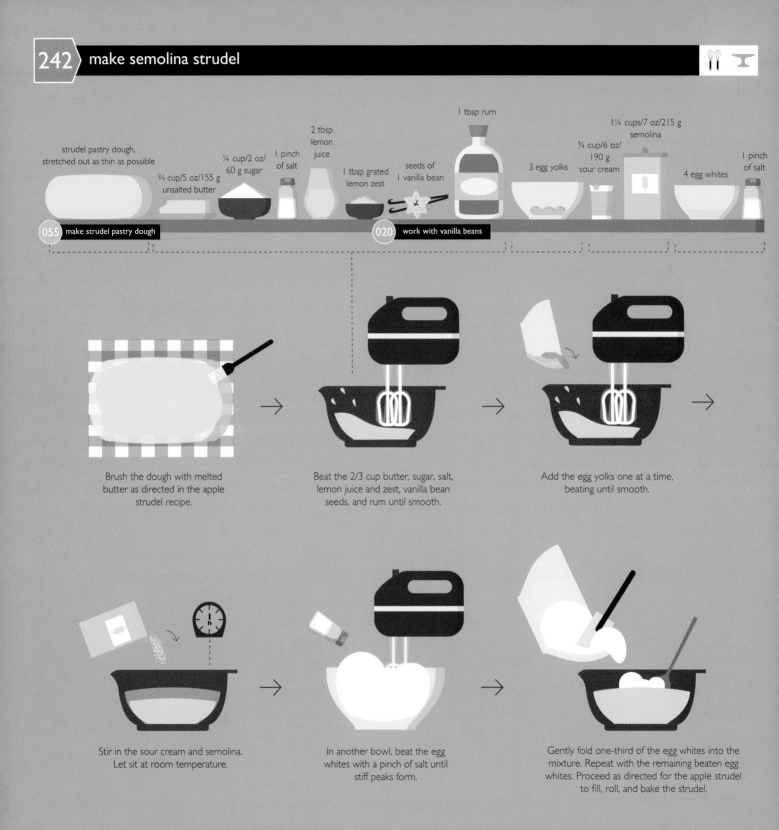

strudel pastry dough, stretched out as thin as possible

⅔ cup/5 oz/155 g unsalted butter

¼ cup/2 oz/ 60 g sugar

1 pinch of salt

2 tbsp lemon juice

1 tbsp grated lemon zest

seeds of 1 vanilla bean

1 tbsp rum

3 egg yolks

¾ cup/6 oz/ 190 g sour cream

1¼ cups/7 oz/215 g semolina

4 egg whites

1 pinch of salt

055 make strudel pastry dough

020 work with vanilla beans

Brush the dough with melted butter as directed in the apple strudel recipe.

Beat the 2/3 cup butter, sugar, salt, lemon juice and zest, vanilla bean seeds, and rum until smooth.

Add the egg yolks one at a time, beating until smooth.

Stir in the sour cream and semolina. Let sit at room temperature.

In another bowl, beat the egg whites with a pinch of salt until stiff peaks form.

Gently fold one-third of the egg whites into the mixture. Repeat with the remaining beaten egg whites. Proceed as directed for the apple strudel to fill, roll, and bake the strudel.

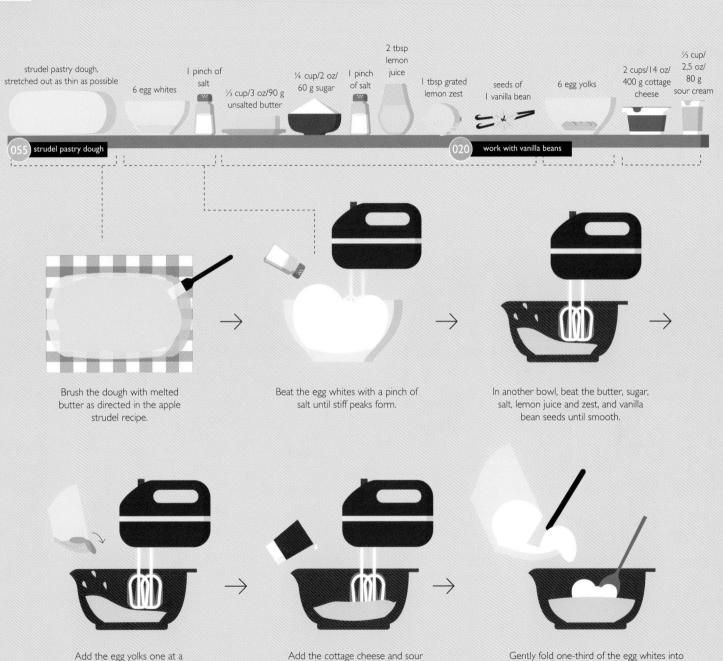

strudel pastry dough, stretched out as thin as possible

6 egg whites

1 pinch of salt

⅓ cup/3 oz/90 g unsalted butter

¼ cup/2 oz/ 60 g sugar

1 pinch of salt

2 tbsp lemon juice

1 tbsp grated lemon zest

seeds of 1 vanilla bean

6 egg yolks

2 cups/14 oz/ 400 g cottage cheese

⅓ cup/ 2,5 oz/ 80 g sour cream

055 strudel pastry dough

020 work with vanilla beans

Brush the dough with melted butter as directed in the apple strudel recipe.

Beat the egg whites with a pinch of salt until stiff peaks form.

In another bowl, beat the butter, sugar, salt, lemon juice and zest, and vanilla bean seeds until smooth.

Add the egg yolks one at a time, beating until smooth.

Add the cottage cheese and sour cream, and beat until smooth.

Gently fold one-third of the egg whites into the mixture. Repeat with the remaining beaten egg whites. Proceed as directed for the apple strudel to fill, roll and bake the strudel.

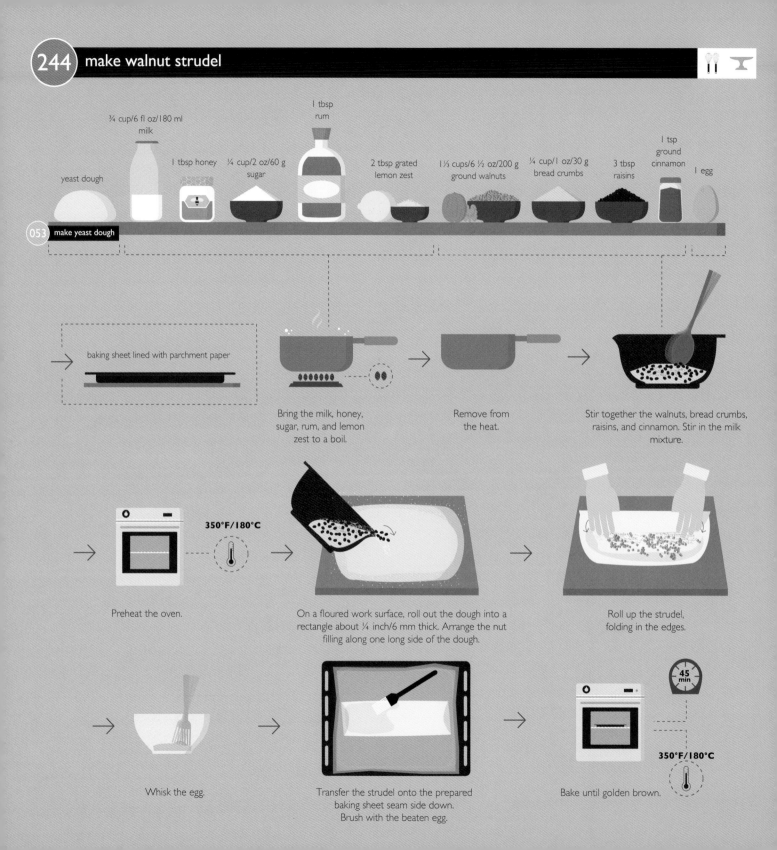

¾ cup/6 fl oz/180 ml milk

1 tbsp rum

1 tbsp honey

¼ cup/2 oz/60 g sugar

2 tbsp grated lemon zest

1⅓ cups/6 ½ oz/200 g ground walnuts

¼ cup/1 oz/30 g bread crumbs

3 tbsp raisins

1 tsp ground cinnamon

1 egg

yeast dough

053 make yeast dough

baking sheet lined with parchment paper

Bring the milk, honey, sugar, rum, and lemon zest to a boil.

Remove from the heat.

Stir together the walnuts, bread crumbs, raisins, and cinnamon. Stir in the milk mixture.

350°F/180°C

Preheat the oven.

On a floured work surface, roll out the dough into a rectangle about ¼ inch/6 mm thick. Arrange the nut filling along one long side of the dough.

Roll up the strudel, folding in the edges.

Whisk the egg.

Transfer the strudel onto the prepared baking sheet seam side down. Brush with the beaten egg.

Bake until golden brown.

45 min

350°F/180°C

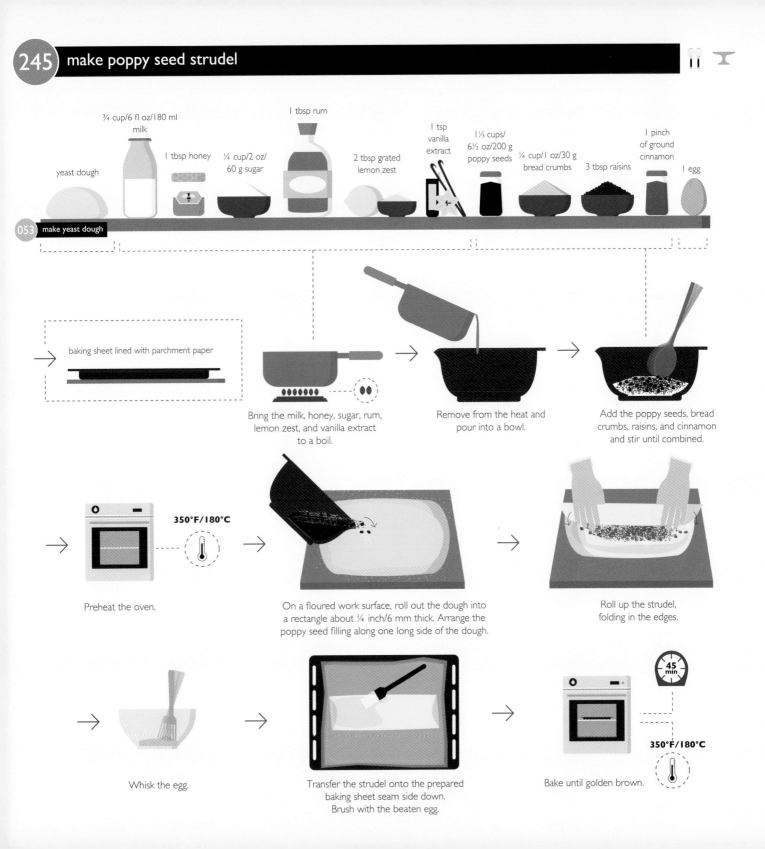

¾ cup/6 fl oz/180 ml milk

1 tbsp rum

1 tsp vanilla extract

1⅓ cups/ 6½ oz/200 g poppy seeds

1 pinch of ground cinnamon

yeast dough

1 tbsp honey

¼ cup/2 oz/ 60 g sugar

2 tbsp grated lemon zest

¼ cup/1 oz/30 g bread crumbs

3 tbsp raisins

1 egg

053 make yeast dough

baking sheet lined with parchment paper

Bring the milk, honey, sugar, rum, lemon zest, and vanilla extract to a boil.

Remove from the heat and pour into a bowl.

Add the poppy seeds, bread crumbs, raisins, and cinnamon and stir until combined.

Preheat the oven.

**350°F/180°C**

On a floured work surface, roll out the dough into a rectangle about ¼ inch/6 mm thick. Arrange the poppy seed filling along one long side of the dough.

Roll up the strudel, folding in the edges.

Whisk the egg.

Transfer the strudel onto the prepared baking sheet seam side down. Brush with the beaten egg.

Bake until golden brown.

**45 min**

**350°F/180°C**

1 lb/500 g filo dough

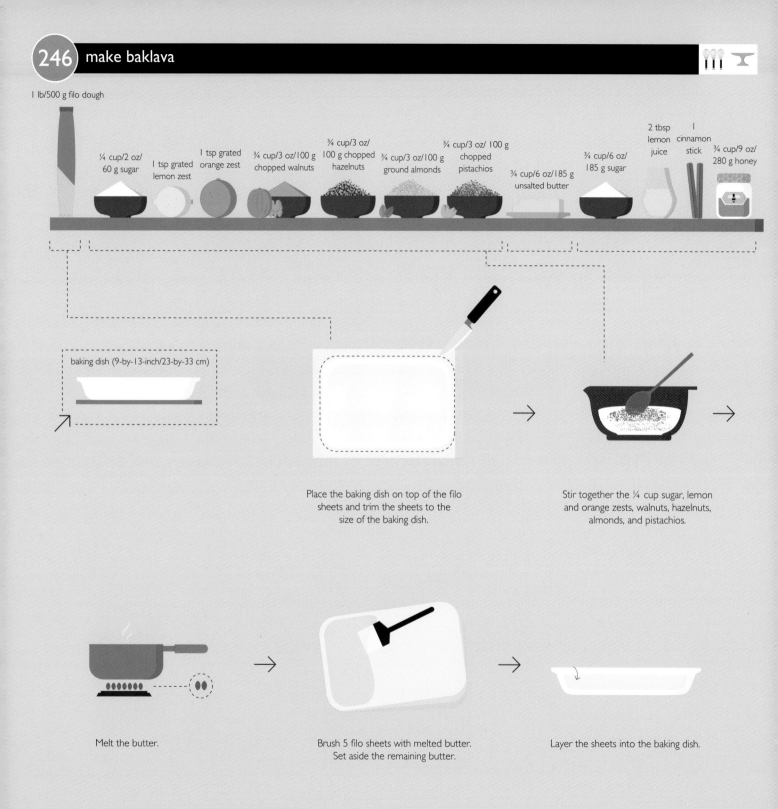

¼ cup/2 oz/ 60 g sugar

1 tsp grated lemon zest

1 tsp grated orange zest

¾ cup/3 oz/100 g chopped walnuts

¾ cup/3 oz/ 100 g chopped hazelnuts

¾ cup/3 oz/100 g ground almonds

¾ cup/3 oz/ 100 g chopped pistachios

¾ cup/6 oz/185 g unsalted butter

¾ cup/6 oz/ 185 g sugar

2 tbsp lemon juice

1 cinnamon stick

¾ cup/9 oz/ 280 g honey

baking dish (9-by-13-inch/23-by-33 cm)

Place the baking dish on top of the filo sheets and trim the sheets to the size of the baking dish.

Stir together the ¼ cup sugar, lemon and orange zests, walnuts, hazelnuts, almonds, and pistachios.

Melt the butter.

Brush 5 filo sheets with melted butter. Set aside the remaining butter.

Layer the sheets into the baking dish.

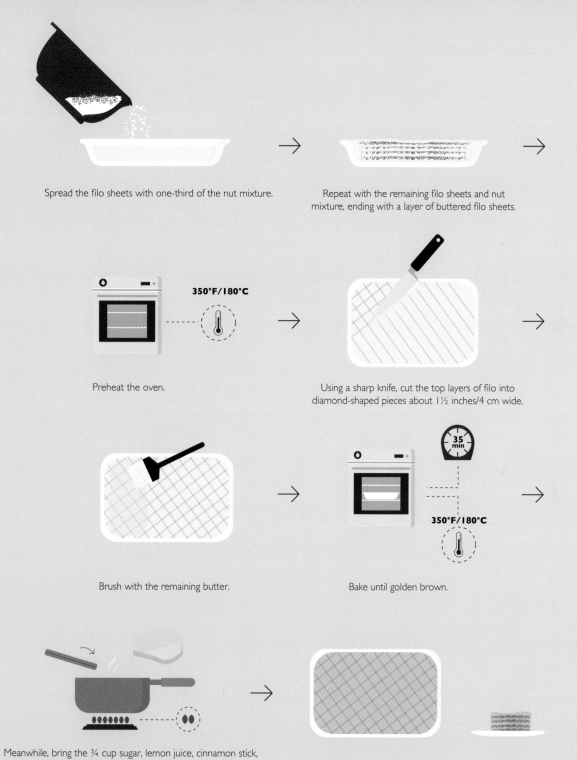

Spread the filo sheets with one-third of the nut mixture.

Repeat with the remaining filo sheets and nut mixture, ending with a layer of buttered filo sheets.

350°F/180°C

Preheat the oven.

Using a sharp knife, cut the top layers of filo into diamond-shaped pieces about 1½ inches/4 cm wide.

Brush with the remaining butter.

35 min

350°F/180°C

Bake until golden brown.

Meanwhile, bring the ¾ cup sugar, lemon juice, cinnamon stick, and honey to a boil with 1 cup/8 fl oz/250 ml water. Cook, stirring, until the sugar dissolves. Discard the cinnamon stick.

Cut the baklava into diamonds, then pour the syrup over the top.

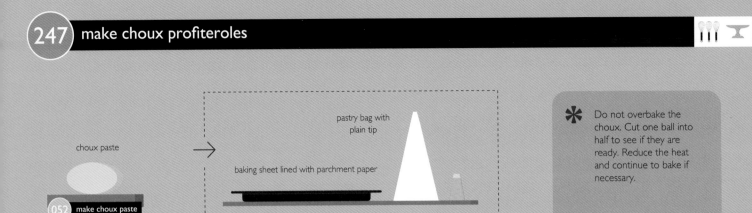

choux paste

052 make choux paste

baking sheet lined with parchment paper

pastry bag with plain tip

✱ Do not overbake the choux. Cut one ball into half to see if they are ready. Reduce the heat and continue to bake if necessary.

400°F/200°C

Preheat the oven.

Fill a pastry bag fitted with a plain tip with the choux paste.

Pipe small balls onto the baking sheet, spacing them about 2 inches/5 cm apart.

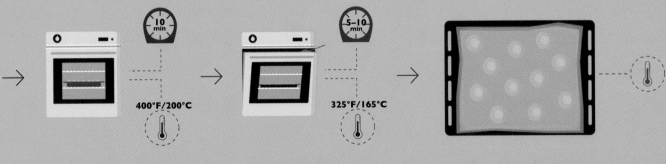

10 min

400°F/200°C

Bake until puffed and lightly brown. Reduce the temperature.

5–10 min

325°F/165°C

Use a wooden spoon to prop open the oven door and continue to bake.

Let the balls cool completely, then fill.

## 248 | make profiteroles with ice cream

1¼ cups/
10 fl oz/300 ml
vanilla ice cream       chocolate sauce

**295** make chocolate sauce

Cut the profiteroles almost through. Fill each ball with a small scoop of vanilla ice cream. Top with warm chocolate sauce.

## 249 | make profiteroles with pastry cream

2 tbsp
confectioner's sugar

pastry cream

**292** make pastry cream

Fill a pastry bag fitted with a small plain tip with pastry cream and fill each ball.

Dust with confectioner's sugar.

## 250 | make profiteroles with jam filling

¾ cup/7½ oz/230 g
apricot jam

2 tbsp
confectioner's sugar

1 tbsp lemon
juice

Stir together the jam and lemon juice.

Fill a pastry bag fitted with a small plain tip with the jam mixture and fill each ball. Dust with confectioner's sugar.

## 251 | make profiteroles with baileys cream

⅓ cup/3 fl oz/80 ml Baileys

1 cup/7 oz/200 g
whipped cream

**015** whip cream

Gently stir the Baileys into the whipped cream.

Fill a pastry bag fitted with a small plain tip with Baileys cream and fill each ball.

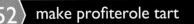

30 baked choux profiteroles

1 cup/7 oz/200 g heavy cream

2 tbsp confectioners' sugar, sifted

chocolate sauce

295 make chocolate sauce

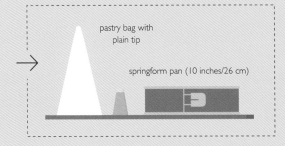

pastry bag with plain tip

springform pan (10 inches/26 cm)

Beat the cream and sugar until medium peaks form.

Cut the profiteroles almost through.

Fill a pastry ball fitted with a small plain tip with the whipped cream and fill each ball.

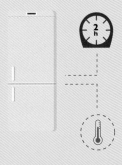

Place the filled profiteroles into the springform pan.

Cover with warm chocolate sauce. The chocolate should cover the profiteroles completely.

Refrigerate before serving.

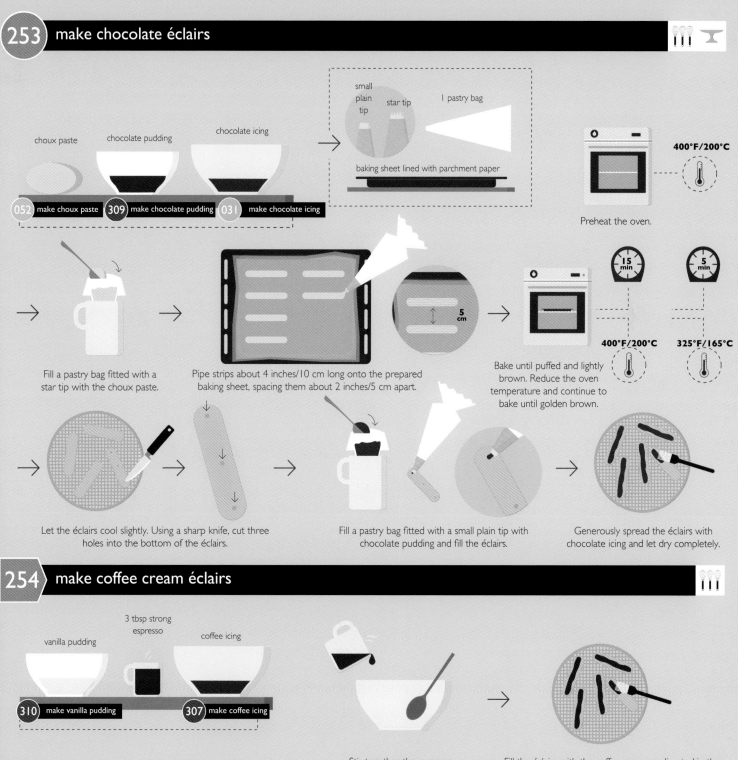

## 253 make chocolate éclairs

choux paste

chocolate pudding

chocolate icing

052 make choux paste   309 make chocolate pudding   031 make chocolate icing

small plain tip   star tip   1 pastry bag

baking sheet lined with parchment paper

400°F/200°C

Preheat the oven.

Fill a pastry bag fitted with a star tip with the choux paste.

Pipe strips about 4 inches/10 cm long onto the prepared baking sheet, spacing them about 2 inches/5 cm apart.

5 cm

15 min   5 min

400°F/200°C   325°F/165°C

Bake until puffed and lightly brown. Reduce the oven temperature and continue to bake until golden brown.

Let the éclairs cool slightly. Using a sharp knife, cut three holes into the bottom of the éclairs.

Fill a pastry bag fitted with a small plain tip with chocolate pudding and fill the éclairs.

Generously spread the éclairs with chocolate icing and let dry completely.

## 254 make coffee cream éclairs

vanilla pudding

3 tbsp strong espresso

coffee icing

310 make vanilla pudding   307 make coffee icing

Stir together the espresso and vanilla pudding.

Fill the éclairs with the coffee cream as directed in the chocolate éclairs recipe. Spread the éclairs with coffee icing.

choux paste

2 tbsp slivered almonds

½ cup/4 fl oz/ 125 ml heavy cream

2 tbsp confectioners' sugar

2 tbsp sour cream

I tbsp grated lemon zest

royal icing

baking sheet lined with parchment paper

052   make choux paste

305   make royal icing

**400°F/200°C**

Preheat the oven.

Divide the choux paste into 4 portions and form them into balls.

Press them into flat circles and, using a paring knife, make a hole in the middle.

Place the rings on the prepared baking sheet. Sprinkle the pastry rings with the slivered almonds.

**20 min**

**400°F/200°C**

Bake until puffed and lightly browned.

**15 min**

**325°F/165°C**

Reduce the temperature. Use a wooden spoon to prop open the oven door and continue to bake until golden brown. Let cool completely.

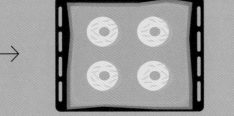

Beat the heavy cream and sugar until soft peaks form. Beat in the sour cream and lemon zest until stiff peaks form.

Split the almond rings horizontally, spread with the lemon whipped cream and put them back together.

Decorate with royal icing.

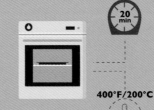

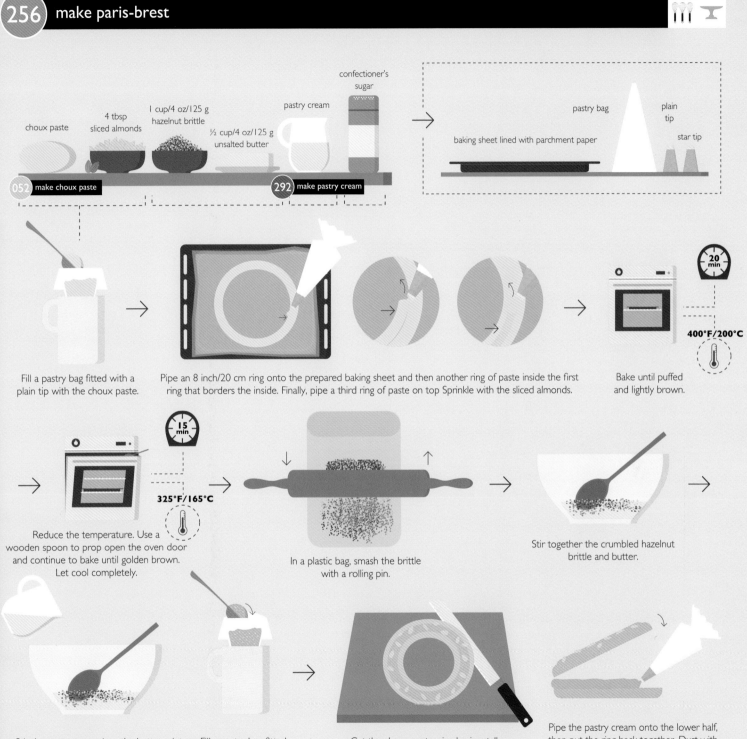

choux paste

4 tbsp
sliced almonds

1 cup/4 oz/125 g
hazelnut brittle

½ cup/4 oz/125 g
unsalted butter

pastry cream

confectioner's
sugar

pastry bag

plain
tip

baking sheet lined with parchment paper

star tip

052 make choux paste

292 make pastry cream

Fill a pastry bag fitted with a
plain tip with the choux paste.

Pipe an 8 inch/20 cm ring onto the prepared baking sheet and then another ring of paste inside the first
ring that borders the inside. Finally, pipe a third ring of paste on top Sprinkle with the sliced almonds.

20 min

400°F/200°C

Bake until puffed
and lightly brown.

15 min

325°F/165°C

Reduce the temperature. Use a
wooden spoon to prop open the oven
door and continue to bake until golden brown.
Let cool completely.

In a plastic bag, smash the brittle
with a rolling pin.

Stir together the crumbled hazelnut
brittle and butter.

Stir the pastry cream into the butter mixture. Fill a pastry bag fitted
with a star tip with the pastry cream mixture.

Cut the choux pastry ring horizontally
into two parts.

Pipe the pastry cream onto the lower half,
then put the ring back together. Dust with
confectioner's sugar and serve.

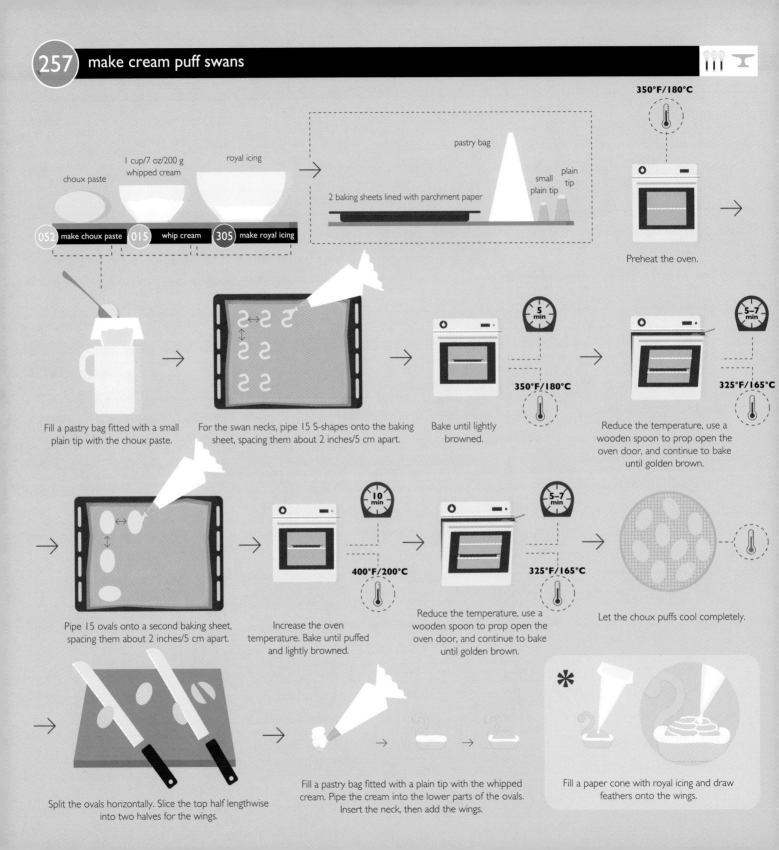

choux paste

1 cup/7 oz/200 g whipped cream

royal icing

052 make choux paste  015 whip cream  305 make royal icing

pastry bag

2 baking sheets lined with parchment paper

small plain tip

plain tip

350°F/180°C

Preheat the oven.

Fill a pastry bag fitted with a small plain tip with the choux paste.

For the swan necks, pipe 15 S-shapes onto the baking sheet, spacing them about 2 inches/5 cm apart.

Bake until lightly browned.

5 min

350°F/180°C

Reduce the temperature, use a wooden spoon to prop open the oven door, and continue to bake until golden brown.

5–7 min

325°F/165°C

Pipe 15 ovals onto a second baking sheet, spacing them about 2 inches/5 cm apart.

Increase the oven temperature. Bake until puffed and lightly browned.

10 min

400°F/200°C

Reduce the temperature, use a wooden spoon to prop open the oven door, and continue to bake until golden brown.

5–7 min

325°F/165°C

Let the choux puffs cool completely.

Split the ovals horizontally. Slice the top half lengthwise into two halves for the wings.

Fill a pastry bag fitted with a plain tip with the whipped cream. Pipe the cream into the lower parts of the ovals. Insert the neck, then add the wings.

* Fill a paper cone with royal icing and draw feathers onto the wings.

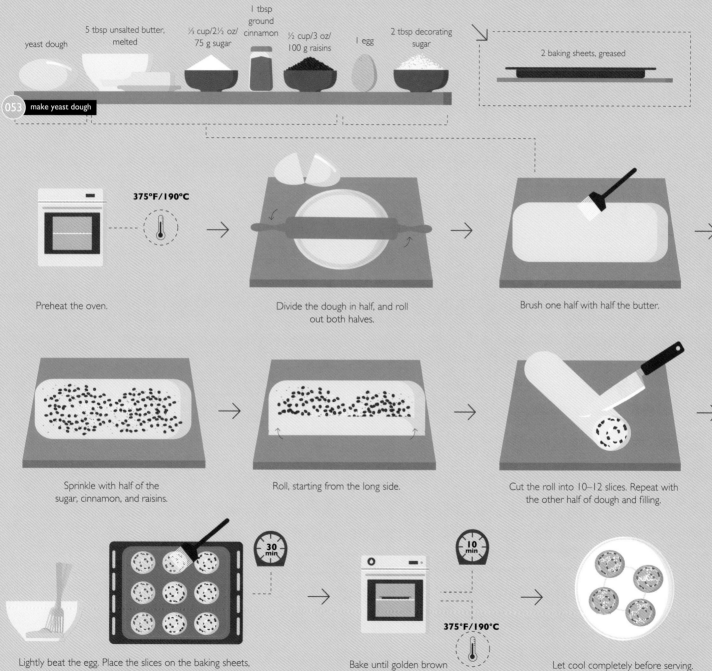

yeast dough

5 tbsp unsalted butter, melted

⅓ cup/2½ oz/ 75 g sugar

1 tbsp ground cinnamon

½ cup/3 oz/ 100 g raisins

1 egg

2 tbsp decorating sugar

2 baking sheets, greased

053 make yeast dough

375°F/190°C

Preheat the oven.

Divide the dough in half, and roll out both halves.

Brush one half with half the butter.

Sprinkle with half of the sugar, cinnamon, and raisins.

Roll, starting from the long side.

Cut the roll into 10–12 slices. Repeat with the other half of dough and filling.

30 min

Lightly beat the egg. Place the slices on the baking sheets, cut side up, brush with the beaten egg, sprinkle with decorating sugar and let proof until doubled in size.

10 min

375°F/190°C

Bake until golden brown and cooked through.

Let cool completely before serving.

½ recipe cake batter

1½ oz/45 g cream cheese, at room temperature

**046** prepare chiffon cake batter

½ recipe cake batter

1½ oz/45 g cream cheese, at room temperature

2 tbsp cocoa powder

**046** prepare chiffon cake batter

loaf pan (8 inches/20 cm), greased

**350°F/180°C**

Preheat the oven.

15 min

**350°F/180°C**

Pour the cake batter into the pan and bake until golden brown. Let cool.

Remove the cake from the pan. Cut away the hard edges from the crust.

Stir the cocoa powder into the cake batter.

15 min

**350°F/180°C**

Pour the cake batter into the pan and bake until golden brown. Let cool.

Crumble the cake into fine crumbs by hand. Add the cream cheese and stir to combine.

1 h

Wrap the mixture in plastic wrap and chill.

Remove the cake from the pan. Cut away the hard edges from the crust.

Crumble the cake into fine crumbs by hand. Add the cream cheese and stir to combine.

30 min

Form small tablespoon-sized balls. Place on a baking sheet and refrigerate.

Insert skewers into the bottom of each cake ball, pressing it halfway through.

1 h

Wrap the mixture in plastic wrap and chill.

30 min

Form small tablespoon-sized balls. Place on a baking sheet and refrigerate.

Insert skewers into the bottom of each cake ball, pressing it halfway through.

## 261 ice cake pops

royal icing

For colored cake pops, stir a few drops of food coloring into the royal icing.

gel food coloring

305 make royal icing

Dip the cake pops into the royal icing to coat completely. Stand up in a glass until the icing sets.

## 262 ice cake pops with chocolate and a face

chocolate icing     royal icing

043 make a paper cone

031 make chocolate icing     305 make royal icing

Dip the cake pops into the chocolate icing to coat completely. Stand up in a glass until the icing sets.

Fill a paper cone with royal icing and pipe a face onto the cake pop.

## 263 decorate cake pops with colored sugar

4 tbsp colored sanding sugar

royal icing

305 make royal icing

Dip the cake pops into the royal icing to coat completely.

Sprinkle with the colored sugar and let dry in a glass.

## 264 color cake pops

royal icing

043 make a paper cone

gel food coloring

305 make royal icing

Use the food coloring to color the royal icing.

Dip the cake pops into the icing to coat completely. Pipe decorative patterns onto the cake pops.

soufflés and custards

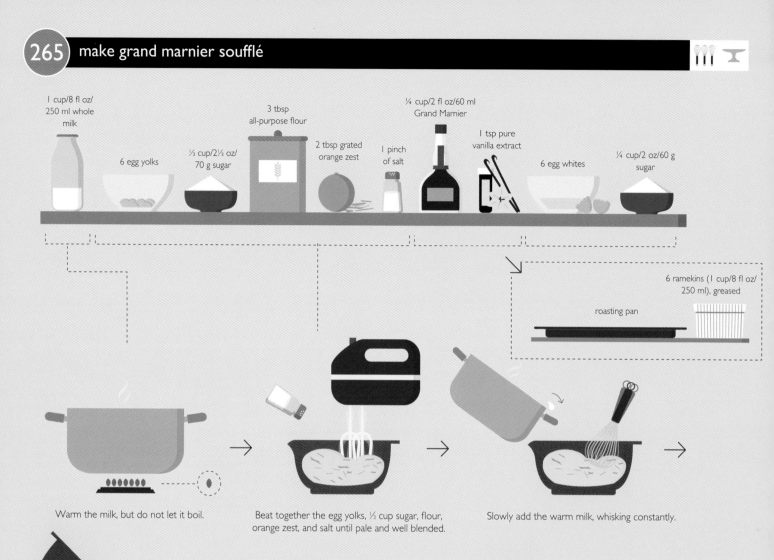

1 cup/8 fl oz/ 250 ml whole milk

6 egg yolks

⅓ cup/2⅓ oz/ 70 g sugar

3 tbsp all-purpose flour

2 tbsp grated orange zest

1 pinch of salt

¼ cup/2 fl oz/60 ml Grand Marnier

1 tsp pure vanilla extract

6 egg whites

¼ cup/2 oz/60 g sugar

6 ramekins (1 cup/8 fl oz/ 250 ml), greased

roasting pan

Warm the milk, but do not let it boil.

Beat together the egg yolks, ⅓ cup sugar, flour, orange zest, and salt until pale and well blended.

Slowly add the warm milk, whisking constantly.

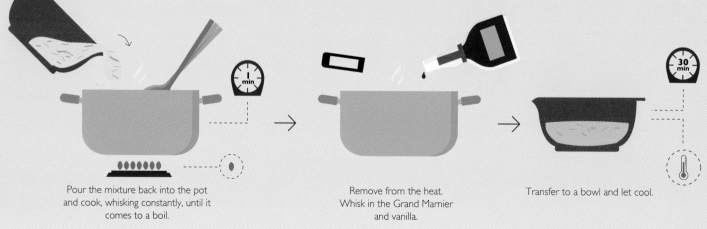

Pour the mixture back into the pot and cook, whisking constantly, until it comes to a boil.

Remove from the heat. Whisk in the Grand Marnier and vanilla.

Transfer to a bowl and let cool.

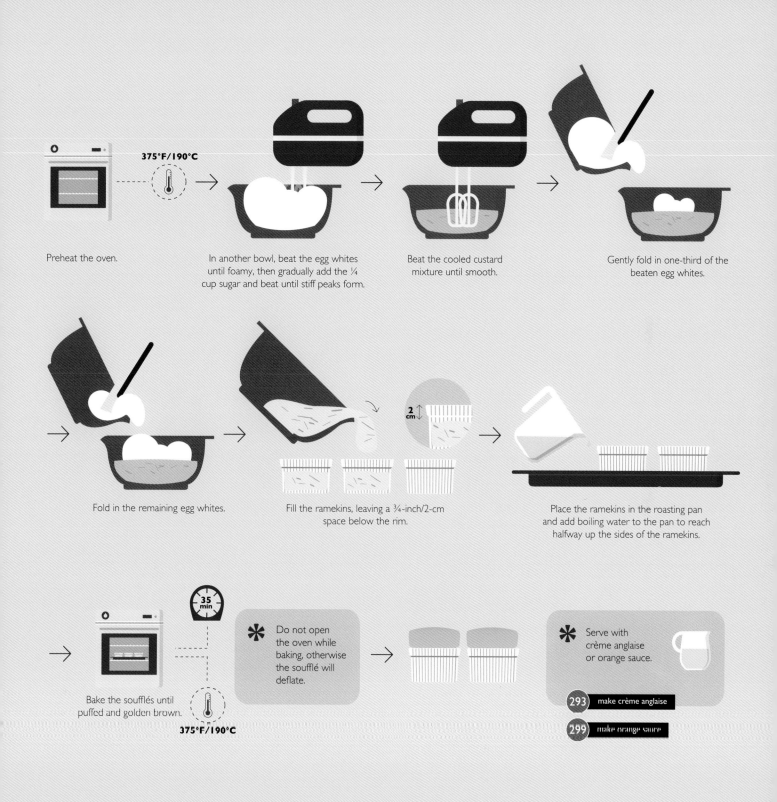

Preheat the oven.

375°F/190°C

In another bowl, beat the egg whites until foamy, then gradually add the ¼ cup sugar and beat until stiff peaks form.

Beat the cooled custard mixture until smooth.

Gently fold in one-third of the beaten egg whites.

Fold in the remaining egg whites.

2 cm

Fill the ramekins, leaving a ¾-inch/2-cm space below the rim.

Place the ramekins in the roasting pan and add boiling water to the pan to reach halfway up the sides of the ramekins.

35 min

Bake the soufflés until puffed and golden brown.

375°F/190°C

\* Do not open the oven while baking, otherwise the soufflé will deflate.

\* Serve with crème anglaise or orange sauce.

293  make crème anglaise

299  make orange sauce

2 tbsp dry white wine

3 apples, peeled, cored, and cut into eighths

6 egg whites

I pinch of salt

I tsp lemon juice

⅓ cup/3 oz/90 g sugar

I soufflé dish (6 cups/48 fl oz/1.5 l), greased

Use the egg yolks for crème anglaise.

293 make crème anglaise

400°F/200°C

25 min

Cook the apples in the wine until they soften and the liquid evaporates.

Transfer to a bowl and, using an immersion blender, purée until smooth.

Preheat the oven.

In another bowl, beat the egg whites until foamy, then slowly add the salt, lemon juice, and sugar. Beat until stiff peaks form.

Gently fold in the apple purée.

2 cm

Fill the soufflé dish, leaving a ¾-inch/2-cm space below the rim.

30 min

400°F/200°C

Bake the soufflé until puffed and golden brown.

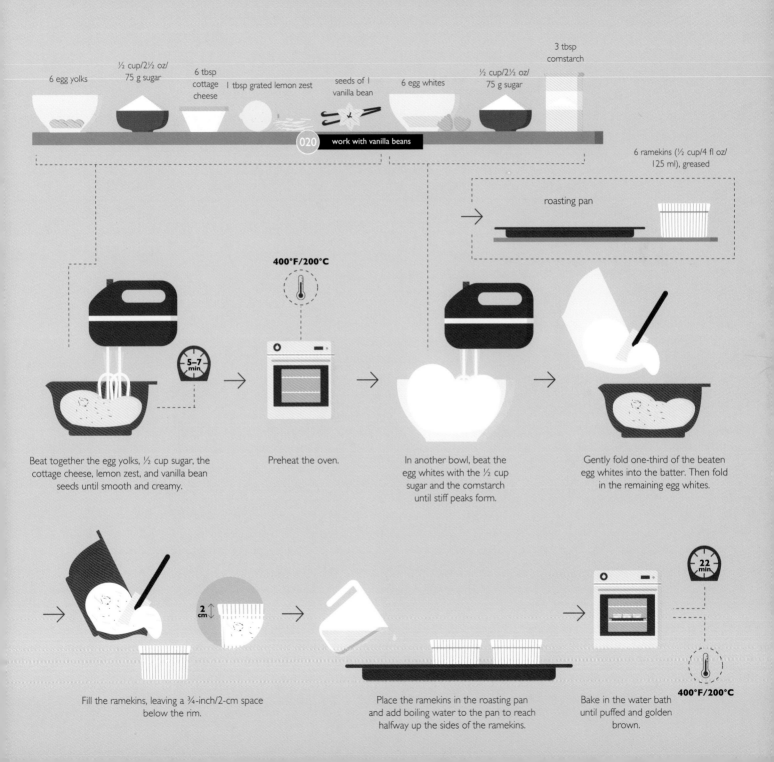

6 egg yolks

½ cup/2½ oz/ 75 g sugar

6 tbsp cottage cheese

1 tbsp grated lemon zest

seeds of 1 vanilla bean

6 egg whites

½ cup/2½ oz/ 75 g sugar

3 tbsp cornstarch

020 work with vanilla beans

6 ramekins (½ cup/4 fl oz/ 125 ml), greased

roasting pan

400°F/200°C

5–7 min

Beat together the egg yolks, ½ cup sugar, the cottage cheese, lemon zest, and vanilla bean seeds until smooth and creamy.

Preheat the oven.

In another bowl, beat the egg whites with the ½ cup sugar and the cornstarch until stiff peaks form.

Gently fold one-third of the beaten egg whites into the batter. Then fold in the remaining egg whites.

2 cm

22 min

400°F/200°C

Fill the ramekins, leaving a ¾-inch/2-cm space below the rim.

Place the ramekins in the roasting pan and add boiling water to the pan to reach halfway up the sides of the ramekins.

Bake in the water bath until puffed and golden brown.

2 eggs

2 egg yolks

3 tbsp sugar, plus sugar for the ramekins

1 pinch of salt

3½ oz/100 g dark chocolate, chopped

5 tbsp/2½ oz/75 g unsalted butter

½ cup/2½ oz/75 g flour

6 ramekins (½ cup/4 fl oz/ 125 ml), greased

roasting pan

Beat the eggs, egg yolks, sugar, and salt until smooth and fluffy.

Melt the chocolate and butter, stirring until smooth. Remove from the heat and let cool slightly.

Preheat the oven.

**375°F/190°C**

Gently stir the chocolate mixture into the egg mixture.

Stir in the flour.

Coat the ramekins with sugar.

Fill the ramekins, leaving a ¾-inch/2-cm space below the rim.

2 cm

Place the ramekins in the roasting pan and add boiling water to the pan to reach halfway up the sides of the ramekins.

Bake until puffed.

10 min

**375°F/190°C**

The centers should still be soft. Do not overbake.

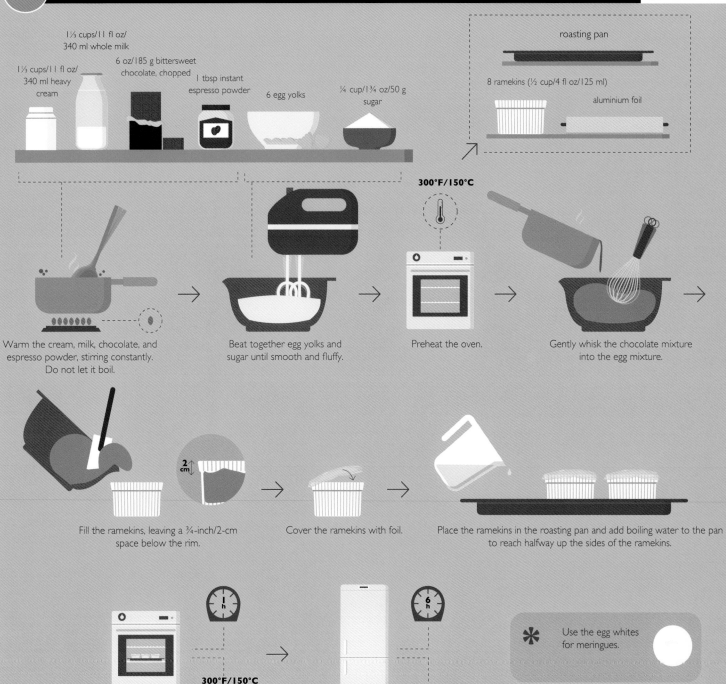

1⅓ cups/11 fl oz/ 340 ml whole milk

1⅓ cups/11 fl oz/ 340 ml heavy cream

6 oz/185 g bittersweet chocolate, chopped

1 tbsp instant espresso powder

6 egg yolks

¼ cup/1¾ oz/50 g sugar

roasting pan

8 ramekins (½ cup/4 fl oz/125 ml)

aluminium foil

**300°F/150°C**

Warm the cream, milk, chocolate, and espresso powder, stirring constantly. Do not let it boil.

Beat together egg yolks and sugar until smooth and fluffy.

Preheat the oven.

Gently whisk the chocolate mixture into the egg mixture.

Fill the ramekins, leaving a ¾-inch/2-cm space below the rim.

**2 cm**

Cover the ramekins with foil.

Place the ramekins in the roasting pan and add boiling water to the pan to reach halfway up the sides of the ramekins.

**300°F/150°C**

Bake in the water bath until the custards are set.

Remove the ramekins from the water bath. Refrigerate until cold.

※ Use the egg whites for meringues.

221 | make meringues

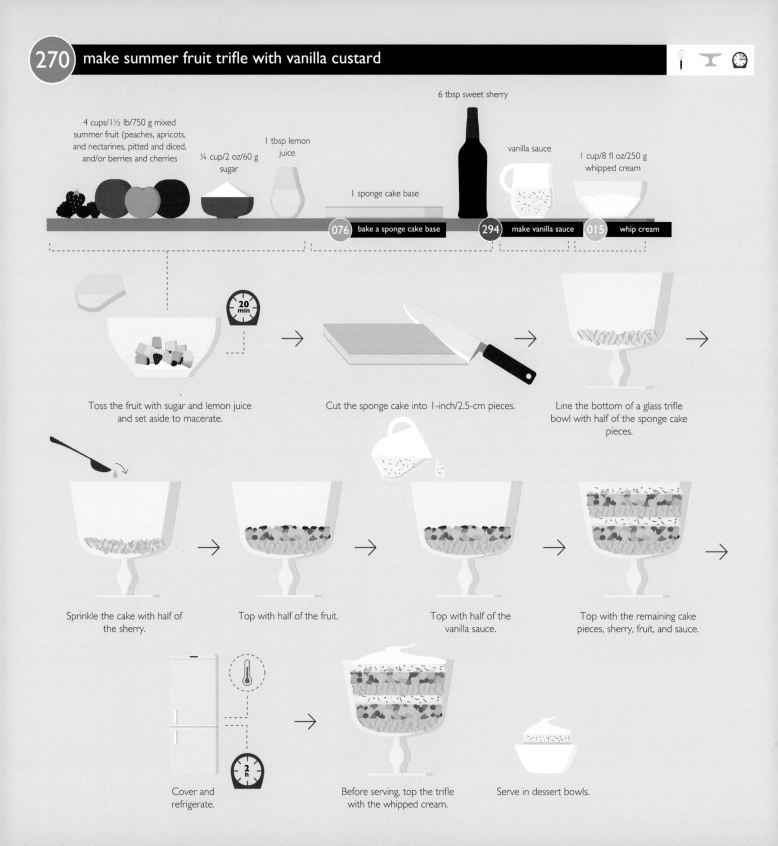

6 tbsp sweet sherry

4 cups/1½ lb/750 g mixed summer fruit (peaches, apricots, and nectarines, pitted and diced, and/or berries and cherries)

¼ cup/2 oz/60 g sugar

1 tbsp lemon juice

vanilla sauce

1 cup/8 fl oz/250 g whipped cream

1 sponge cake base

**076** bake a sponge cake base

**294** make vanilla sauce

**015** whip cream

**20 min**

Toss the fruit with sugar and lemon juice and set aside to macerate.

Cut the sponge cake into 1-inch/2.5-cm pieces.

Line the bottom of a glass trifle bowl with half of the sponge cake pieces.

Sprinkle the cake with half of the sherry.

Top with half of the fruit.

Top with half of the vanilla sauce.

Top with the remaining cake pieces, sherry, fruit, and sauce.

Cover and refrigerate.

Before serving, top the trifle with the whipped cream.

Serve in dessert bowls.

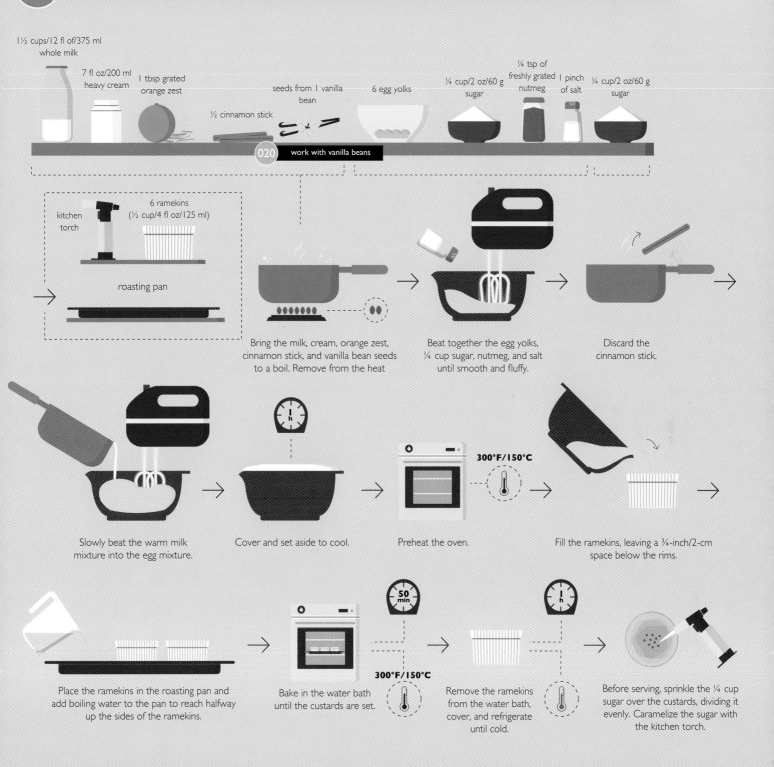

1½ cups/12 fl of/375 ml whole milk

7 fl oz/200 ml heavy cream

1 tbsp grated orange zest

½ cinnamon stick

seeds from 1 vanilla bean

6 egg yolks

¼ cup/2 oz/60 g sugar

¼ tsp of freshly grated nutmeg

1 pinch of salt

¼ cup/2 oz/60 g sugar

020 work with vanilla beans

kitchen torch

6 ramekins (½ cup/4 fl oz/125 ml)

roasting pan

Bring the milk, cream, orange zest, cinnamon stick, and vanilla bean seeds to a boil. Remove from the heat

Beat together the egg yolks, ¼ cup sugar, nutmeg, and salt until smooth and fluffy.

Discard the cinnamon stick.

Slowly beat the warm milk mixture into the egg mixture.

Cover and set aside to cool.

Preheat the oven. 300°F/150°C

Fill the ramekins, leaving a ¾-inch/2-cm space below the rims.

Place the ramekins in the roasting pan and add boiling water to the pan to reach halfway up the sides of the ramekins.

Bake in the water bath until the custards are set. 50 min 300°F/150°C

Remove the ramekins from the water bath, cover, and refrigerate until cold.

Before serving, sprinkle the ¼ cup sugar over the custards, dividing it evenly. Caramelize the sugar with the kitchen torch.

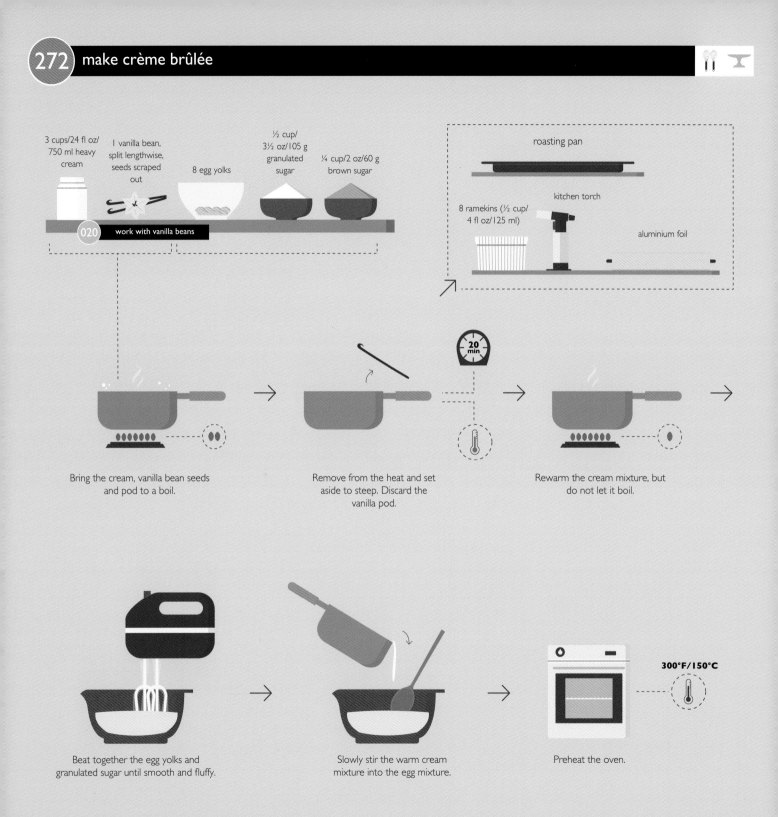

3 cups/24 fl oz/ 750 ml heavy cream

I vanilla bean, split lengthwise, seeds scraped out

8 egg yolks

½ cup/ 3½ oz/105 g granulated sugar

¼ cup/2 oz/60 g brown sugar

020 work with vanilla beans

roasting pan

8 ramekins (½ cup/ 4 fl oz/125 ml)

kitchen torch

aluminium foil

20 min

Bring the cream, vanilla bean seeds and pod to a boil.

Remove from the heat and set aside to steep. Discard the vanilla pod.

Rewarm the cream mixture, but do not let it boil.

Beat together the egg yolks and granulated sugar until smooth and fluffy.

Slowly stir the warm cream mixture into the egg mixture.

Preheat the oven.

300°F/150°C

Return the mixture to the saucepan, cook, stirring constantly, until the custard has thickened.

Fill the ramekins, leaving a ¾-inch/2-cm space below the rims.

Cover the ramekins with foil.

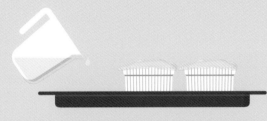

Place the ramekins in the roasting pan and add boiling water to the pan to reach halfway up the sides of the ramekins.

Bake in the water bath **300°F/150°C** until the custards are set.

Remove the ramekins from the water bath.

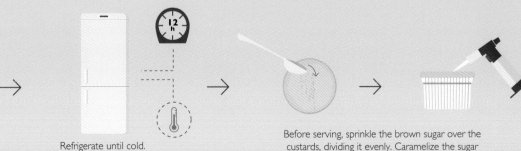

Refrigerate until cold.

Before serving, sprinkle the brown sugar over the custards, dividing it evenly. Caramelize the sugar with the kitchen torch.

## 273 › make crème brûlée with rosemary

Prepare the crème brûlée as directed, but add
2 sprigs of rosemary to the cream mixture,
discard with the vanilla bean.

## 274 › make coffee crème brûlée

1 tsp instant
espresso
powder

Prepare the crème brûlée as directed, but add
instant espresso powder instead of the vanilla bean.

## 275 › make chocolate crème brûlée

1 tbsp cocoa
powder

Prepare the crème brûlée as directed, but add
cocoa instead of the vanilla bean.

## 276 › make orange crème brûlée

⅓ cup/3 fl oz/80 ml
Cointreau

2 tbsp grated
orange zest

Prepare the crème brûlée as directed, but add
orange zest and Cointreau instead of the vanilla
bean. Strain the cream mixture before using.

## 277 › make chocolate-chile crème brûlée

½ cup/2½ oz/75 g
chopped bittersweet
chocolate    1 small
jalapeño chile

Prepare the crème brûlée as directed, but add the chile
instead of the vanilla bean. Discard the chile. Melt the
chocolate in the cream.

## 278 › make crème brûlée with whisky

⅓ cup/3 fl oz/80 ml
sweet whisky

Prepare the crème brûlée as directed. Stir in
the whisky just before dividing the custard
between the ramekins.

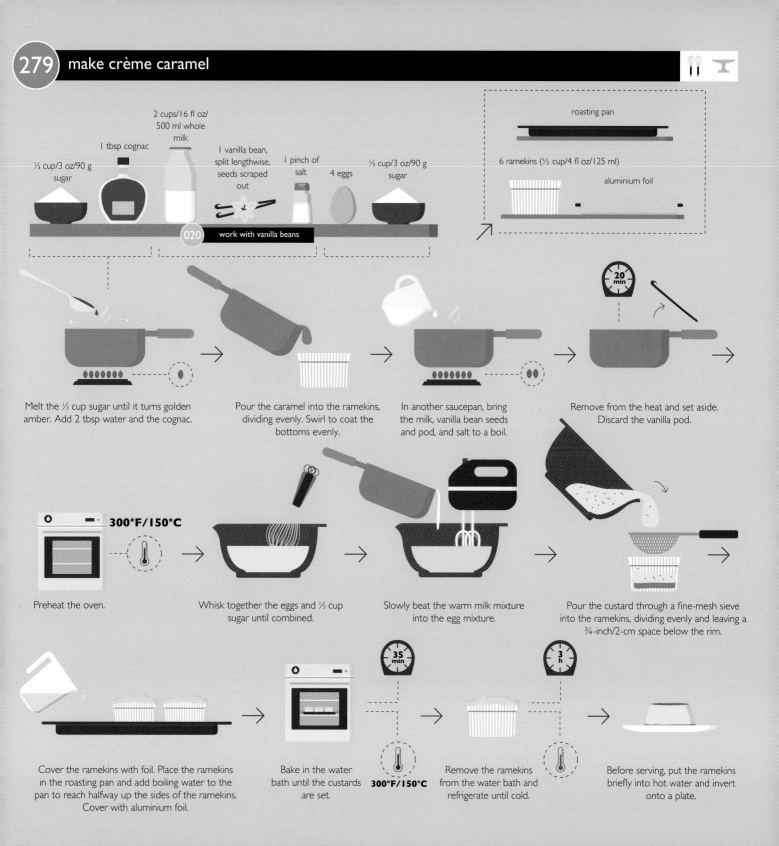

⅓ cup/3 oz/90 g sugar

1 tbsp cognac

2 cups/16 fl oz/ 500 ml whole milk

1 vanilla bean, split lengthwise, seeds scraped out

1 pinch of salt

4 eggs

⅓ cup/3 oz/90 g sugar

roasting pan

6 ramekins (½ cup/4 fl oz/125 ml)

aluminium foil

020 work with vanilla beans

Melt the ⅓ cup sugar until it turns golden amber. Add 2 tbsp water and the cognac.

Pour the caramel into the ramekins, dividing evenly. Swirl to coat the bottoms evenly.

In another saucepan, bring the milk, vanilla bean seeds and pod, and salt to a boil.

Remove from the heat and set aside. Discard the vanilla pod.

300°F/150°C

Preheat the oven.

Whisk together the eggs and ⅓ cup sugar until combined.

Slowly beat the warm milk mixture into the egg mixture.

Pour the custard through a fine-mesh sieve into the ramekins, dividing evenly and leaving a ¾-inch/2-cm space below the rim.

Cover the ramekins with foil. Place the ramekins in the roasting pan and add boiling water to the pan to reach halfway up the sides of the ramekins. Cover with aluminium foil.

Bake in the water bath until the custards are set.

300°F/150°C

Remove the ramekins from the water bath and refrigerate until cold.

Before serving, put the ramekins briefly into hot water and invert onto a plate.

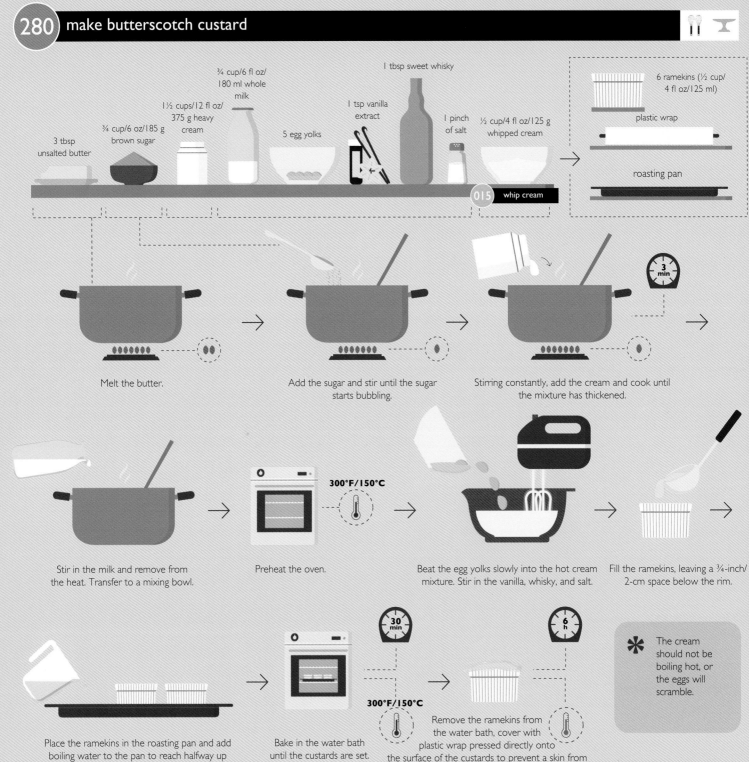

3 tbsp unsalted butter

¾ cup/6 oz/185 g brown sugar

1½ cups/12 fl oz/375 g heavy cream

¾ cup/6 fl oz/180 ml whole milk

5 egg yolks

1 tsp vanilla extract

1 tbsp sweet whisky

1 pinch of salt

½ cup/4 fl oz/125 g whipped cream

6 ramekins (½ cup/4 fl oz/125 ml)

plastic wrap

roasting pan

015 whip cream

Melt the butter.

Add the sugar and stir until the sugar starts bubbling.

Stirring constantly, add the cream and cook until the mixture has thickened.

3 min

Stir in the milk and remove from the heat. Transfer to a mixing bowl.

Preheat the oven. 300°F/150°C

Beat the egg yolks slowly into the hot cream mixture. Stir in the vanilla, whisky, and salt.

Fill the ramekins, leaving a ¾-inch/2-cm space below the rim.

Place the ramekins in the roasting pan and add boiling water to the pan to reach halfway up the sides of the ramekins.

Bake in the water bath until the custards are set. 300°F/150°C

30 min

6 h

Remove the ramekins from the water bath, cover with plastic wrap pressed directly onto the surface of the custards to prevent a skin from forming, and refrigerate. Serve with whipped cream.

* The cream should not be boiling hot, or the eggs will scramble.

12 oz/375 g day-old white bread

4 eggs

½ cup/4 oz/125 g brown sugar

¾ tsp vanilla extract

1 tsp ground cinnamon

1 pinch of freshly grated nutmeg

1 pinch of salt

4 cups/32 fl oz/1 l whole milk

¼ cup/1½ oz/45 g dried raisins

confectioner's sugar for garnish

roasting pan

baking dish (8 cups/64 fl oz/2 l), greased

Cut the bread into ¾-inch/2-cm cubes.

Whisk together the eggs, sugar, vanilla, cinnamon, nutmeg, salt, and milk.

Spread the bread cubes in the baking dish and scatter the raisins evenly over the bread.

Pour the egg mixture over the bread cubes and let sit.

**20 min**

**350°F/180°C**

Preheat the oven.

Place the baking dish in the roasting pan and add boiling water to the pan to reach halfway up the sides of the dish.

**40 min**

**350°F/180°C**

Bake in the water bath until the custard is set.

Before serving, dust with confectioners' sugar.

✳ Serve the bread pudding with fruit sauce or vanilla sauce.

298  make fruit sauce

294  make vanilla sauce

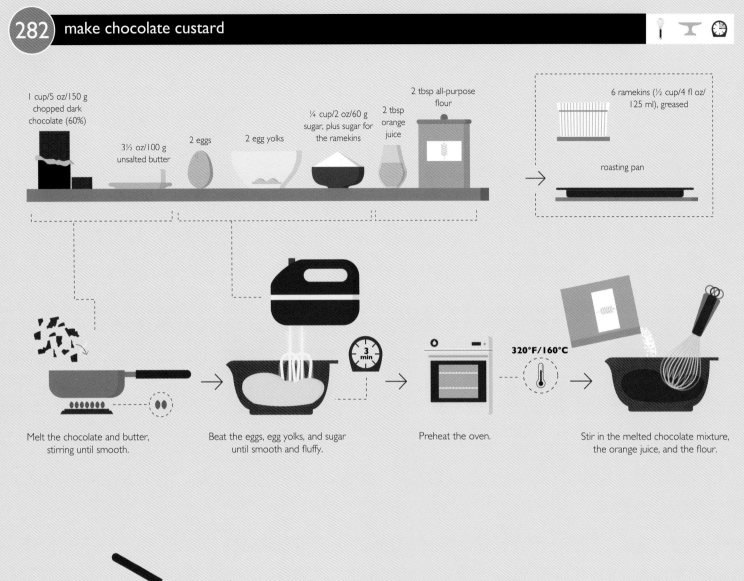

1 cup/5 oz/150 g chopped dark chocolate (60%)

3½ oz/100 g unsalted butter

2 eggs

2 egg yolks

¼ cup/2 oz/60 g sugar, plus sugar for the ramekins

2 tbsp orange juice

2 tbsp all-purpose flour

6 ramekins (½ cup/4 fl oz/ 125 ml), greased

roasting pan

Melt the chocolate and butter, stirring until smooth.

Beat the eggs, egg yolks, and sugar until smooth and fluffy.

3 min

Preheat the oven.

320°F/160°C

Stir in the melted chocolate mixture, the orange juice, and the flour.

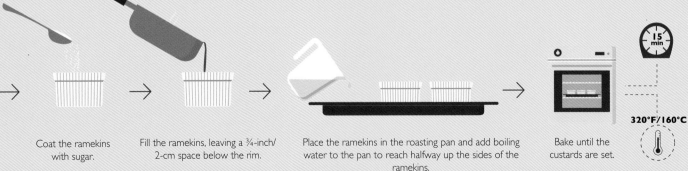

Coat the ramekins with sugar.

Fill the ramekins, leaving a ¾-inch/ 2-cm space below the rim.

Place the ramekins in the roasting pan and add boiling water to the pan to reach halfway up the sides of the ramekins.

Bake until the custards are set.

15 min

320°F/160°C

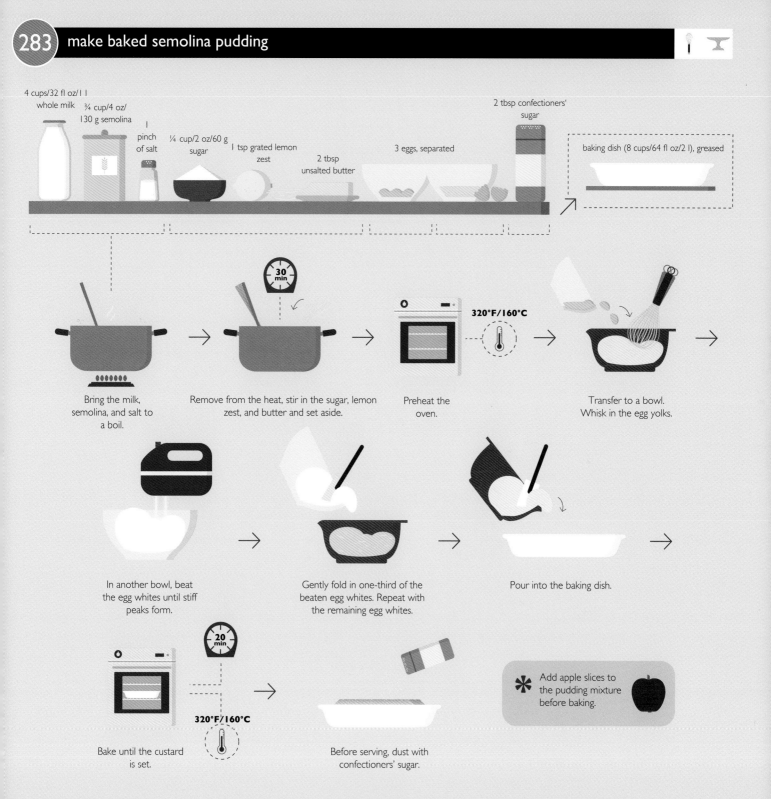

4 cups/32 fl oz/1 l whole milk

¾ cup/4 oz/130 g semolina

1 pinch of salt

¼ cup/2 oz/60 g sugar

1 tsp grated lemon zest

2 tbsp unsalted butter

3 eggs, separated

2 tbsp confectioners' sugar

baking dish (8 cups/64 fl oz/2 l), greased

Bring the milk, semolina, and salt to a boil.

Remove from the heat, stir in the sugar, lemon zest, and butter and set aside.

30 min

Preheat the oven.

320°F/160°C

Transfer to a bowl. Whisk in the egg yolks.

In another bowl, beat the egg whites until stiff peaks form.

Gently fold in one-third of the beaten egg whites. Repeat with the remaining egg whites.

Pour into the baking dish.

Bake until the custard is set.

20 min

320°F/160°C

Before serving, dust with confectioners' sugar.

✳ Add apple slices to the pudding mixture before baking.

¾ cup/5½ oz/170 g
Arborio rice

4 cups/32 fl oz/1 l
whole milk

½ cup/4 oz/125 g
sugar

1 tsp ground
cinnamon

grated zest of
½ orange

1 pinch
of salt

2 egg yolks

baking dish (8 cups/64 fl oz/2 l), greased

Bring the rice, milk, sugar, cinnamon,
orange zest, and salt to boil.

Reduce the heat to low and simmer,
stirring constantly.

Remove from the heat,
transfer to a bowl, and
let cool.

Preheat the oven.

320°F/160°C

Stir in the egg yolks.

Pour into the baking dish.

Bake until the pudding is
creamy and the rice is tender.

320°F/160°C

Let cool. The mixture will thicken
as it cools. Cover and refrigerate.

Stir the baked risotto pudding.

Serve in little bowls.

✳ Serve with fruit
sauce.

298 make fruit sauce

4 egg whites

4 egg yolks

⅔ cup/5 oz/150 g sugar

2 cups/1 lb/500 g cottage cheese

¾ cup/3 oz/90 g all-purpose flour

¼ cup/1⅓ oz/ 45 g semolina

1 pinch of salt

2 tbsp lemon juice

1 tbsp grated lemon zest

6 tbsp/3 fl oz/100 ml whole milk

3 tbsp unsalted butter, diced

confectioner's sugar for garnish

baking dish (8 cups/64 fl oz/2 l), greased

Beat the egg whites until stiff peaks form.

In another bowl, beat the egg yolks and sugar until smooth and fluffy.

Add the cottage cheese, flour, semolina, salt, lemon juice, and lemon zest and beat together until well blended.

Preheat the oven.

**350°F/180°C**

Gently fold one-third of the beaten egg whites into the mixture. Fold in the remaining egg whites.

Put the milk and butter into the baking dish. Pour in the pudding mixture and spread evenly.

Bake until golden brown.

**35 min**

**350°F/180°C**

Before serving, dust with confectioner's sugar.

3 egg yolks

1 cup/8 oz/250 g sugar

½ cup/2½ oz/75 g all-purpose flour

1 pinch of salt

1 tbsp grated lemon zest

juice of 2 lemons

1⅓ cups/11 fl oz/330 ml whole milk

3 egg whites

8 ramekins (½ cup/ 4 fl oz/125 ml), greased

roasting pan

350°F/180°C

Beat the egg yolks and sugar until smooth and fluffy.

Stir in the flour and salt and beat until very thick.

Preheat the oven.

Stir in the lemon zest, juice, and milk.

In another bowl, beat the egg whites until stiff peaks form.

Gently fold one-third of the beaten egg whites into the lemon mixture. Fold in the remaining egg whites.

Fill the ramekins, leaving a ¾-inch/2-cm space below the rim.

2 cm

Place the ramekins in the roasting pan and add boiling water to the pan to reach halfway up the sides of the ramekins.

45 min

Bake in the water bath until set and puffed.

350°F/180°C

20 min

Let cool in the water bath, then serve.

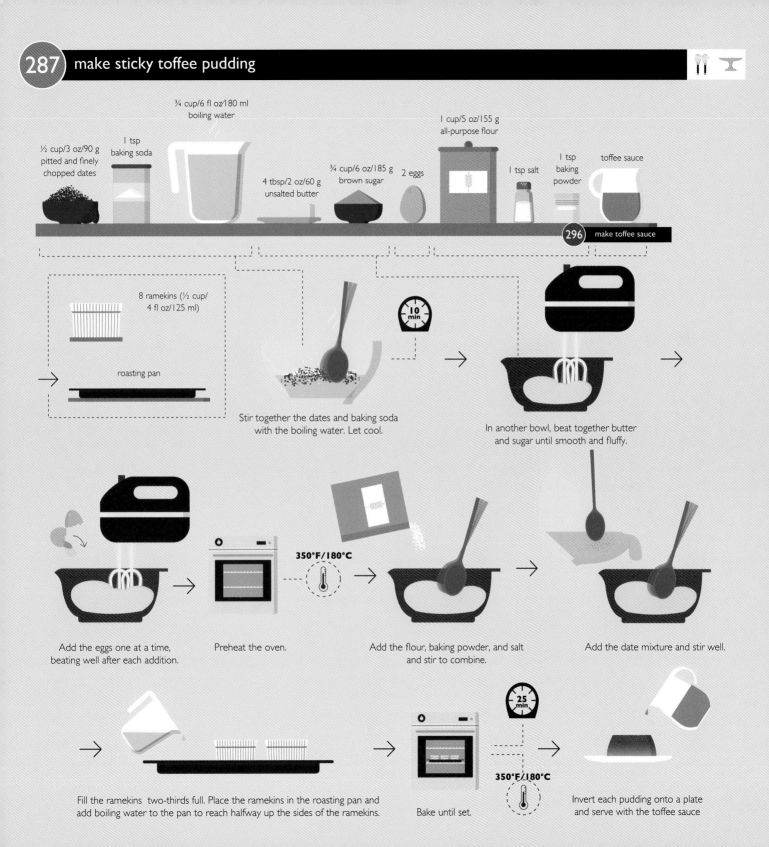

½ cup/3 oz/90 g pitted and finely chopped dates

1 tsp baking soda

¾ cup/6 fl oz/180 ml boiling water

4 tbsp/2 oz/60 g unsalted butter

¾ cup/6 oz/185 g brown sugar

2 eggs

1 cup/5 oz/155 g all-purpose flour

1 tsp salt

1 tsp baking powder

toffee sauce

296 make toffee sauce

8 ramekins (½ cup/ 4 fl oz/125 ml)

roasting pan

10 min

Stir together the dates and baking soda with the boiling water. Let cool.

In another bowl, beat together butter and sugar until smooth and fluffy.

Add the eggs one at a time, beating well after each addition.

Preheat the oven.

350°F/180°C

Add the flour, baking powder, and salt and stir to combine.

Add the date mixture and stir well.

Fill the ramekins two-thirds full. Place the ramekins in the roasting pan and add boiling water to the pan to reach halfway up the sides of the ramekins.

Bake until set.

25 min

350°F/180°C

Invert each pudding onto a plate and serve with the toffee sauce

sauces,
glazes, and
toppings

6 peaches
(about 1½ lb/650 g)

¼ cup/2 oz/60 g
sugar

1 tsp lemon juice

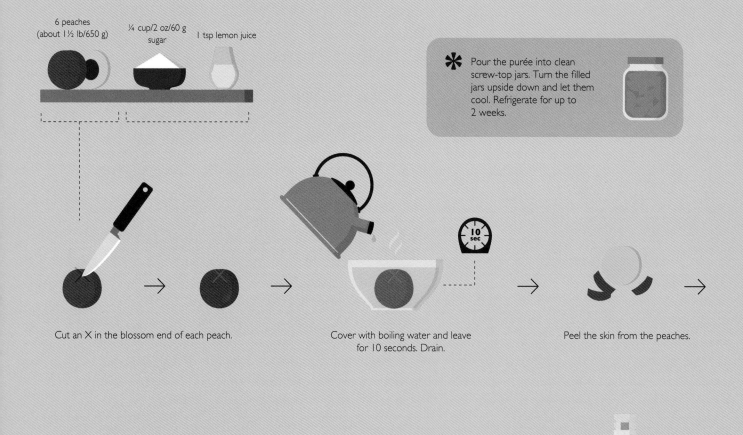

✳ Pour the purée into clean
screw-top jars. Turn the filled
jars upside down and let them
cool. Refrigerate for up to
2 weeks.

Cut an X in the blossom end of each peach.

Cover with boiling water and leave
for 10 seconds. Drain.

Peel the skin from the peaches.

Cut the peeled peaches from the pits.

Bring the peaches, sugar, lemon juice and 2 tbsp
water to a boil and remove from the heat.

Purée until smooth.

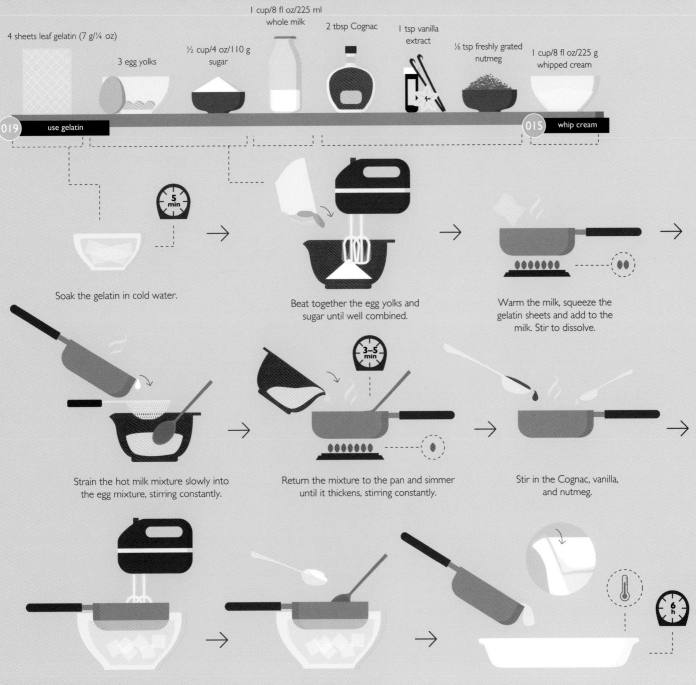

4 sheets leaf gelatin (7 g/¼ oz)

3 egg yolks

½ cup/4 oz/110 g sugar

1 cup/8 fl oz/225 ml whole milk

2 tbsp Cognac

1 tsp vanilla extract

⅛ tsp freshly grated nutmeg

1 cup/8 fl oz/225 g whipped cream

019 | use gelatin

015 | whip cream

Soak the gelatin in cold water.

Beat together the egg yolks and sugar until well combined.

Warm the milk, squeeze the gelatin sheets and add to the milk. Stir to dissolve.

Strain the hot milk mixture slowly into the egg mixture, stirring constantly.

Return the mixture to the pan and simmer until it thickens, stirring constantly.

Stir in the Cognac, vanilla, and nutmeg.

Set the pan in a larger bowl filled with ice water and whisk until the mixture cools and starts to set.

Gently fold in the whipped cream.

Pour the custard into a baking dish and place a piece of plastic wrap directly on the surface. Refrigerate until set.

1 cup/8 oz/250 g
unsalted butter

⅔ cup/5 oz/150 g
sugar

2 egg yolks

**\*** To store the buttercream, put it in a bowl and gently press a piece of plastic wrap directly onto the surface to prevent a skin from forming.

Remove the butter and eggs from the refrigerator and let stand at room temperature for 2 hours.

Beat the butter and sugar until creamy.

Add the egg yolks, one at a time, and beat until combined.

7 min

1 cup/8 oz/
250 g
unsalted
butter

⅔ cup/5 oz/150 g
sugar

2 egg yolks

1 cup/2½ oz/150 g
chopped bittersweet
chocolate

Prepare the basic buttercream.

In the top of a double boiler, melt the chocolate, let cool to room temperature, then add to the buttercream and beat until well combined.

3 egg yolks

5 tbsp/2½ oz/70 g sugar

1 cup/8 fl oz/225 ml whole milk

2 tbsp cornstarch

1 tsp vanilla extract

Do not let the cream boil, or the eggs will scramble. Always work with low heat. Refrigerate for up to 4 days.

Beat together the egg yolks and sugar until smooth.

In another bowl, whisk together 2 tbsp of the milk and the cornstarch.

Whisk the cornstarch mixture into the egg yolk mixture.

Warm the remaining milk.

Pour the hot milk into the egg yolk mixture in a slow, steady stream, whisking constantly.

6–8 min

Return the mixture to the pan, add the vanilla and cook until the mixture thickens, whisking constantly.

Pour into a bowl.

6–8 h

Press a piece of plastic wrap directly on the surface and refrigerate until cold.

1 cup/8 fl oz/250 ml whole milk

¾ cup/6 fl oz/180 ml heavy cream

1 vanilla bean, split lengthwise and seeds scraped

⅓ cup/3 oz/90 g sugar

4 egg yolks

Refrigerate for up to 2–3 days.

020 work with vanilla beans

Bring the milk, cream, vanilla pod and seeds, and sugar to a simmer.

Remove from the heat and let cool; discard the vanilla pod.

Beat the egg yolks until smooth.

Whisk half of the milk mixture into the egg yolks.

Pour the egg mixture back into the saucepan with the remaining milk mixture.

Cook, stirring constantly, until the sauce thickens.

Transfer to a mixing bowl and let cool, stirring frequently.

Press a piece of plastic wrap directly on the surface and refrigerate until cold.

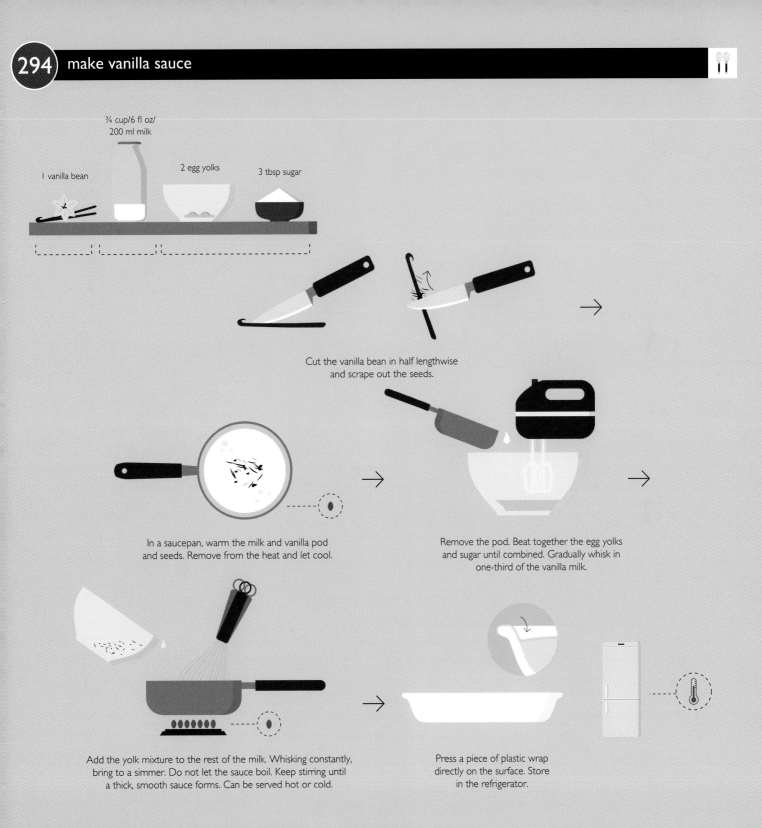

¾ cup/6 fl oz/
200 ml milk

1 vanilla bean

2 egg yolks

3 tbsp sugar

Cut the vanilla bean in half lengthwise
and scrape out the seeds.

In a saucepan, warm the milk and vanilla pod
and seeds. Remove from the heat and let cool.

Remove the pod. Beat together the egg yolks
and sugar until combined. Gradually whisk in
one-third of the vanilla milk.

Add the yolk mixture to the rest of the milk. Whisking constantly,
bring to a simmer. Do not let the sauce boil. Keep stirring until
a thick, smooth sauce forms. Can be served hot or cold.

Press a piece of plastic wrap
directly on the surface. Store
in the refrigerator.

⅓ cup/3 fl oz/ 75 ml milk

¾ cup/ 3½ oz/100 g heavy cream

3½ oz/100 g dark chocolate

In a small saucepan, bring the milk and cream to a boil, then remove from the heat.

Break the chocolate into small pieces

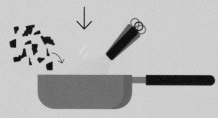

Add the chocolate and stir until it has melted.

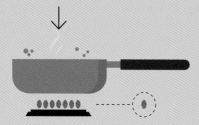

Heat until warm, then serve.

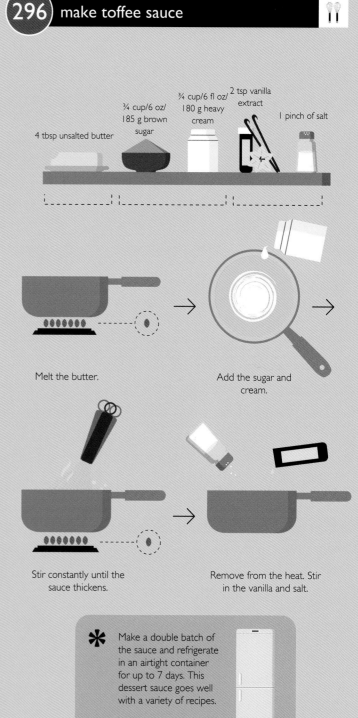

4 tbsp unsalted butter

¾ cup/6 oz/ 185 g brown sugar

¾ cup/6 fl oz/ 180 g heavy cream

2 tsp vanilla extract

1 pinch of salt

Melt the butter.

Add the sugar and cream.

Stir constantly until the sauce thickens.

Remove from the heat. Stir in the vanilla and salt.

✳ Make a double batch of the sauce and refrigerate in an airtight container for up to 7 days. This dessert sauce goes well with a variety of recipes.

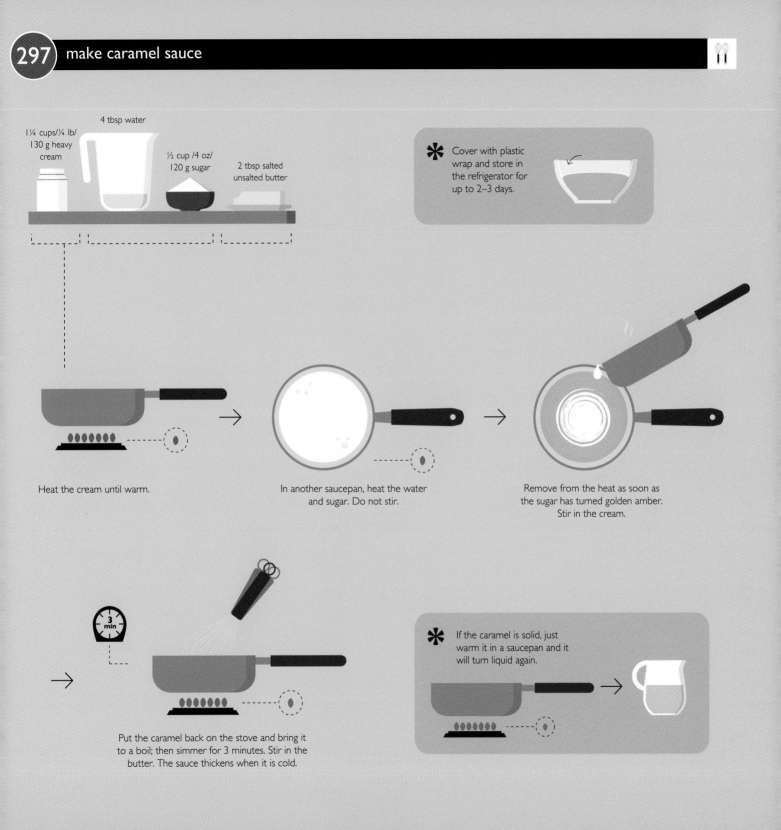

1¼ cups/¼ lb/ 130 g heavy cream

4 tbsp water

½ cup /4 oz/ 120 g sugar

2 tbsp salted unsalted butter

Heat the cream until warm.

In another saucepan, heat the water and sugar. Do not stir.

Remove from the heat as soon as the sugar has turned golden amber. Stir in the cream.

* Cover with plastic wrap and store in the refrigerator for up to 2–3 days.

3 min

Put the caramel back on the stove and bring it to a boil; then simmer for 3 minutes. Stir in the butter. The sauce thickens when it is cold.

* If the caramel is solid, just warm it in a saucepan and it will turn liquid again.

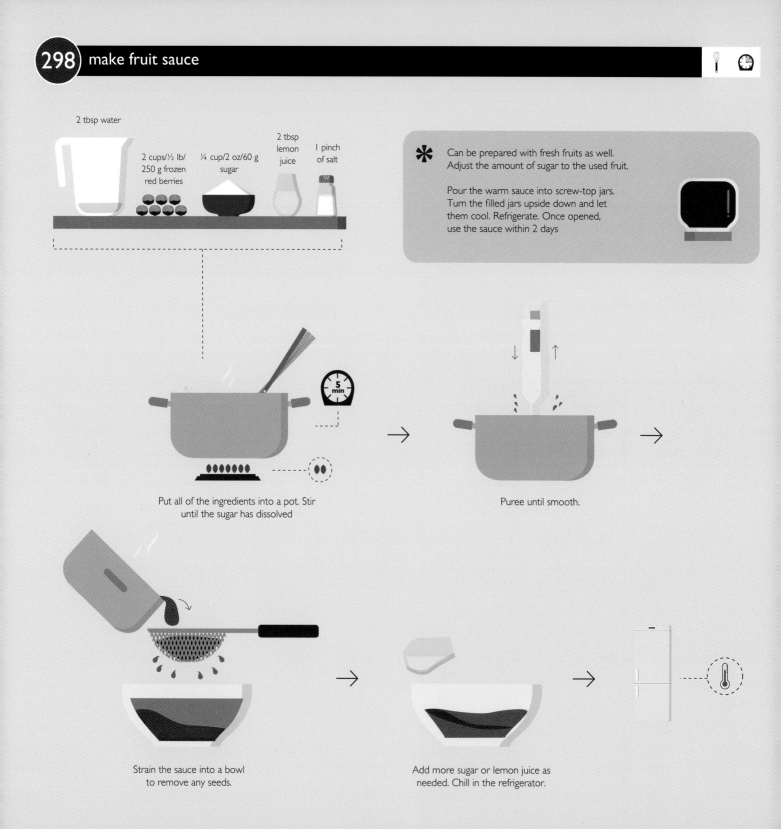

2 tbsp water

2 cups/½ lb/ 250 g frozen red berries

¼ cup/2 oz/60 g sugar

2 tbsp lemon juice

1 pinch of salt

**\*** Can be prepared with fresh fruits as well. Adjust the amount of sugar to the used fruit.

Pour the warm sauce into screw-top jars. Turn the filled jars upside down and let them cool. Refrigerate. Once opened, use the sauce within 2 days

Put all of the ingredients into a pot. Stir until the sugar has dissolved

Puree until smooth.

Strain the sauce into a bowl to remove any seeds.

Add more sugar or lemon juice as needed. Chill in the refrigerator.

3 tbsp Grand Marnier

3½ oz/110 g
sugar

¼ cup/2oz/60 g
unsalted butter,
in cubes

¾ cup/6 fl oz/
180 ml orange
juice

2 tbsp
lemon juice

2 tbsp grated
orange zest

* Pour the sauce into
a screw-top jar and
store in the refrigerator.

5 min

Cook the sugar without
stirring until it melts and
caramelizes.

Add the butter, orange juice, and
lemon juice and bring to a boil.

Add the orange zest and
cook, stirring, until
the caramel dissolves.

Remove from the heat and
add the Grand Marnier.

⅓ cup/3 fl oz/
80 ml lemon
juice

3 eggs

zest of 1 lemon

½ cup/4 oz/
125 g sugar

½ cup/4 oz/125 g
butter, in chunks

* To prevent the curd
from getting lumpy,
do not let it boil.

10 min

Whisk together
the eggs.

Add the eggs to the top of a double boiler
and add the lemon juice, lemon zest,
and sugar. Whisk to combine.

Gradually add the butter, stirring
until it melts. Continue stirring
until thickened.

Fill sterilized jars and seal them.
The curd can be stored in the
refrigerator for up to 2 weeks.

## 301 | make wine sabayon

1 cup/8 fl oz/250 ml
Gewürztraminer or Riesling

4 egg yolks

⅓ cup/3 oz/90 g
sugar

lemon juice
to taste

✳ Do not let the cream boil,
or the eggs will scramble.
Always work with low heat.

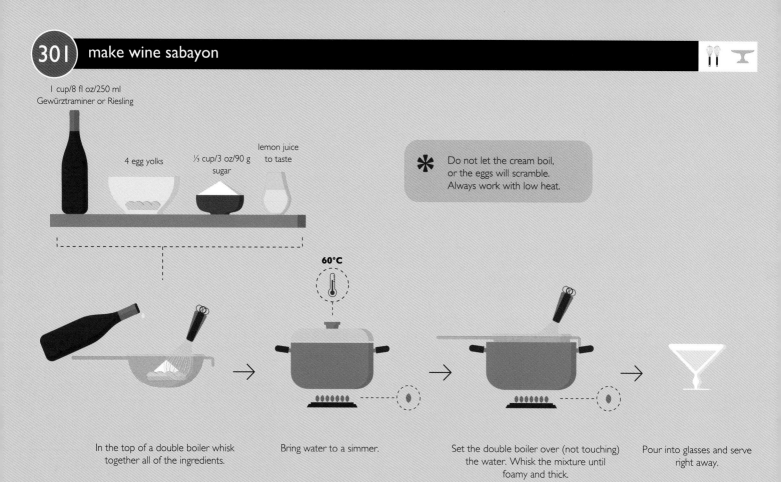

60°C

In the top of a double boiler whisk
together all of the ingredients.

Bring water to a simmer.

Set the double boiler over (not touching)
the water. Whisk the mixture until
foamy and thick.

Pour into glasses and serve
right away.

## 302 | prepare zabaglione

⅓ cup/3 fl oz/80 ml
Marsala

4 egg yolks

⅓ cup/3 oz/90 g
sugar

lemon juice to
taste

Replace the white wine with Marsala and
prepare like wine sabayon.

2 sheets leaf gelatin (3.5 g/⅛ oz)

1 cup/8 fl oz/ 250 ml milk

1 pinch of salt

6 tbsp/3 oz/ 90 g crème fraîche

3 tbsp Amaretto

019 use gelatin

Soak the gelatin in cold water.

Warm the milk with the salt. Squeeze the gelatin sheets, add to the pan, and let dissolve in the milk.

Pour the mixture into a bowl.

Stir in the crème fraîche and Amaretto.

Pour through a fine-mesh sieve into a clean bowl.

Let cool completely.

Pour the Amaretto mixture into a whipped cream canister and refrigerate until cold.

Just before serving, shake the canister well.

Spray the foam onto a dessert.

2 sheets leaf gelatin (3.5 g/⅛ oz)

¾ cup/3 oz/90 g sliced almonds

1 cup/8 fl oz/ 250 ml milk

1 pinch of salt

6 tbsp/3 oz/90 g crème fraîche

Soak the gelatin in cold water.

Dry roast the sliced almonds, stirring constantly, until golden.

Add the milk and salt to the pan with the almonds and bring to a boil.

Remove from the heat and let cool.

Stir in the crème fraîche.

Pour through a fine-mesh sieve set over a bowl and discard the almonds.

Heat ½ cup/4 fl oz/125 ml of the almond milk. Squeeze the gelatin sheets, add to the milk mixture, and let dissolve. Stir into the remaining almond milk.

Let cool completely.

Pour the mixture into a whipped cream canister and refrigerate until cold.

Just before serving, shake the canister well.

Spray the foam onto a dessert.

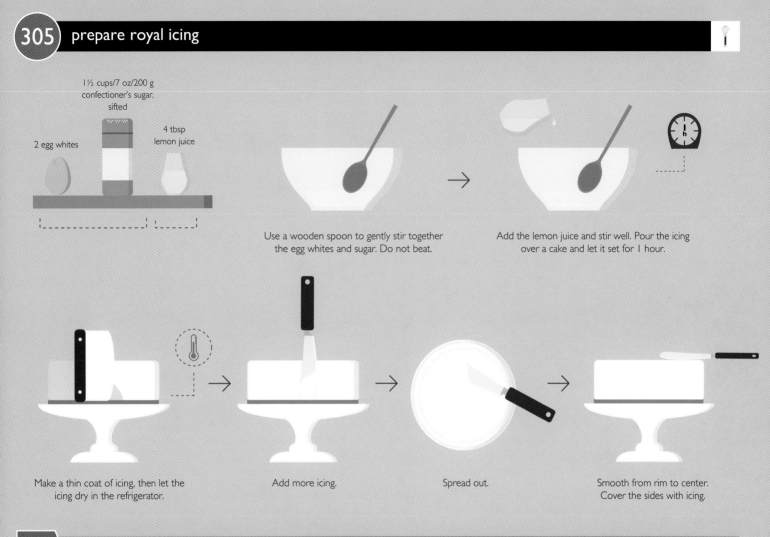

1½ cups/7 oz/200 g confectioner's sugar, sifted

2 egg whites

4 tbsp lemon juice

Use a wooden spoon to gently stir together the egg whites and sugar. Do not beat.

Add the lemon juice and stir well. Pour the icing over a cake and let it set for 1 hour.

Make a thin coat of icing, then let the icing dry in the refrigerator.

Add more icing.

Spread out.

Smooth from rim to center. Cover the sides with icing.

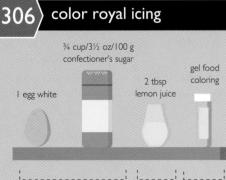

¾ cup/3½ oz/100 g confectioner's sugar

1 egg white

2 tbsp lemon juice

gel food coloring

Prepare the icing as directed. Add 2–4 drops of food coloring and stir to combine. Use as directed.

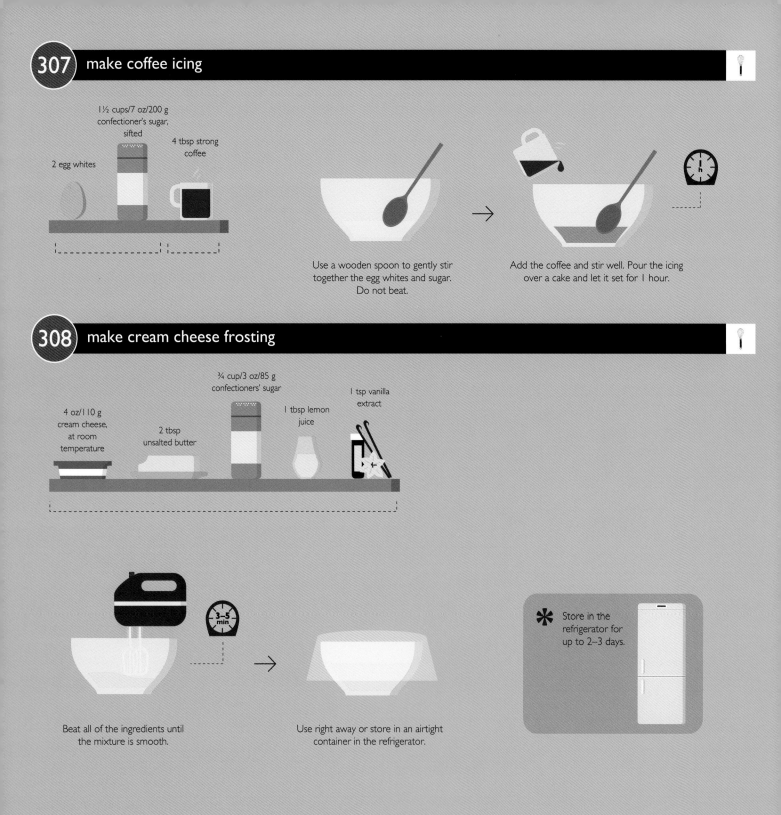

## 307 | make coffee icing

1½ cups/7 oz/200 g confectioner's sugar, sifted

4 tbsp strong coffee

2 egg whites

Use a wooden spoon to gently stir together the egg whites and sugar. Do not beat.

Add the coffee and stir well. Pour the icing over a cake and let it set for 1 hour.

## 308 | make cream cheese frosting

4 oz/110 g cream cheese, at room temperature

2 tbsp unsalted butter

¾ cup/3 oz/85 g confectioners' sugar

1 tbsp lemon juice

1 tsp vanilla extract

Beat all of the ingredients until the mixture is smooth.

Use right away or store in an airtight container in the refrigerator.

✳ Store in the refrigerator for up to 2–3 days.

2 cups/16 fl oz/
500 ml milk

1½ oz/50 g
bittersweet
chocolate,
broken into
pieces

1 tbsp cocoa
powder

3 tbsp sugar

2 tbsp
cornstarch

Warm 1¼ cups/10 fl oz/300 ml
milk, add the chocolate, and
stir until it is melted.

Whisk together the remaining
¾ cup/6 fl oz/200 ml milk,
cocoa, sugar, and cornstarch
just until combined.

Stir into the hot chocolate mixture. Bring to a
boil, whisking constantly. Simmer at low heat
until the mixture thickens.

Ladle into pudding cups, press a piece of plastic wrap
directly on the surface and let cool completely.

2 cups/16 fl oz/
500 ml milk

1 vanilla bean

3 egg yolks

¼ cup /
2 oz/60 g
sugar

¼ cup/2 oz/
30 g cornstarch

Cut the vanilla bean in half lengthwise,
then scrape out the seeds.

Warm the milk and vanilla seeds.

Whisk the egg yolks and
sugar until creamy.

Whisk in the cornstarch and add
5 tbsp of the hot milk mixture.

Whisk the egg yolk mixture into the hot
milk and cook, stirring constantly, until it
comes to a boil and thickens.

Ladle into pudding cups, press a piece
of plastic wrap directly on the surface
and let cool completely.

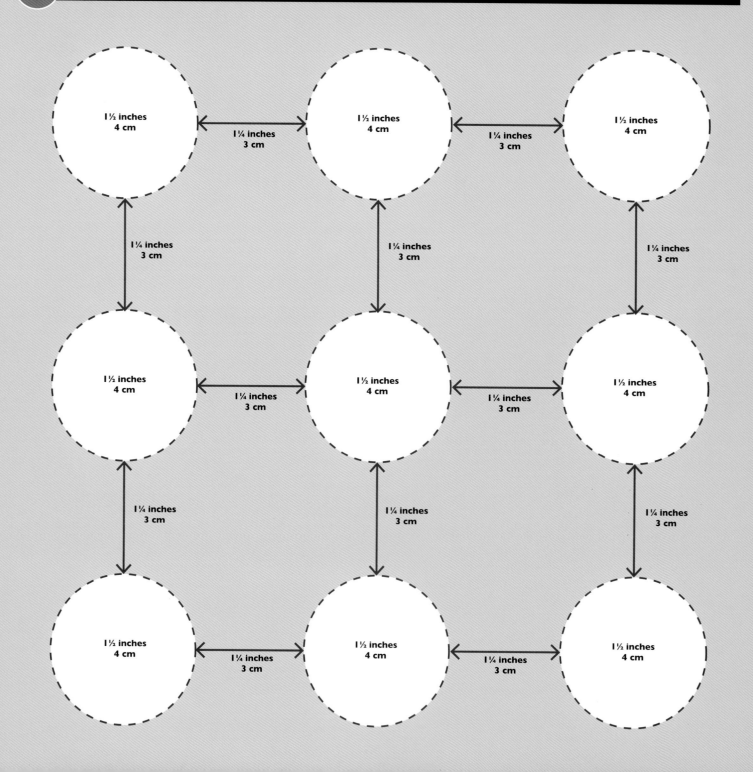

stencil for chocolate chip cookies

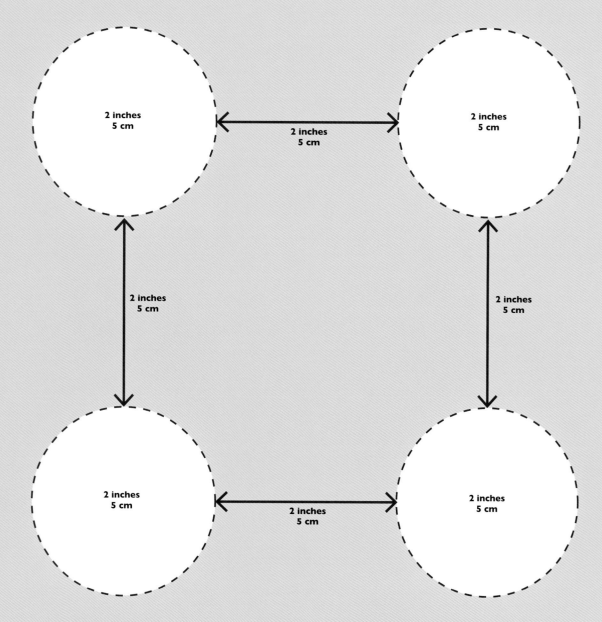

# index

# weldonowen

1045 Sansome Street, San Francisco, California, USA

www.weldonowen.com

## BAKE! THE QUICK-LOOK COOKBOOK

## A WELDON OWEN PRODUCTION

Copyright © 2015 Weldon Owen, Inc.

Printed in China by 1010 Printing International

First printed in 2015

10 9 8 7 6 5 4 3 2 1

Library of Congress Control Number: 2014955733

ISBN 13: 978-1-61628-935-5

ISBN 10: 1-61628-935-X

Weldon Owen is a division of

## BONNIER

## WELDON OWEN, INC.

President  Roger Shaw

Sr. VP, Sales and Marketing  Amy Kaneko

Finance Director  Philip Paulick

Creative Director  Kelly Booth

Cover Designer  Debbie Berne

Production Designer  Monica S. Lee

Associate Publishers  Amy Marr

Project Editor  Kim Laidlaw

Associate Editor  Emma Rudolph

Production Director  Chris Hemesath

Associate Production Director  Michelle Duggan

Author  Gabriela Scolik

Infographics  no.parking, www.noparking.it

Editor  Bettina Dietrich

Team  Kathrin Raminger, Daniela Schmid

A Show Me Now Book.
Show Me Now is a trademark
of Weldon Owen Inc.
www.showmenow.com